Lincoln Christian College

D0153545

Ellenii Christian College

MODERN SOCIOLOGICAL THEORY
An Introduction

Lincoln Christian College

MODERN SOCIOLOGICAL THEORY
An Introduction

M. FRANCIS ABRAHAM

Professor of Sociology
Grambling State University, Grambling, Louisiana

DELHI
OXFORD UNIVERSITY PRESS
BOMBAY CALCUTTA MADRAS
1982

Oxford University Press, Walton Street, Oxford OX2 6DP

LONDON GLASGOW NEW YORK TORONTO
DELHI BOMBAY CALCUTTA MADRAS KARACHI
KUALA LUMPUR SINGAPORE HONG KONG TOKYO
NAIROBI DAR ES SALAAM CAPE TOWN
MELBOURNE AUCKLAND

and associates in

BEIRUT BERLIN IBADAN MEXICO CITY

© Oxford University Press 1982

Printed in India by Dharm Prakash
at Urvashi Press, 49/3 Vaidwara, Meerut 250002
and published by R. Dayal, Oxford University Press
2/11 Ansari Road, Daryaganj, New Delhi 110002

For
Dr G. Ramachandran

67072

Preface

In teaching a course in modern sociological theory I have always confronted several problems. Most of the available texts are organized around either men or ideas. Either they seek to touch on all the major contributions of leading theorists or to analyse different *perspectives* on the most significant sociological concepts. The texts that deal with theoretical systems *per se* are usually brief and sketchy. I have attempted to present a comprehensive overview of the major schools of sociological theory incorporating diverse perspectives and illustrations drawn from different cultural contexts.

Several considerations have guided my pursuit. First, I wanted to understand the essence of the various schools of sociological theory so that I can present them more effectively to my undergraduate students. Second, I wanted the students to understand the basic disagreement on the meaning of sociological theory itself; the first chapter, therefore, contains a fairly long list of definitions and arguments. Third, I responded to the need to emphasize the necessity of incessant interchanges between theory and methodology, a theme that is often left out of theory texts. Fourth, a number of theoretical orientations on the nature, function and change of social structure—the central focus of sociological theory—had to be analysed. This consideration prompted the inclusion of several themes that are not usually dealt with in textbooks on sociological theory. Systems theory, theories of anomie and alienation, structural versus behavioural perspectives, and evolutionary theory fall in this category. With these innovations and systematic analysis of major schools of theory, the serious student will, I hope, find this book illuminating as I found my research for this rewarding and enriching.

Now, I should like to acknowledge my gratitude to a number of people who have directly or indirectly lent me a helping hand. I am grateful to Dr John Henry Morgan who contributed the chapter on phenomenology and ethnomethodology, collaborated with me on the chapter on symbolic interactionism and made significant editorial changes in other chapters. I am deeply indebted to

Dr William McIntosh, Dean of the College of Arts and Sciences,
and Dr Birdex Copeland, Jr, Chairman of the Department of
Sociology at Grambling State University for their intellectual
support and for providing an ideal environment to pursue this
work. My thanks are also due to two of my graduate assistants,
Lillian Portis and Sheila Hendrix, who provided invaluable assistance in getting the manuscript ready and on time.

M. FRANCIS ABRAHAM

Grambling
20 December 1981

Contents

CHAPTER 1

What is Sociological Theory?

Scholarship in the social and philosophical sciences through the ages has shown a persistent interest in theories about human behaviour and has produced an abundant crop of literature. Although the broad spectrum of social theories touches on all aspects of behaviour, personality and social processes and institutions, only a small and relatively recent portion of this literature is essentially sociological in form and substance. Before we attempt a precise definition of sociological theory, we need to look at the various interpretations of theory *per se*.

Theory means different things to different people. It is a much abused term in popular speech, philosophical discourse and scientific treatises alike. The proponent of every theory has his own definition of what constitutes a theory. To many, a theory could be an apparently intelligent statement about anything, about our tastes and distastes, our value-orientations, our failures and accomplishments, our strategies and convictions, a wild hypothesis about life on some far away planet, or life after death. Sometimes a theory is used to mean a speculative statement that is not, or even cannot be, supported by evidence. 'In scope, it (a theory) may be as broad as all thought or as narrow as a single thought. The word may be applied to the thinking process *per se* or only to its results and conclusions. In form, it may vary from complete conjecture to solid confirmation, from unarticulated impression to precisely defined prediction.'[1] Theory, as employed in this text, will be defined as a conceptual scheme designed to explain observed regularities, or relationships between two or more variables. In the words of Abraham Kaplan:

A theory is a way of making sense of a disturbing situation so as to allow us most effectively to bring to bear our repertoire of habits, and even more important, to modify habits or discard them altogether, replacing them by new ones as the situation demands. In the reconstructed logic, accordingly, theory will appear as the device for interpreting, criticizing, and unifying established laws, modifying them to fit data unanticipated in their formulation, and guiding the enterprise of discovering new and more powerful generalizations. To engage in theorizing means not just to learn by experience but to take thought about what is there to be learned. To speak loosely, lower animals grasp scientific laws but never rise to the level of scientific theory. They learn *by* experience but not *from* it, for *from* learning requires symbolic constructions which can provide vicarious experience never actually undergone.[2]

Today sociologists use theory to mean any or all of the following:[3]

1. Concept—conceptual ordering—construct—constructed type;
2. Frame of reference—conceptual scheme—perspective;
3. Intelligent hunch—hypothesis—theorem—postulate—systematized assumption;
4. Proposition—axiom—law—generalization;
5. Model—logico-deductive scheme—mathematical formulations;
6. Ideal type—paradigm—typology—continuum.

Whereas to some sociologists, a 'theory is an explanation of the relationships between phenomena which is not as solidly established as a law, but is more than a mere hypothesis'[4], to others '(1) theories should be stated more formally; (2) theories should be testable; and (3) predictive power should be the primary criterion for assessing theories.'[5] However, sociological theories differ considerably in terms of such characteristics as verifiability, precision, scope, predictive power or the radius of the explanatory shell. And Robert Merton is justified in stating that six different types of work are 'often lumped together as comprising sociological theory: (1) methodology; (2) general sociological orientations; (3) analysis of sociological concepts; (4) *post factum* sociological interpretations; (5) empirical generalizations in sociology, and (6) sociological theory.'[6]

It seems only fitting to quote the definitions of sociological theory provided by three of the most outstanding sociologists of today:

PARSONS: A theoretical system in the present sense is a body of logically interdependent generalized concepts of empirical reference. Such a system tends, ideally, to become 'logically closed', to reach such a state of logical integration that every logical implication of any combination of propositions in the system is explicitly stated in some other propositions in the same system.[7]

MERTON: . . . the term sociological theory refers to logically inter-connected sets of propositions from which empirical uniformities can be derived.[8]

HOMANS: It consists, first, of a set of concepts or conceptual scheme. Some of the terms in the scheme I call descriptive concepts, serving to show what the theory is about... Others I call operative concepts or properties of nature ... A theory consists, second, of a set of propositions, each stating a relationship .... between at least two of the properties and the propositions form a deductive system ... Third, some of the propositions of a scientific theory must be contingent, in the sense that experience is relevant to their truth or falsity or to that of propositions derived from them. The propositions in a deductive system need not always differ in generality, but often they do ....[9]

Thomas Ward analysed twenty-seven definitions of sociological theory and, synthesizing their common ingredients, arrived at this definition: '. . . a theory is a logical deductive-inductive system of concepts, definitions, and propositions which states a relationship between two or more selected aspects of phenomena from which testable hypotheses can be derived.'[10]

Zetterberg finds two different interpretations of social theory in two different traditions of sociology:[11]

1. Within the humanistic tradition of sociology, social theory means two related but different things:
   (a) Classical works or 'all of the better sociological writings of the older vintage' which could more appropriately be termed as 'sociological classics', that is, the great works of the founding fathers of sociology.
   (b) Sociological criticism or 'a commentary on sociological writings', usually from a historical perspective, tracing continuities in the accumulation of knowledge through developments and re-interpretations.
2. Within the scientific tradition of sociology, social theory refers to two different but related enterprises:
   (a) Sociological taxonomy or a system of definitions based on an orderly schema of defining concepts and relationships in the sociological vocabulary;
   (b) 'Systematically-organized, law-like propositions about society that can be supported by evidence.'

According to Zetterberg, only the fourth definition can be appropriately attributed to sociological theory; the first three interpretations should not be dignified by the label 'social theory'.

The position that empirically verifiable, law-like propositions alone constitute sociological theory, is open to question. Imagine a textbook in sociological theory listing only law-like propositions. And, how many law-like propositions are there in sociology? Again, should all theoretical propositions be supported by evidence?

In the first place, if we accept Zetterberg's definition, we do not have a single full-fledged textbook in sociological theory to date, except, of course, works which abound in empirical generalizations and mathematical models, because much of the accumulated literature in sociological theory encompasses mainly sociological classics, sociological criticism and sociological taxonomy, all of which Zetterberg has rejected as being non-theory. Secondly, the available scholarship in sociological theory does not require that every social theory be empirically verifiable in the rigorous fashion of the physical sciences. Social contract theory, social Darwinism, the protestant ethic and the spirit of capitalism, Marxian theory of class war, Sorokin's theory of social and cultural dynamics, Parson's theory of social action, and Durkheim's theory of religion have been influential sociological theories although none of them can be verified in their entirety. And if these are not theories, what are they?

The dominant mainstream in social thought, as well as the greater proportion of current literature in contemporary sociological theory, views theory as composed of three major realms:

1. Main currents in sociological thought, especially as manifested in the works of great masters like Comte, Spencer, Durkheim, Weber, Pareto, Simmel, Toennies and others;

2. General modes of sociological analysis like evolutionary theories, structural-functionalism, conflict theory and the system theory which generate a host of propositions concerning the society as a whole;

3. A large number of theoretical perspectives, paradigms, empirical generalizations, deductive-inductive systems and typologies which deal with the relationships between units within society.

A theory is a plausible explanation about social phenomena or a class of social phenomena, logically construed and systematically organized, that underscores the relationship between two well-defined variables. It is more than a hypothesis or speculative reasoning but far from a social law that is supported by evidence. A theory is thus contrasted with a fact, law and practice. A fact is an empirically verifiable observation whereas a theory is a systematized relationship between facts. And a theory cannot be derived from empirical observations and generalizations merely by means of rigorous induction. A theory is a symbolic construction and theory-building is a matter of creative achievement. A theory is thus an abstract conceptual scheme that reaches out beyond itself, transcending the observable realm of empirical reality into a higher level of abstraction by means of a symbolic construction. 'In this sense it stands for the symbolic dimension of experience, as opposed to the apprehension of brute fact.'[12]

Characteristics of Sociological Theory

Thomas Ward[13] surveyed some one hundred popular texts in the social sciences published since 1950 and undertook a content analysis of 27 definitions of sociological theory. His findings with regard to the characteristics of a theory are most instructive. The vast majority of the definitions studied—89 per cent to be exact—mentioned that a theory has a systematic structure and 74 per cent of them suggested that it should be possible for a theory to generate hypotheses which are empirically verifiable (*not* that the theory itself should be verifiable). In 70 per cent of the cases, the structure of the theory was defined as being logically connected. The term 'proposition' appeared in 59 per cent of the definitions, and 44 per cent defined theory as a logical-deductive system. Only 19 per cent of the definitions mentioned 'laws', 'generalizations' or 'definitions'. Postulates and axioms are even more infrequent, having been mentioned in only 15 per cent of the definitions surveyed. Ward's analysis is a good indication of what sociologists think of a theory.

In the words of Timasheff:

A theory is a set of propositions complying, ideally, with the following conditions: one, the propositions must be couched in terms of exactly defined concepts; two, they must be consistent with each other; three, they must be such that from them the existing generalizations could be deductively derived; four, they must be fruitful—show the way to further observations and generalizations increasing the scope of knowledge.[14]

Concepts and propositions, definitions and hypotheses constitute the essential ingredients of a theory. Sociological concepts, which provide an orderly schema for the classification and description of a class of social phenomena or a singular aspect of some social reality, undergo considerable refinement before they enter into a theoretical scheme. Not only does a theory refine the concepts it uses, but a new theory may generate its own new concepts. Similarly, the propositions or laws that enter into a theory must not only be well defined, they also are necessarily 'altered by being brought into systematic connection with one another, as marriage relates two people who are never the same again. Each law takes up into itself something of the substance of the others. It is generalized, reformulated, or at any rate, reinterpreted.[15]

The basic question concerning the characteristics of a theory is whether it should be verifiable or not. Some theorists equate sociological theories with the scientific laws in the mature sciences like physics and biology and assert that social theories are no more than speculative exercises unless they correspond to well defined propositions or laws that can be empirically tested. But the fact is that this state of maturity is a distant goal for the infant discipline of sociology. Moreover, the development of sociology since its very inception has been characterized by a large number of conflicting theories and perspectives. Sociologists have not developed a single inductive procedure or mathematical model that could 'test' their theories and validate them as applicable to all groups and societies. Sociological theories fall between the two extremes of an empirical law and purely speculative reasoning. Indeed, to some sociologists, even a simple hypothesis is a minor theory and every speculative ideal can be classed as a theory if it generates at least one fruitful hypothesis that is logically sound. It 'is not to deny the need for any form of verification. A theory 'is considered, verified in a preliminary way, if no known fact or generalization seems to contradict it. If there is contradiction, the tentative theory must be rejected, or at least modified.'[16] When conflicting theories seem to explain the same social phenomena as in the case of the rise of capitalism which is differently interpreted by Marx and Weber, the situation calls for a critical observation whereby a theory which is supported by an overwhelming array of 'evidence' is pronounced more fruitful. However, the critical observation is, by no means, a final test since conflicting theories involve conditions which can never be fulfilled because of the idealizations involved. Yet they will continue to be influential theories. Thus, sociological theories need not be verified in the fashion of the theories in physics; however, they need to fit a syndrome of facts that have a bearing on the class of phenomena being theorized about. This is validation in the simple correspondence, not verification in the statistical sense; and to that, sociological theories can aspire, for now at least.

It is then obvious that sociological theories are not necessarily social laws. Whereas a scientific law is a confirmed summation of relationships between empirically observable phenomena, a sociological theory is primarily a heuristic device. Laws are 'discovered' by observing patterned relationships; theories are invented by creative ingenuity. Granted, sociologists can, to some extent, formulate laws concerning human behaviour in society; nevertheless, the search for such laws is not the *raison d'être* of the discipline. To consider the quest for social laws to be an end in itself or even the primary objective of sociology is to nip 'sociological imagination' in the bud, and to reduce sociology to sterile 'abstracted empiricism'. The truth is that, in sociology, a rigorous inductive procedure or a logical deductive format may not yield fruitful sociological insights. On the other hand, a theory may establish a systematic connection between isolated laws and transcend them into a more meaningful conceptual scheme inspiring new empirical studies, theoretical laws and frames of reference. In short, a sociological theory could be a logically construed impressionistic generalization or an intuitive statement intermediate in degree of verification between a law and an hypothesis. And in the words of Abel, 'All theories fall between the two extremes of a simple explanatory principle and a deductive system with an abstract relational structure formed by theoretical postulates.'[17]

To summarize, a sociological theory may be said to have the following characteristics:

1. A theory is couched in terms of well defined concepts and logically inter-connected propositions.
2. A theory is a systematized symbolic construction and does not share the ineluctability of fact. Theory-building is a creative achievement and involves a qualitative jump beyond evidence.
3. A theory is provisional in character; it is always open to revision depending on new insights and evidences. It is neither necessary nor desirable for a sociological theory to be a final formulation.
4. It is verifiable in a preliminary way, that is, consistent with the body of known facts and available evidences.

5. It is systematized formulation that seeks to reconcile the needs of a humanistic tradition (speculative, creative, etc.) with the demands of a scientific tradition (measurement, rigorous induction, predictive power, etc.).

Types of Theories

In a volume entitled *Modern Sociological Theory*, Boskoff refers to two types of social theory: *non-social, reductionist* explanations of social phenomena with reference to environmental and physical factors as well as natural forces (e.g., geographic determinism), and 'proto-sociology', which was marked by 'a growing emancipation from most of the concepts and orientations of the physical and biological sciences'[18] and 'conceived as an intellectual synthesis of data and generalizations supplied by the specialized social disciplines.'[19]

Homans identifies two types of general theory: (1) the normative, and (2) the non-normative. 'To speak very roughly, normative theories explain how men ought to behave if they are to accomplish certain results, and non-normative theories explain how they actually do behave.'[20] The normative theories fall into two categories— the one-sided and the two- or many-sided. While the former seeks to explain how a particular social actor or social group ought to behave in order to attain certain goals, the latter is concerned with interaction between two or more persons who behave normatively towards one another. Theories of applied sociology fall into the first category; the theory of Games illustrates the second type. According to Homans, there are three types of non-normative theories: structural, functional and psychological.

Structural theories explain the existence of some element of social behaviour; however, 'element' may be defined by its relations to other elements and the relations of these elements to one another in some configuration, a social structure or social system. In functional theories, the highest-order propositions say that a society or other social unit will not survive, remain in equilibrium, or reach its goals unless a certain element or combination of elements of behaviour occurs in the unit. In psychological theories the highest-order propositions say that some variable in the behaviour of individual men as members of a species—not the behaviour of societies or groups as such—is a more or less specific function of some other variable in the behaviour of individual men or of the physical environment. I do not think that any one of these types of theories often occurs in its pure form in sociological writings; it is usually mixed with other types.'[21]

Helmut Wagner classifies sociological theory into three main categories:[22]

1. Positive sociological theories, whose authors consider, or actually treat, sociology as a natural science. Neo-positivism, human ecology, structural functionalism, social behaviourism and bio-psychological theory of culture fall in this category.

2. Interpretative sociologies, whose authors consider, or actually treat, sociology as a social science in contradistinction to the natural sciences. Theories of cultural understanding, interpretative sociology of action and interaction, interpretative social psychology and social phenomenology represent this class of sociological theories.

3. Non-scientific or evaluative social theories, whose authors neither value nor consider nor actually treat sociology as a positive or interpretative science. The examples are social-philosophical theory, ideological social theory and humanitarian reform theory.

Boskoff, Homans and Wagner have used definitionally specific criteria for their classification; they have lumped together extremely divergent theories under the same category. And the value of attempts to classify sociological theories as reductionist and non-reductionist, or evaluative and scientific is highly questionable. Therefore, using three general criteria, let us differentiate between three alternate schemes of classification.

Speculative vs. Grounded Theories

Speculative theory refers to an abstract impressionistic approach rooted in the philosophical system. The great encyclopedic minds of Comte and Spencer have synthesized the findings of a variety of disciplines to formulate a formidable array of impressive theoretical systems to explain social processes and organizations. But grounded theory is based on the findings of empirical research and in the words of Glaser and Strauss, 'generating grounded theory is a way of arriving at theory, suited to its supposed uses. We shall contrast this position with theory generated by logical deduction from *a priori* assumptions.'[23] A speculative theory corresponds to a conceptual ordering whereas grounded theory corresponds to an empirical generalization. The former generates a host of assumptions, philosophical and methodological, as well as theoretical entities and conceptual schema; the latter produces specific sociological laws, principles and empirical generalizations. Speculative theories usually give rise to theoretical laws, and grounded theories to empirical laws. Speculative theories usually rely on historical method whereas grounded theories make use of positive methods and mathematical procedures.

Grand Theory vs. Miniature Theory

A grand theory is a broad conceptual scheme with systems of interrelated propositions that provide a general frame of reference for the study of social processes and institutions. It differs from the speculative theory only in that its propositions are somewhat anchored—although not solidly—in the empirical world, whereas the propositions emanating from the speculative theories are essentially assumptions rooted in the philosophical system. The difference is only a matter of degree, not of kind. A grand theory is a comprehensive formulation generating a host of propositions and provides a master scheme of general sociological orientations. Grand theories abound in jargon, tendency-statements and intuitive generalizations. Parson's general system theory and Sorokin's theory of socio-cultural dynamics are examples of grand theories.

Miniature theories are partial theories, rather than inclusive theories. They are what Merton calls 'theories of the middle range: theories intermediate to the minor working hypotheses evolved in abundance during the day-to-day routines of research, and the all-inclusive speculations comprising a master conceptual scheme from which it is hoped to derive a very large number of empirically observed uniformities of social behavior.'[24] They are more specific and their frame of reference is considerably limited; they generate a manageable number of propositions concerning specific units within society. They are less pretentious than the high-sounding all-inclusive grand theories. Merton's theory of anomie, Homans's theory of elementary social behaviour, Pareto's theory of the circulation of the elites and Festinger's theory of cognitive dissonance are examples of theories of the middle range.

Macro vs. Micro Theories

On the basis of the radius of their explanatory shell, theories may be classified as macro or micro or molar and molecular theories. Macro theories are broader in scope and encompass an extended range of laws. Micro theories have a narrow frame of reference and focus on a limited range of phenomena. The early masters of social thought were almost exclusively concerned with grand, cosmic issues or total societal patterns. Theories of society, culture and institutions constitute the tradition of macro-sociology and Emile Durkheim is its major exponent. Micro-sociology is concerned with 'interactions among the atoms of society' and German nominalists like Weber and Simmel are its principal architects. Psychological reductionism, role theory and small group theories represent the micro tradition in contemporary sociology. The distinction between the two types of theories is based on the size of the unit of analysis rather than the level of analysis. Macro theorists, for example, study the factory as a social system; micro theories, on the other hand, seek to analyse workers' behaviour within the industrial establishment. The former delineate the social structure; the latter explain social roles and individual behaviour that mediates the structure. Macro theories deal with society as a whole; micro theories deal with the subsystems that make up the whole. Parsons's general systems theory is of the molar type whereas Homans's exchange theory is of the molecular type. Macro theories are a species of grand theories and can be verified only in a preliminary fashion. Micro theories belong to the tribe of the miniature theories and can be 'tested' in the 'scientific' sense. This is why many scientists claim that micro theories are intrinsically more satisfactory and fruitful in the pursuit of scientific inquiry. According to them, 'It is often felt that only the discovery of a micro-theory affords real scientific understanding of any type of phenomenon, because only it gives us insight into the inner mechanisms of the phenomenon, so to speak. Consequently, classes of events for which no micro theory was available have frequently been viewed as not actually understood.'[25] However, this position is entirely untenable in the social sciences. Money cannot be reduced to coin; nor can social phenomena be reduced to individual phenomena. Society is more than an aggregate of individuals because of the qualitative jump involved in the transformation of the unit into the system. There are many sociological phenomena for which molecular theories cannot provide any satisfactory explanation because of the multiplicity of the variables included and the complexity of their interrelationships. Hence, we choose between types of theories depending on the social phenomena and the range of variables involved.

Functions of Theories

Morris Cohen's perceptive statement epitomizes the importance of theory: 'Purely theoretical contributions to astronomy and mathematics, by increasing the precision of navigation, saved more lives at sea than any possible improvements in the carpentry of lifeboats.'[26]

The major functions of sociological theory may be summarized as follows:

1. Theory suggests potential problems and produces new investigative studies. A fruitful theory is a storehouse of meaningful hypotheses and a continuous source of inspiration to the process of sociological inquiry. And many empirical investigations lead to theory-building just as they proceed from well-formulated theories.

2. Theory predicts facts. Based on intuitive knowledge, historical analysis and observation of social uniformities, a theoretical system often provides a secure ground for prediction. Usually expressed as tendency-statements, such theoretical postulates increase the fruitfulness of research by providing leads for further inquiry.

3. Theory systematizes matters and their relationships into convenient conceptual schema. Not only does it explain observed regularities and social uniformities, it also simplifies laws and establishes order in congeries of facts. A 'mental shorthand' so to speak, theory summarizes relationships between variables in a conceptual framework.

4. Theory establishes a linkage between specific empirical findings and general sociological orientations, thus enhancing the meaningfulness of research. Unrelated findings of isolated studies suddenly assume new meanings when they are put in the proper sociological perspective. Theory mediates between specific empirical generalizations and broad sociological orientations rooted in the intellectual tradition.

5. In providing meaning, the theory also attests to truth. A hypothesis may be as much confirmed by fitting it into a theory as by fitting it into the facts. For it then enjoys the support provided by the evidence for all the other hypotheses of that theory. Just as a law is not only confirmed by the factual data but also helps give the data factual status, so a theory is not only supported by established laws but also plays a part in establishing them..[27]

6. Theory guides research and narrows down the range of facts to be studied. Theory supplies hypotheses, povides direction to the investigation and helps the researcher look for certain variables and overlook others. Oppenheimer puts it succinctly: 'In order for us to understand anything, we have to fail to perceive a great deal that is there. Knowledge is always purchased at the expense of what might have been seen and learned and was not. . . . It is a condition of knowledge that somehow or the other we pick the clues which give us insight into what we are to find out about the world.'[28]

7. Theories serve as tools of inquiry. They aid in the formulation of a research design, in conducting experiments, making measurements and quantifying data. This function corresponds to the instrumentalist view of theories.

8. Theory points to gaps in our knowledge and seeks to fill them with intuitive, impressionistic or 'extensional generalizations.' 'What is important is that laws propagate when they are united in a theory: theory serves as matchmaker, midwife and godfather all in one. This service is what is delicately known as the "heuristic function of theory." '[29]

Theories and Models

It is unfortunate that in much of the current sociological literature theories and models are used interchangeably. However, there are significant differences between them. Theories are substantive, symbolic, speculative, imaginative, impressionistic and intrinsically beautiful; they represent a jump beyond evidence, are the product of creative achievement and could have their moorings entirely in the humanistic tradition. A model is a formal theory, a product of logical derivation and abstract formulations; it is concerned with form rather than substance. 'Whereas the rules of deduction create the logical form, the substance of an explanation has to do with the extralogical terms in the constituent statements.'[30] Model building involves rigorous logico-deductive schemes and excludes argumentation. Moreover, models are isomorphs of one another. As Brodbeck points out, 'Two theories whose laws have the same form are isomorphic or *structurally similar* to each other. If the laws of one theory have the same form as the laws of another theory, then one may be said to be a *model* for the other.'[31] And Kaplan seeks to distinguish:

five different senses in the confusing and often confused usage of the term 'model': (1) any theory more strictly formulated than is characteristic of the literary, academic, or heuristic cognitive styles, one presented with some degree of mathematical exactness, and logical rigour; (2) a semantical model, presenting a conceptual analogue to some subject-matter; (3) a physical model, a nonlinguistic system analogous to some other being studied; (4) a formal model, a model *of* a theory which presents the latter purely as a structure of uninterpreted symbols; (5) an interpretive model, providing an interpretation *for* a formal theory.[32]

From the maze of terminological confusion, we may single out two different types of models commonly used in sociology: substantive models and statistical or physical science models.

Substantive Models: This is indeed a contradiction in terms. How could a model, devoid of any argumentation, be substantive? Yet several sociologists have equated some of the discipline's most substantive theories with models. Inkeles, for example, has classed evolutionary theories, structural-functionalism, and conflict theories as models. He uses the term 'model' to refer to a rather general image of the main outline of some major phenomenon, including certain leading ideas about the nature of the units involved and the pattern of their relations. A theory we take to be a heuristic device for organizing what we know, or think we know, at any particular time about some more or less explicitly posed question or issue. A theory would, therefore, be more limited and precise than a model. A theory can ordinarily be proved wrong. In the case of the model, it can usually only be judged incomplete, misleading or unproductive.[33] Thus, according to Inkeles, a model is greater in scope and range than a theory and it may indeed encompass a host of theories. These statements are certainly misleading for they confuse models with grand theories. To confuse general sociological orientations with models could lead to serious errors of judgement. Theoretical perspectives are frames of reference, not statistical systems. Argumentation constitutes the very essence of grand theories which are essentially substantive, whereas models which are purely mathematical formulations exclude any argumentation. However, many theories of the middle range lend themselves to model-building. Theories such as the theory of relative deprivation, exchange theory, norm of reciprocity and coalition theory could be expressed in rigorous models although such expressions may not necessarily enhance the value of these theories. In short, substantive models consist of postulates, propositions, principles and axioms derived from more substantive theories transformed into more abstract mathematical formulations. These models borrow their propositions from substantive theories and subject them to rigorous logico-deductive formalizations.

Physical Science or Statistical Models

Whereas substantive models start with the propositions of established miniature theories, statistical models start with empirical findings. An observed—or observable—relationship between variables or a newly ascertained social uniformity is taken to correspond to a pattern in the physical or mathematical sciences. The correspondence is quickly noted and immediately translated into the appropriate formulation. Lundberg, Dodd and others have insisted that all social phenomena can and must be explained in terms of the laws from the physical sciences. The movements of a man fleeing from a mob can be explained by the same laws in physics which explain the flight of a piece of paper before the wind, they contend. Other sociologists use a mathematical model or a statistical technique to explain a relationship or social pattern they have discovered. The theory of probability and set theory are often used to describe many aspects of the social world. The assumption, of course, is that all social phenomena can be quantified and subjected to precise measurement. Neither the great speculative postulates rooted in the humanistic tradition nor the contemporary theoretical perspectives on the nature of social institutions and processes would support this assumption.

Even if we can give meaningful content to the concepts drawn from physics, there is no reason to assume that the relations between the analogous elements in the social world will be the same as in the physical world. Indeed, there is every reason to doubt that they will. Therefore, no particular benefit is gained by the laborious process of translating sociological problems into the language of physics and chemistry.[34]

The social world and human behaviour within it are so complex that any simplistic model can only distort reality. This is not to argue that model-building or measurement has no place in sociology. The point is that the contention that every social phenomenon must be quantified is neither acceptable nor desirable. And the contribution of statistical models to the development of the discipline in general, and to the growth of the sociological imagination in particular, has been negligible to date.

James Beshers identifies two contrasting approaches to theory construction in the behavioural sciences: the 'simplicity' criterion approach and the interdependence postulate approach. They correspond roughly to the physical science or statistical models and substantive models described above. Research-oriented social scientists who consider theory to be a system of empirically verifiable propositions prefer the simplicity approach. 'The interdependence postulate approach places the processes of model-building and measurement in the central position in theory construction. Interdependence adherents argue that the true relationships may be determined by measurement, and that these relationships constitute parts of models that must be included in all theories dealing with these data.'[35] The models as well as their methodologies are quite different in these two approaches to theory construction. The simplicity criterion approach, commonly employed by small group theorists, consists of measurements on a set of discrete elements such as unit acts or traits and their summation in the final analysis. The interdependence approach, characteristic of systems' theorists, is essentially holistic, consisting of 'measurement in reference to inferred properties of organization or complex relationships.'

Studies in micro-sociology are more amenable to model-building; the interdependence approach is at once the most efficient and often indispensable when the data demand holistic analysis. Hence, both approaches are valid, and the choice of one over the other depends on the nature of sociological data.

In summary, a model is a formalized theory expressed either in a mathematical formula or a physical science analogue. It essentially involves quantification and measurement and is hence testable or verifiable in the fashion of the more exact natural sciences. Therefore, it claims greater predictive power and validity than substantive theories which are more argumentative.

The Myth of True Theory

In the behavioural sciences, the quest for a true theory could be a futile intellectual exercise; every theory holds some pieces to the picture puzzle of the social world. A complete picture of social phenomena emerges only through the integration of a variety of social theories. Quine has put it very effectively: 'Knowledge normally develops in a multiplicity of theories, each with its limited utility .... These theories overlap very considerably, in their so-called logical laws and in much else, but that they add up to an integrated and consistent whole is only a worthy ideal and happily not a prerequisite of scientific progress.'[36]

No theory is absolutely true, for there is *no absolute truth in the first place.* And no theory is a final formulation because new knowledge is pouring in all the time which modifies or even repudiates existing theories. Even the theories that remain downright repudiated today had their days of glory. Unilinear evolutionary theory is a case in point. Ever since Comte expounded the theory, generations of early sociologists—and, to some extent, contemporary experts in modernization—have used it to describe the dynamics of evolution and progress in total societies.

A theory is not judged productive or otherwise solely in terms of the answers it gives; equally, indeed, the value of a theory lies in the number of questions raised. A productive theory must suggest potential problems, generate fruitful hypotheses, provide new perspectives and guide sociological inquiry. In this sense, theories may very well be ends in themselves, just as they may be means to other ends.

Theoretical bias is one of the common ailments afflicting social scientists. This borders on scientific ideology of some sort, either a fixed point of view or a rigid frame of reference. Theoretical bias creeps in when sociologists grow too fond of a particular theory and become identified with it so deeply as to preclude considerations of

other factors and perspectives. This colours their vision of the
social world and they develop resistance to new ideas or theories.
Not infrequently, some of the greatest sociologists of today have
displayed their bias in the analysis of social processes and systems.
Selective perception, however, is inevitable and useful. All theories
are not applicable to all situations at all times. Sociologists must
choose between—sometimes conflicting—theories depending on the
themes and contexts of their inquiry. The danger lies not in selective perception which is essential, but in sociologists' tendency
'toward dogged intellectual loyalties, favouring one or another
approach to the exclusion of all others.'[37]

Sociologists can—and must—learn to live with diversity. It is not
the existence of diverse theories but their abuses that must concern
us. The weakness of the discipline lies not in the multiplicity of
theories, but rather, in the sociologists' eagerness to be defensive
about them, for it betrays their pious hope for a true theory
some day. Knowledge about social universe grows in myriad ways.
A product of creative achievement and intellectual sophistication,
sociological theories must reflect the thought processes of the
imaginative mind.

NOTES

1. Calvin Larson, *Major Themes in Sociological Theory* (New York, David McKay Company, 1973), p. 4.
2. Abraham Kaplan, *The Conduct of Inquiry* (SanFrancisco, Chandler Publishing Company, 1964), p. 295.
3. Larson, op. cit., p. 5, adapted and expanded.
4. Clement S. Mihanovich *et al.*, *Glossary of Sociological Terms* (Milwaukee, Bruce Publishing Co., 1957), p. 24.
5. Jack Gibbs, *Sociological Theory Construction* (Hinsdale, The Dryden Press, 1972), p. 4.
6. Robert K. Merton, *Social Theory and Social Structure* (Glencoe, Free Press, 1957), p. 86.
7. Talcott Parsons, *Essays in Sociological Theory* (Glencoe, Free Press, 1954), pp. 212–13.
8. Merton, op. cit., p. 39.
9. George C. Homans, 'Contemporary Theory in Sociology', pp. 951–77 in R. E. L. Faris (ed.), *Handbook of Modern Sociology* (Chicago, Rand McNally & Co., 1964), pp. 951–2.
10. Thomas J. Ward, 'Definitions of Theory in Sociology', in R. Serge Denisoff *et al.* (eds.), *Theories and Paradigms in Contemporary Sociology* (Ithaca, F. E. Peacock Publishers, 1974), p. 39.

11. Hans L. Zetterberg, *On Theory and Verification in Sociology* (New York, The Bedminster Press, 1965), see chapters 1 and 2.
12. Kaplan, op. cit., p. 294.
13. Ward, op. cit., p. 28.
14. Nicholas S. Timasheff and George A. Theodorson, *Sociological Theory* (New York, Random House, 1976), fourth edition, p. 10.
15. Kaplan, op. cit., p. 897.
16. Timasheff, op. cit., p. 10.
17. Theodore Abel, *The Foundation of Sociological Theory* (New York, Random House, 1970), p. 8.
18. Alvin Boskoff, 'From Social Thought to Sociological Theory', in Howard Becker and Alvin Boskoff (eds.), *Modern Sociological Theory* (New York, Holt, Rinehart and Winston, 1957), p. 6.
19. ibid., p. 6.
20. Homans, op. cit., p. 960.
21. ibid., p. 961.
22. Helmut R. Wagner, *Types of Sociological Theory*, in Denisoff *et al.*, p. 42.
23. Larson, op. cit., p. 2.
24. Merton, op. cit., pp. 5–6.
25. Quoted by Kaplan, op cit., p. 300.
26. Morris Cohen, *Reason and Nature: An Essay on the Meaning of Scientific Method* (New York, Macmillan, 1931).
27. Kaplan, op. cit., p. 302.
28. Robert Oppenheimer, 'Tradition and Discovery', *ACLS Newsletter* (October, 1959), p. 7.
29. Kaplan, op. cit., p. 303.
30. Gibbs, op. cit., p. 30.
31. See Llewellyn Gross (ed.), *Symposium on Sociological Theory* (New York, Harper and Row, 1959), p. 379.
32. Kaplan, op. cit., pp. 267–8.
33. Alex Inkeles, *What is Sociology?* (Englewood Cliffs, Prentice-Hall, Inc., 1964), p. 28.
34. ibid., p. 40.
35. James M. Beshers, 'Models and Theory Construction', *American Sociological Review*, 22 (February, 1957), pp. 32–8. Also reprinted in Milton L. Barron (ed.), *Contemporary Sociology* (New York, Dodd, Mead and Company, 1972), p. 595.
36. Quoted in Kaplan, op. cit. pp. 309–10.
37. Inkeles, op. cit., p. 45.

CHAPTER 2

Theory and Sociological Inquiry

Conflict between Theory-building and Empiricism

The interplay between theory and research is taken for granted in most scientific enterprises. Ideally, the relationship may be summarized as follows: Theory suggests potential problems for empirical inquiry; empirical findings are then incorporated into the theoretical system; the theory itself stands validated, revised or rejected according to the findings uncovered by research; and theory establishes a meaningful relationship between discrete facts and suggests new hypotheses for further inquiry.

However, sociology has never approached this ideal situation. The rift between empiricists and theorists is as old as the discipline itself. When, in the mid-nineteenth century, the great encylopedic minds of Comte and Spencer developed grand conceptual schemes on social organization and institutions, there was already a growing opposition to speculative social theories devoid of empirical reference. As early as 1838, the first issue of the *Journal of the Empirical Society of London* lamented 'a growing distrust of mere hypothetical theory and *a priori* assumption, and the appearance of a general conviction that, in the business of social science, principles are valid for application only inasmuch as they are legitimate induction from facts, accurately observed and methodically classified.'[1]

The conflict between theorists and researchers or, in the words of Weber, 'interpretive specialists' and 'subject matter specialists' has persisted to the present day prompting C. Wright Mills to dub the two types in the 'derogatory' terms of 'grand theory' and 'abstracted empiricism'. It is true that sociological theory is to a great extent developed independently of any body of continuing research and, similarly, empirical research has seldom concerned itself with theoretical interests. The result is a deep hiatus between empirically minded 'workers' and theoretically oriented 'scholars'. What is worse is the erroneous assumption that 'figure of speech' and 'fact gathering' are two mutually exclusive realms and that theorists and researchers owe their allegiance to only one of the two schools. A division of labour between men who are primarily concerned with the analytical theories of society and those who are primarily interested in ascertaining social facts in the empirical realm is understandable—and essential. What is disquieting is the mutual distrust and animosity between the two. The empiricists have seldom attempted to contribute to theory and are often antitheoretical. 'They consider any work in theoretical fields as positively pernicious and contrary to the canons of science. It is speculation, sterile dialectic, metaphysics or even mysticism.'[2] The theorists, on the other hand, have shown little concern for empirical work but betray 'a sovereign disdain for the arduous difficulties of the empirical fields.'

What accounts for the persistent conflict between theory and empiricism? In the first place, sociology is an outgrowth of social philosophy. Early masters of social thought were speculative philosophers who never bothered to establish any empirical base for great conceptual schemes they expounded. The philosophical and humanistic orientation still persists in sociology with a characteristic disdain for empirical work.

Secondly, sociological theories seem to be divided into mutually exclusive and antagonistic schools. If there is no agreement on 'relevant' theories, how could the researchers be expected to be guided by them, ask the empiricists. George Homans even claims that sociology has no good 'theory that will explain and predict a number of known facts'.[3] Hyman, however, does not see any reason to be discouraged by the presence of conflicting theories. He argues that the competition between rival systems of theory for the allegiance of research workers is a good safeguard against the danger that it will all turn out negatively. Moreover, such a competition is likely to encourage the researchers to test one system vs. the other and in that process refine the testing procedure itself.

A third source of conflict is the empiricists' overemphasis on measurement—the assumption that anything can and must be quantified, or else it is devoid of any scientific value. They point to the extreme importance of measurement in physics and contend that sociology can claim the status of a science only by developing precise instruments of measurement. This line of argument is unacceptable to theorists who claim that in the realm of human social interaction, everything that counts cannot be counted, and everything that is counted does not count. As Parsons points out, 'numerical data are far less scientifically important until they can be so fitted into analytical categories. I venture to say that this is true of the vast majority of such data in the social fields.'[4] He also contends that 'measurement as such is not logically essential to science.' According to him, measurement is only a special case of a broader category, classification, which may be arrived at by the logical structure of an analytical scheme by establishing the determinate relationship between the variables; the classification arrived at by measurement could be all too simplistic and incapable of explaining the complex values of variables and their relationships.

Fourth, empiricists are often disillusioned by the plethora of broad theoretical orientations which appear in the guise of sociological theories. Some of the propositions derived from deterministic theories (e.g., social organization is determined by technological factors) or evolutionary theories are so vague and general that no amount of human ingenuity can 'test' them in any systematic manner. The undue emphasis on such broad generalizations has been responsible for at least part of the controversy between theorists and researchers.

Fifth, Parsons points out that empiricists find it hard to accept the particular brands of theory proposed by contemporary sociologists, for many of their features inhibit the potential usefulness of theory for empirical research. Here the question is not whether the theory is 'relevant' or generally agreed upon; rather the archaic form and the clumsy theoretical scheme often discourage attempts at empirical verification.

Finally, theorists have been disenchanted by the 'marked discontinuities of empirical research' and the abundance of facts, discrete empirical generalizations and *post factum* interpretations. Merton, for instance, decries the 'marked dispersion of empirical inquiries, oriented toward a concrete field of human behaviour, but lacking a central theoretic orientation.'[5] Facts are amassed and 'suitable' explanations provided but meaningful relationships between complex variables are seldom established.

The afore-mentioned controversy is reflected in the writings of a number of scholars. Let us look at some of their arguments more closely.

Hyman feels that things conspire to make systematic methods

appealing and useful to the research worker while they conspire against the utilization of systematic theory. He lists a number of factors that facilitate the application of systematic methods to research. In addition to gains in validity, reliability, precision, and the like, a good method is efficient; it is appealing to the investigators and fits in the rhythm of their work. Also, there are a number of research organizations and institutes which train the individuals in the routines and skills of particular methods. A social scientist interested in a particular method can simply buy it, and there are several 'how-to-do-it' manuals. But there are no institutes that train scholars in theorizing or books that tell them how to theorize on a specific problem.

Blumer's essay on variable analysis, or, 'the scheme of sociological analysis which seeks to reduce human group life to variables and their relations',[6] is pertinent here. The thrust of his argument is that contemporary sociological analysis is primarily an analysis of discrete variables with little substantive theoretical orientation. Blumer enumerates the limitations of variable analysis as follows:

1. The 'chaotic condition that prevails in the selection of variables' indicates that just about anything may be selected as a variable, however specific, general or vague.

2. There are no proper guidelines or theoretical considerations for the selection of variables which may be prompted by 'some specious impression of what is important' or 'an imaginative ingenuity'.

3. There is a 'disconcerting absence of generic variables, that is, variables that stand for abstract categories', and 'without generic variables, variables yield only separate and disconnected findings'.

4. The assumption that in actual social life 'the independent variable automatically exercises its influences on the dependent variable is a basic fallacy'.

5. Variable analysis is concerned with two or more variables and cannot deal with what lies between them.

6. Variable analysis is characterized by striking indifference to the process of interpretation. Blumer deplores 'the inevitable tendency to work with truncated factors and, as a result, to conceal or misrepresent the actual operations in human group life.' Interpretation in theoretical terms is essential to give meaning and 'qualitative constancy' to research.

Robert Bierstedt has mentioned five undesirable consequences of 'blinded empiricism' in sociology:

(1) It places an inappropriate emphasis upon, what T. H. Marshall calls 'an aimless assembly of facts'; (2) it determines the kinds of research that are pursued and particularly exaggerates the scientific, as separate from the practical, importance of community studies; (3) it illogically reverses the roles of theory and research in sociology, and (4) it places an undue burden upon the writers of textbooks; and (5) it makes of sociology a disorderly science in which principles, generalizations, and laws are distinguished by their scarcity.[7]

C. Wright Mills deplores the ahistorical bias among empiricists, that is, their tendency to deal mainly with contemporaneous events for which they are likely to get the kind of data they need. And John McKinney has outlined five limiting consequences of empiricism:

First, it has contributed to a specific form of methodological naivete. Although empiricism has eliminated some surface forms of subjectivity, it certainly has not eliminated certain more subtle and tenacious forms. . . . Second, a great many recent sociological investigations have closely resembled mere collections of facts and hence have not even approximated the scientific model ostensibly subscribed to by the empiricists. . . . Third, the roles of theory and research have been reversed in empirical method as compared to standard scientific practice. Instead of evaluating research in terms of its contribution to theory, empiricists tend to evaluate theory solely in terms of its current utility in research. . . . Fourth, radical empiricism has led to random, helter-skelter, petty, uncodified research. Moreover, its adherents have emphasized immediate rather than long-range accomplishments because they distrust theory as a guideline. This concern for immediacy seems inevitably to produce the 'practical' and undoubtedly leads away from basic research. . . . Fifth, the deemphasizing of systematic theory for the sake of empirical 'free enterprise' has increased the difficulty of extracting sociological principles and generalizations from the mass of ideographic facts.'[8]

McKinney goes on to argue that resistance to radical empiricism has developed mainly along three lines. The first was the growing emphasis on *system*. The structural-functional approach and systematic sociology relegated empiricism to the background and pushed the concept of system and analytical schema to the forefront. Secondly, the 'continued emphasis on conceptual apparatus in the form of constructed types, mathematical models, and conceptual schemes, began to stress the indispensability of theory in any scientific enterprise.' Thirdly, 'emphasis was placed on research design within the *logic* of the experimental method.' Although an aspect of empirical science, experimental method with its emphasis on logic and rationality has led to significant modification of extreme empiricism.

The Role of Theory in Social Research

Robert Merton's perceptive analysis of the interrelationship between theory and research has helped to clarify a number of misconceptions. He has indicated five ways in which theory influences research.

1. It provides general orientations. Theory suggests potential problems and fruitful hypotheses; it points to the variables that are relevant and important and indicates the dimensions of key variables. Theory helps in the selection of cases, facts, and data. We never investigate 'all of the facts' relative to the phenomena in question but only those which we think are 'important'. This selection among the wide range of possible facts is guided by some prior notions or theories about the nature of the phenomena being studied. Admit it or not, every researcher who makes the crucial selection of cases or variables is invariably guided by their relevance to the logical structure of a theoretical scheme. Parsons asserts that:

the alternative for the scientist in the social or any other field is not as between theorizing and not theorizing, but as between theorizing explicitly with a clear consciousness of what he is doing with the greater opportunity that gives of avoiding the many subtle pitfalls of fallacy, and following the policy of the ostrich, pretending not to theorize and thus leaving one's theory implicit and uncriticized, thus almost certainly full of errors.[9]

However, this position is not accepted by all. Homans, for instance, considers the claim that theory ought to guide research 'presumptuous', for, according to him, sociology does not have a 'good' theory. It is easy, he contends, to suggest that researchers should investigate the effects of 'theoretically relevant variables' but the question is 'relevant to what theory?' Homans argues:

There are few cases in sociology in which a developed deductive system has actually guided research. The reason is that there are few such deductive systems and still fewer among 'general' theories. Let the sociologist feel guilty about that if he likes, but not about the fact of theoretical guidance. It makes sense to have theory guide research only if there is some reason for having confidence in the theory, and the theorist's own assertion is not sufficient reason. In the absence of such confidence, the researcher should feel free to do anything he pleases, so long as he studies men. Indeed, he could do worse than indulge in mere data collection.[10]

Homans's is an extreme position. The assertion that there are no sociological theories that could effectively guide empirical research is highly debatable. Of course, theorists are divided. But to be able to guide research theories need not command general agreement. Conflicting theories could generate contradictory hypotheses and propositions and it is the responsibility of the empiricists to test their validity. The researcher who is guided by a particular theoretical scheme may first find that his propositions derived from the theory are discredited by the array of facts. There is nothing to prevent him from repeating the crucial experiment with the proposition from an opposing theoretical system. Theoretical consideration also enables the researcher to narrow the range of inquiry by pinpointing potentially significant and relevant variables, thereby saving time, money and other resources. The researcher need not be discouraged by the multiplicity of theories which provided different perspectives; he should, rather, abandon the demand for a true theory, for if we already have a number of sociological theories that can explain and predict all the known facts, then the scope of empirical research is very much limited. What is the need for elaborate research if the existing theories can explain and predict all significant social phenomena? The reciprocal relationship between theory and research may be summarized thus: theory guides research, research goads theory.

Of course there are merits in Homans's argument that 'the researcher should feel free not to accept theoretical guidance'. Even if the researcher allows himself to be guided by false or inadequate theories, his work may not necessarily suffer; indeed, he may benefit from it. Homans contends that good theories do not necessarily lead to good researches. However, it cannot be denied that theoretical guidance reduces the chance that the researcher will be groping in the dark and that it increases manifold the fruitfulness of research.

2. Developing sociological concepts. Concepts are essential ingredients of theory; they specify the form and content of the variables. Researchers translate labels into appropriate indices. For example, Durkheim defined different types of social integration conceptually but it is left to the empiricists to construct different

indices to measure it. Similarly, Parsons's pattern variables have been effectively utilized in the empirical analysis of the process of modernization. In short, theories provide interpretive definitions of concepts, while empiricism provides operational definitions of concepts.

3. Furnishes *post factum* sociological interpretations. The data are first collected and then subjected to interpretive analysis. This process seeks to explain discovery, rather than test a predesignated hypothesis. The trouble with this method is that explanations are always consistent with the particular set of observations; if they cannot be explained for some reason, the surprising finding is explained away by shifting the blame on to a research tool or technique, sample error or a bad definition of concepts. In any case, *post factum* explanations cannot furnish any compelling evidence, they remain at the level of *plausibility* because of the 'failure to provide distinctive tests of the interpretations apart from their consistency with the initial observations. The analysis is fitted to the facts, and there is no indication of just which data would be taken to contravene the interpretations. As a consequence, the documentary evidence merely illustrates rather than tests the theory.[11]

Curiously this is the function of theory that Homans applauds most: *codification*, or the 'strategy by which deductive systems are inductively arrived at'. This, to him, illustrates the role of theory in organizing and systematizing empirical findings. The process begins with a number of empirical generalizations; then we proceed to reduce their number by the process of elimination, definition, comparison to other similar propositions, by crucial observation to see if they could be derived from a higher level of generality and by inventing higher order propositions if necessary. However, an ardent advocate of psychological reductionism in sociology, Homans feels sociologists do not have to invent such higher order propositions since they are already invented for them in behavioural psychology. The whole process of codification, according to him, centres around *ex-post facto* explanation. He hastens to add that there is nothing 'illegitimate' about *ex-post facto* explanations. 'All science begins with *ex-post facto* explanations and without them could not get off the ground.'[12]

4. Formulates empirical generalizations. A major function of social theory in empirical research is to summarize observed uniformities of relationship between variables and to synthesize them

with reference to existing conceptual schemes. It is not enough to state isolated propositions dealing with relationships between discrete facts: there must be an interpretive synthesis which seeks to compare the new findings with prevailing theories in order to understand their larger significance. Alfred Marshall put it succinctly: 'The most reckless and treacherous of all theorists is he who professes to let the facts and figures speak for themselves.'[13] Whatever procedures are used, the research process itself will prove fruitful only if it interprets the empirical data by incorporating them into the more general principles and theories of the conceptual scheme. Testing a specific hypothesis is only one of the initial steps in the research process; the central aim of any research enterprise ought to be to test the *ideas* with which the research began—to elaborate, specify, modify, confirm or abandon the conceptual model that inspired the empirical work.

In a similar vein, Parsons argues that no scientifically oriented empiricist is 'content to state bald, discrete facts'; he seeks to bring forth causal relations. His illustration:

It is stated not merely that the steam railroad was developed and certain kinds of industrial developments took place, but that without the invention of the railroad these developments *could not* have taken place—that the invention of the railroad was a *causal factor* in industrial development. Now I wish to assert that such an imputation of causal relationship cannot be proved without reference to generalized theoretical categories. If it is asserted, the assertion is logically dependent on these categories whether they are explicit or implicit.[14]

5. Further development of sociological theory. Theory prods research, and empirical findings, in turn, elaborate theory. A seemingly isolated uniformity points up to a meaningful relationship between apparently discrete variables. This leads to a modification of original conceptual framework to make allowance for new relations and patterns. The formulation and testing of new hypotheses leads to cumulation of both theory and research as well as 'increases the fruitfulness of research through the successive exploration of implications.' Merton claims: 'By providing a rationale, the theory introduces a ground for prediction which is more secure than mere empirical extrapolation from previously observed trends . . . . The atheoretic empiricist would have no alternative, however, but to predict on the basis of extrapolation.'[15]

Above all, the performance of the aforesaid function makes

theory more *precise* and *determinate*, improves *testability*, supplies a measure of confirmation, and 'enhances the likelihood of approximating a "crucial" observation of experiment.' Successive exploration of new leads in empirical inquiry and resultant modification of initial theories, as well as 'formalized derivation' and 'codification' make empirical studies more theory-oriented and substantive theories more empirically sound.

Nevertheless, there is not always the need for such an established order as theory before research. The researcher who begins with a theory or a set of propositions derived from a theory usually works from model to data; he gathers data in order to test a hypothesis or validate a theory. But the researcher may also work from data to model. In this case, the researcher may start with an observed regularity (for example, consistently higher rates of suicide in a given social group), collect data from different social contexts, examine relationships between different variables and arrive at certain generalizations or 'higher order propositions' or even a general theory.

Parsons believes that all the controversy about the role of theory in social research stems from the sociologists' failure to recognize the great potential of the new brand of analytical theory (probably his own): 'a body of logically inter-related generalized concepts (logical universals) the specific facts corresponding to which (particulars) constitute statements describing empirical phenomena.' It is no longer possible to contend, as Homans does, that sociology does not have a sound theory to guide research effectively. The analytical theory, which is highly abstract, is capable of guiding research by establishing logical relationships between interdependent systems. Parsons summarized the principal functions of analytical theory for research as follows:

- In the vast welter of miscellaneous facts we face it provides us with selective criteria as to which are important and which can safely be neglected.
- It provides a basis for coherent organization of the factual material thus selected without which a study is unintelligible.
- It provides a basis not only of selection and organization of known facts, but in a way which cannot be done otherwise reveals the *gaps* in our existing knowledge and their importance. It thus constitutes a crucially important guide to the direction of fruitful research.

Through the mutual logical implications of different analytical systems for each other it provides a source of cross fertilization of related fields of the utmost importance. This often leads to very important developments within a field which would not have taken place had it remained theoretically isolated.[16]

The Consequences of Research for Theory

So far we have dealt primarily with the role of theory in social research. Let us now turn to the consequences of research for theory. The principles of methodology are not peculiar to sociology. They are common to all scientific enterprises, and indeed, they transcend any body of substantive theory. 'In short, methodology essentially answers the question of "how"; substantive theory answers the question of "what".'[17] But from its very inception, sociology has been dominated by a large bulk of general theoretical orientations and conceptual analyses without any empirical reference. Later revolt against systematic and speculative theorizing unsustained by empirical test led to a marked interest in research as well as the development of methodology. And John McKinney has summarized the consequences of empiricism as follows:

First, the refreshing contrast of empirical research with the apriorism of the classical writers discredited the completely speculative approach. Second, empiricism established the necessity of controlled observation and research design as components of scientific investigation. Third, the necessity of keeping theory in touch with evidence and relating it to the bedrock of accumulative fact is basically an empirical contribution. Fourth, empiricism made an outstanding contribution to the procedural rules of research. It is the empirically oriented who to a great extent have codified the research rules and practices. Fifth, the empiricists have accomplished an enormous amount of investigation, much of it trivial but most of it arduous.'

Robert Merton has made a seminal contribution to the understanding of the consequences of research for social theory. He has summarized the 'bearing of empirical research on sociological theory' as follows:

1. The serendipity pattern, that is, the unanticipated, anomalous and strategic datum exerts pressure for initiating theory. Surprising or unexpected facts or even those considered inconsistent with prevailing theory become meaningful in the process of empirical inquiry and lead to fresh hypotheses unanticipated at the time of formulating the research design. Successive exploration of new leads may

prompt development of a new theory or extension of existing theories. For example, note how the theory of relative deprivation and reference group theory emerged from anomalies in detailed quantitative findings or in the course of puzzling over paradoxical findings. Hyman lays great stress on serendipity patterns and even advocates 'a programme of training for serendipity' which he believes will enable the research worker to experience serendipity with greater frequency and stimulate him to new and better theorizing.

2. The recasting of theory, that is, new data exert pressure for the elaboration of a conceptual scheme. Repeated observation of hitherto neglected facts and new variables so far considered irrelevant may prompt a re-evaluation of theory—and even a substantial revision. 'Whereas the serendipity pattern centres in an apparent inconsistency which presses for resolution, the reformulation pattern centres in the hitherto neglected but relevant fact which presses for an extension of the conceptual scheme'.[19]

3. The refocusing of theoretic interest, that is, new methods of empirical research exert pressure for new foci of theoretical interest. Empirical work invents new procedures and techniques which facilitate the collection of new and pertinent and previously unavailable facts, which may now stimulate fresh hypotheses. Also old theories should be put to test with the help of new techniques. Instead of indulging in speculative philosophy, theorists are now forced to focus attention on 'areas in which there is an abundance of pertinent statistical data'.

4. The classification of concepts, that is, empirical research exerts pressure for clear concepts. It is in an attempt to operationalize concepts, that researchers have developed indices of variables such as morale, social cohesion, etc.,—often defined loosely in the conceptual scheme—which, in turn, have led to greater conceptual clarity of key elements in the theoretical system. Research cannot proceed without first defining the concepts with sufficient clarity, however vague the concepts may be in the theoretical scheme, a process that enhances the fruitfulness of conceptual analysis.

Despite all these clarifications concerning the interplay between theory and research, controversy between 'collectionalists' and theorists has engaged the attention of a number of scholars. Clarence and Sylvia Sherwood have sought to arbitrate between raw empiricism and sociological theory and they have suggested the following ways in which a mutually rewarding association between the two schools may be established.[20]

1. A clear distinction must be made and maintained between empirical (descriptive) and theoretical (explanatory) constructs.
2. Relationships between variables (Blumer's variable analysis and Bierstedt's excessive empiricism) are the sociological *subject matter* which it is the objective of sociological theory to explain . . . .
3. Explanation is a function of the *implication-power* of a set of theoretical concepts and propositions, the extent to which the set implies two or more empirical relationship propositions . . . .
4. An acceptable theory in any set of concepts that explains—implies—two or more empirically verified (statistically probable) propositions which assert a relationship between two or more variables and do not simultaneously imply false (statistically improbable) propositions.
5. Implied empirical propositions concerning which there is no evidence one way or the other constitute an important testing ground for the theory, the set of concepts and propositions from which the empirical propositions are deducted . . . .
6. There is no natural order of research before theory or *vice-versa*. Every verified empirical proposition—relationship between variables—presents theory with an explanatory task. And, every theory must 'face the facts' of its own implications in that it must not imply a proposition that has been found to be false. Theory may suggest research in that it implies one or more propositions concerning which there is no existing evidence. Verified relationships may suggest new theories or modifications in old ones . . . .
7. Propositions are *legitimate hypotheses* for research only if they are theorems, that is, propositions which have been reduced from a set of theoretical propositions.

In recent years there have been strong pressures toward a convergence of theory and research. Increasingly sociologists have become aware of the futility of assigning exclusive domains for either theory or research. As Merton puts it:

The stereotype of the social theorist high in the empyrean of pure ideas uncontaminated by mundane facts is fast becoming no less outmoded than the stereotype of the social researcher equipped with the questionnaire and pencil and hot on the isolated and meaningless statistic. For in building the mansion of sociology during the last decades, theorist and empiricist have learned to work together. What is more, they have learned to talk to one another in the process. At times, this means only that a sociologist has learned to talk to himself since increasingly the same man has taken up both theory and research. Specialization and integration have developed hand in hand. All this has led not only to the realization that theory and empirical research *should* interact but to the result that they *do* interact[21].

Parsons and other analytical theorists feel compelled to demonstrate the validity of their theories. The advocates of raw empiricism are forced to develop a sociological orientation in the interpretative analysis of specific relations between discrete variables. Grand theories have left the high pedestal for empirical reference; abstracted empiricism has become infused with more substantive orientation.

And in his essay entitled 'The Quest for Universals in Sociological Research', Ralph Turner evaluates the limitations imposed on theory building by the exclusive reliance upon *either* analytic induction *or* enumerative induction. Analytic induction yields universally applicable generalizations but provides no basis for empirical prediction which 'always requires some statistical or probability statements, because there is some uncertainty or lack of uniformity in the *way* in which the intrusive factors will activate the causal system.'[22] Enumerative induction, on the other hand, is primarily concerned with the measurement of association between variables, and mere statements of correlations among variables provide an insufficient basis for theory. Turner concludes:

'Analytic induction fails to carry us beyond identifying a number of closed systems and enumerative induction fails to go beyond the measurement of associations. The functions of the two methods are not only distinct; they are complementary. When the two methods are used together *in the right combination*, they produce the type of findings which satisfies the canons of scientific method.'

Theory and research: the reciprocal relationship

The interplay between theory and research may be summarized as follows:

1. A theoretical system suggests a number of problems and hypotheses which need to be investigated. Substantive, speculative or intuitive conceptual schemes and analytical theories concerning social uniformities provide insights into the inner working of social mechanisms and patterned regularities in the social world. An empirically minted sociologist can contribute substantially to our knowledge of the social universe by investigating these leads. In the process of his inquiry, the researcher may uncover new, relevant variables and new relationships as well as pursue new leads.

2. Theoretical considerations enter into empirical inquiry at several points; they guide research, facilitate the selection of key variables and relevant cases and help delimit the scope of inquiry by pinpointing significant facts.

3. Empirical inquiry tests, validates or repudiates theories. Propositions derived from sociological theories are tested in different social contexts and their fruitfulness or otherwise ascertained. As Hyman puts it: 'Methodologists reduce the danger that theorists will waste their time building plausible theories out of fallacious findings or will reject a fine theory because of apparently contradictory, but fallacious, findings.'[23]

4. Research helps theory-building. Empirical findings may suggest new hypotheses and relationships as well as point to hitherto unknown uniformities, leading to the formation of brand new theories or the modification or elaboration of existing ones.

5. Empirical research develops and refines sociological concepts, the essential building blocks of sociological theory. Operationalization, construction of indices and the formalization of research findings enhance the clarity of theoretical constructs and the variables.

6. Theory facilitates an effective summation of empirical findings. It compares and contrasts the findings of isolated studies and establishes their larger significance. Specific relationships between discrete variables are analysed in relation to general theoretical system and by enabling replication of studies, theory enhances the effectiveness of particular investigation. Gunnar Myrdal contends,

Facts come to mean something only as ascertained and organised in the frame of a theory. Indeed, facts as part of scientific knowledge have no existence outside such a frame. Questions must be asked before answers can be obtained and, in order to make sense, the questions must be part of a logically coordinated attempt to understand social reality as a whole. A non-theoretical approach is, in strict logic, unthinkable.[24]

7. The interplay between theory and research is a matter of striking a balance between quality and quantity. The emptiness of speculative theory without substantiating data and the blindness of raw empiricism without substantive theory have been talked about much in sociological writing. Empiricists have sought to measure anything and everything; theorists shunned empiricism as mere fact-gathering. In between, model builders sought to formalize every theory in mathematical terms. The three-pronged attack began to shock socio-

logical imagination. The only possible solution to the problem is an increasing interplay between theory and research which will enhance the usefulness of measurement and formalization. And rightly Mc-Kinney observes:

... it has now become a commonplace that, no matter how precise measurement may be, what is measured remains a *quality*. Quanti-fication is a tremendous asset insofar as it achieves greater reliability and precision in measuring the *qualities that are theoretically signifi-cant*. The indispensable working partner of quantifying procedures is obviously the theory that determines what is to be measured.[25]

8. Finally, empirical work enhances the predictive power, preci-sion, validity and verifiability of sociological theories. By the discovery—and successive refinement—of new tools and techniques of methodology, more and more theories are enabled to develop higher order propositions with greater predictive power.

In his essay entitled 'Reflections on the Relation between Theory and Research', Hyman has put forth three suggestions to establish as well as strengthen a mutually rewarding association between theory and research:

1. Greater emphasis on theories of middle range rather than grand theories. According to Hyman, 'middle range theories have been built up by codification of existing bodies of empirical data. By contrast, the task of codifying all knowledge relevant to a general theory in the social sciences seems incompatible with the tempera-ment of general theorists, and perhaps beyond anyone's ability at the present time.'[26] Similarly, middle-range theories, once promul-gated, can stimulate subsequent empirical studies. 'It is the happy feature of middle-range concepts that they are specific and concrete enough for the researcher to see their applicability to his specific problem and to sense how they may be translated into operations.'

2. A shift from theory to theorizing. 'Theory implies something finished, intact. Theorizing implies something in process, an activity of one's mind, rather than the past product of other minds.'

3. A programme of training for serendipity. Hyman believes that many exciting theories have emerged out of anomalous and para-doxical findings. He continues:

From the codifications of middle-range theories, the researcher can learn that there are particular anomalous findings which he may follow up and he can, at least, become aware that anomalies do occur and that he should be alert to their occurrence. From his methodological training he develops the skills to search detailed bodies of data which may yield anomalous findings. The varieties of human experience revealed to him by modern large-scale inquiry include unusual and unexpected patterns. We already have some of the building blocks for our training program.

Frank Westie feels that many researchers do empirical work without reference to any theory primarily because there is a high degree of theoretical incoherence in sociology. He then suggests a research procedure which can maintain theoretical relevance despite the multiplicity of conflicting theories. According to Westie:

This procedure involves (a) explicitly listing a comprehensive range of *presupposed empirical relationships*, many of them diametrically opposed to one another, *which might possibly turn up in the research at hand*, and (b) explicitly listing a *range of interpretations*, many of them diametrically opposed to one another, for each possible empirical finding. Then, through empirical investigation the relationships that actually obtain are selected from the morass of 'presupposed empirical relationships' initially listed. All of the other initially proposed empirical relationships are discarded. The array of alternative interpretations attached to them in the original presentation are also eliminated from consideration as interpretations of the findings.[27]

Finally,

'Select, through subsequent empirical investigations, the best interpretations from among the many contradictory interpretations attached to the surviving empirical relationships.'

It is gratifying to note that the heat of the controversy between theorists and empiricists is cooling off. There is a growing awareness of the need for more intimate interplay between theory and research. However, in actual practice, this happy union has not yet matured, although there are increasing signs for optimism. Let us conclude with a quote from C. Wright Mills' essay, 'On Intellectual Craftsmanship':

Be a good craftsman: Avoid any rigid set of procedures. Above all, seek to develop and to use sociological imagination. Avoid the fetishism of method and technique. Urge the rehabilitation of the unpretentious intellectual craftsman, and try to become such a craftsman yourself. Let every man be his own methodologist; let every man be his own theorist; let theory and method again become part of the practice of a craft. Stand for the primacy of the individual scholar; stand opposed to the ascendancy of research teams of

technicians. Be one mind that is on its own confronting the problems
of man and society'[28]

NOTES

1. Nathan Glazer, 'The Rise of Social Research in Europe', in D. Lerner
    (ed.), *The Human Meaning of the Social Sciences* (New York, Meridian,
    1959), p. 50.
2. Talcott Parsons, 'The Role of Theory in Social Research', *American Socio-
    logical Review*, 3 (September, 1938), 13–20.
3. George C. Homans, 'Contemporary Theory in Sociology', pp. 951–77 in
    R. E. L. Faris (ed.), *Handbook of Modern Sociology* (Chicago, Rand Mc-
    Nally & Co., 1964), p. 973.
4. Parsons, op. cit., p. 19.
5. Robert K. Merton, *Social Theory and Social Structure* (Glencoe, Free Press,
    1957), p. 99.
6. Herbert Blumer, 'Sociological Analysis and the "Variable" ', *American
    Sociological Review*, 21 (December, 1956), 683–90).
7. Robert Bierstedt, *Power and Progress* (New York, McGraw-Hill, 1974), p.
    148.
8. John C. McKinney, 'Methodology, Procedures, and Techniques in Socio-
    logy', in Howard Becker and Alvin Boskoff (ed.), *Modern Sociological
    Theory* (New York, Holt, Rinehart and Winston, 1957), pp. 191–92.
9. Parsons, op. cit., p. 15.
10. Homans, op. cit., p. 974.
11. Merton, op. cit., p. 98.
12. Homans, op. cit., p. 975.
13. Quoted in Parsons, op. cit., p. 15.
14. Parsons, ibid., p. 15.
15. Merton, op. cit., p. 98.
16. Parsons, op. cit., p. 20.
17. McKinney, op. cit., p. 186.
18. Ibid., p. 191.
19. Merton, op. cit., p. 108.
20. Clarence and Sylvia Sherwood, 'Raw Empiricism and Sociological
    Theory', 45 (1966), pp. 164–9.
21. Merton, op. cit., p. 102.
22. Ralph H. Turner, 'The Quest for Universals in Sociological Research',
    American Sociological Review, 18 (1953): 604–11. Reprinted in Billy J.
    Franklin and Harold W. Osborne, *Research Methods: Issues and Insights*
    (Belmont, Wadsworth Publishing Company, 1971, p. 36.
23. H. H. Hyman, 'Reflections on the Relation between Theory and Research',
    in Franklin and Osborne, ibid., pp. 40–1.
24. Gunnar Myrdal, *Value in Social Theory* (London, Routledge and Kegan
    Paul, 1958), p. 233.
25. McKinney, op. cit., p. 203.
26. Hyman, op. cit., pp. 42–5.

27. Frank R. Westie, 'Toward Closer Relations between Theory and Research', *American Sociological Review*, 22 (1957), 149–54. Reprinted in Franklin and Osborne, op. cit., pp. 48–9, 53.

28. C. Wright Mills, *The Sociological Imagination* (New York, Oxford University Press, 1970), p. 24.

CHAPTER 3

System Theory

General Systems Theory: An Introduction

The origin of the term 'system' goes back to Greek antiquity, and today it is commonly used in natural, physical and social sciences. A system consists of two or more units that relate to each other in a structural relationship and form an entity whose elements are functionally inter-dependent. In this elementary sense, the electronic system of a transistor radio, the nervous system of the human body and the solar system of the universe are examples. Rapoport defines a system as '(1) something consisting of a set (finite or infinite) of entities (2) among which a set of relations is specified, so that (3) deductions are possible from some relations to others or from the relations among the entities to the behaviour or the history of the system.'[1] Thus a system is simply a bundle of relations among inter-dependent elements that constitute an orderly arrangement characterized by structural integration and relational isomorphisms.

The modern general systems theory owes its development to Henderson's formulation of societal equilibrium, Cannon's principle of homeostasis, Weiner's formulation of cybernetics and von Bertalanffy's concept of the 'open system'.

Following Pareto, Henderson viewed the organism as possessing a self-regulating mechanism whose goal is the maintenance of equilibrium. According to him:

A state such that if a small modification different from that which will otherwise occur is impressed upon a system, a reaction will at once appear tending toward the conditions that would have existed if the modification had not been impressed . . . . Equilibrium is an equilibrium of forces, more or less like the equilibrium, for instance, in a box spring; that a small modification leaves the forces substantially intact; and that the forces tend to re-establish the state that would have existed if no modification had occurred.[2]

Cannon developed the concept of homeostasis, a relatively stable condition an organism strives to maintain. He sought to identify the principles of stabilization that help maintain the homeostasis in the human as well as the social organism. Like the variety of mechanisms that exist in the body to maintain levels of blood sugar, blood pressure, body temperature, etc., there are mechanisms in society such as state, prison, cultural organizations, etc., that deal with the problem of social disruption.

While the work of men like Henderson and Cannon laid the foundations of systems theory, it was Ludwig von Bertalanffy's formulation of the open system which established systems thinking as a major scientific movement. However, he attempted to build the foundations for systems thinking on a biological, rather than a philosophical or merely formalistic basis. Von Bertalanffy considers the substitution of holistic approach, the view of the world as an organization, for the old fragmented approach of analytic atomistic modes of thought, to be the fundamental starting point of system analysis.

This trend is marked by the emergence of a bundle of new disciplines such as cybernetics, information theory, general system theory, theories of games, of decisions, of queuing and others; in practical application, systems analysis, systems engineering, operations research, etc. They are different in basic assumptions, mathematical techniques and aims, and they are often unsatisfactory and sometimes contradictory. They agree, however, in being concerned, in one way or the other, with 'systems', 'wholes' or 'organizations': and in their totality, they herald a new approach.[3]

Von Bertalanffy regards the characteristic state of the living organism as that of an open system which exchanges materials with its environment and maintains itself in a steady state. He observes:

There is first maintenance of a constant ratio of the components in a continuous flow of materials. Second, the composition is independent of, and maintained constant in, a varying import of materials; this corresponds to the fact that even in varying nutrition and at different absolute sizes the composition of the organism remains constant. Third, after a disturbance, a stimulus, the system re-establishes its steady state. Thus, the basic characteristics of self-regulation are general properties of open system.[4]

Whether it is a tendency toward equilibrium, homeostasis or a self-maintaining steady state, the fundamental assumption of the general system theory is that there is an underlying order, pattern, regularity and stabilization in human behaviour. Indeed, the idea of system is simply a conceptual scheme intended to portray the regularization and self-maintenance of behaviour in continual change. Von Bertalanffy believes that all sciences—physical, natural, social and philosophical—will ultimately culminate in a general system theory. According to him:

A first consequence of the existence of general system properties is the appearance of structural similarities or isomorphies in different fields. There are correspondences in the principles, which govern the behaviour of entities that are instrinsically, widely different. This correspondence is due to the fact that they all can be considered, in certain respects, as 'systems', that is, complexes of elements standing in interaction.[5]

Moreover, in an attempt to enhance precision and predictability through more exact theories, the non-physical fields of science have shown, in recent years, an increasing tendency to adopt mathematical forms and models. As Lilienfeld points out, 'a system can be defined mathematically by a system of simultaneous differential equations such that a change of any one measure within the system is a function of all the other measures within the system; conversely, change of any one measure entails change of all the other measures and of the system as a whole.'[5] Thus with the development of isomorphisms and mathematical forms, von Bertalanffy believes that a general system theory will emerge which will cut across different and apparently unrelated fields. And when general systems theory becomes an 'important regulative device in science', it will no longer be necessary to duplicate the discovery of the same principle in a variety of unrelated fields. But 'by formulating exact criteria, general system theory will guard against superficial analogies which are useless in science and harmful in their practical consequences'.[7]

The general systems theory involves the consideration of such issues as the degree of wholeness, nature of subsystems, the cybernetic principles of control, mechanisms of feedback, communication and information processing, goal-seeking, self-regulation, structural integration, adaptation and 'pattern-maintenance'. Von Bertalanffy summarizes the aims of general systems theory as follows:

(a) There is a general tendency towards integration in the various sciences, natural and social.
(b) Such integration seems to be centred in a general theory of systems.
(c) Such theory may be an important means for aiming at exact

theory in the non-physical fields of science.

(d) Developing unifying principles running 'vertically' through the universes of the individual sciences, this theory brings us nearer to the goal of the unity of science.

(e) This can lead to a much-needed integration in scientific education.[8]

Since World War II general systems theory has become popular not only in the physical and natural but also in the social sciences. As Rapoport points out, the task of general systems theory is to find the most general conceptual framework in which a scientific theory or a technological problem can be placed without losing the essential features of the theory or the problem. The proponents of general systems theory see in it the focal point of resynthesis of knowledge.'[9] In sociology, general systems theory has enabled us to relegate vague analogies and atomistic approaches to the background and to develop a scientific explanation of the socio-cultural and psychological phenomena in terms of such analytic constructs as social system, cultural system, and personality system. In the words of Parsons, system

is the concept that refers both to a complex of interdependencies between parts, components, and processes that involves discernible regularities of relationship, and to a similar type of interdependency between such a complex and its surrounding environment. System, in this sense, is therefore the concept around which all sophisticated theory in the conceptually generalizing disciplines is and must be organized.[10]

System Theory in Sociology

Pareto laid the foundation of system analysis in sociology with his formulation of the concept of society as a system in equilibrium. He conceived of system as a whole consisting of interdependent parts. In such a system, change in some part affects other parts as well as the whole.

By 'the social system' he means that state which a society takes both at a specified moment and in the successive transformations which it undergoes within a period of time. The real state of the system is determined by its conditions, which are of such a nature that if some modification in its form is introduced artificially, a reaction will take place tending to restore the changing form to its original state. If that were not the case, the form, with its normal changes, would not be determined but would be a mere matter of chance. More specifically 'equilibrium' is defined as some state X such that, if subjected to some artificial modification different from those it usually undergoes, a reaction at once occurs tending to restore it to its real, normal state.[11]

The set of forces which maintain social equilibrium involves three types of factors: (1) the extra-human environment or physical condition such as climate, soil, vegetation, etc., (2) external conditions such as a given society's previous states and contact with other cultures, and (3) inner elements of the system such as race, interest, knowledge, values, ideologies and sentiments. It was Pareto's belief that if the social system is subjected to pressures of external forces, inner forces will then push toward the restoration of equilibrium, restoring society to its normal state.

Following Pareto, a number of sociologists, particularly Henderson and Parsons, have elaborated the system model and utilized it extensively as a conceptual framework for the analysis of social phenomena. Walter Buckley, the most outspoken exponent of the general system theory in sociology, sees some sort of convergence emerging:

Both sociology and modern systems theory study many scientific problems in common: wholes and how to deal with them as such; the general analysis of organization—the complex and dynamic relations of parts, especially when the parts are themselves complex and changing and the relationships are non-rigid, symbolically mediated, often circular, and with many degrees of freedom; problems of intimate interchange with an environment, of goal-seeking, of continual elaboration and creation of structure, or more or less adaptive evolution; the mechanics of 'control', of self-regulation or self-direction.[12]

In his *Sociology and Modern Systems Theory*, Buckley sought to elaborate such system concepts as cybernetic principles of control, feedback loops, input and output, information, goal-seeking, self-regulation, information-linkage of the parts and the environment and openness, and demonstrate their fruitfulness for sociological theory. He undertook an elaborate survey of contemporary sociological theorizing to demonstrate the emergence of systems thinking. According to him,

The modern systems approach should be especially attractive to sociology because, in sum, it promises to develop:

1. A common vocabulary unifying the several 'behavioural' disciplines;
2. A technique for treating large, complex organizations;
3. A synthetic approach where piecemeal analysis is not possible due to the intricate interrelationships of parts that cannot be treated out of context of the whole;
4. A viewpoint that gets at the heart of sociology because it sees the sociocultural systems in terms of information and communication nets;
5. The study of *relations* rather than 'entities', with an emphasis on process and transition probabilities as the basis of a flexible structure with many degrees of freedom;
6. An operationally definable, objective, non-anthropomorphic study of purposiveness, goal-seeking system behaviour, symbolic cognitive processes, consciousness and self-awareness, and sociocultural emergence and dynamics in general.[13]

Having classified recent contributions to sociological theory under the three main headings of the structural and categorical approach, the collective behaviour approach and the social psychological approach, Buckley argues that the main task of the system theorist is to develop a framework that incorporates these approaches. According to him, exchange theory, symbolic interaction theory and game theory attest to the influence of systems thinking in sociological theory.

Marvin Oslen has presented a capsule summary of the social system model. According to him, 'a system is a bounded and unified set of interrelated, dynamic, stable processes . . . As applied to social phenomena, the social system model is not a substantive theory of social organization. Rather, it is a highly general, content-free conceptual framework within which any number of different substantive theories of social organization can be constructed. Nor does the social system model refer to any particular kind of social organization. It is an analytical model that can be applied to any instance of the process of social organisation. from families to nations.'[14] Olsen identifies five crucial properties of all social system:

1. Open boundaries. Since all real social organizations are subject to the influences of their environments, social systems are described as open systems; but as analytical constructs their boundaries are arbitrarily defined by the social scientist.

2. Input and outputs. In the process of interchange with its environment, an open system 'takes in' such items as raw materials, energy, entering personnel and information and 'sends-out' finished products, wastes, existing personnel and information. The input-output flows may be spontaneous, designed or forced.

3. Feedback and feedforward. Unlike mechanistic systems, social systems are flexible and capable of adapting to changes in their natural and social environments. Feedback is the flow of information and influence from the environment back into the system enabling it to adapt to its environment. The system modifies the patterns of interchange on the basis of positive or negative feedbacks. In feedforward, 'individuals within the system attempt to anticipate the probable consequences of proposed activities for the system and its environment before the enactment of these activities'.[15]

4. Internal ordering. In constructing the system model, a social scientist must not only determine its boundaries but also specify its components, their nature and size, patterns of inter-relationships and the extent of functional autonomy.

5. Key functionaries. Olsen mentions the following functionaries who constitute the centre of power within social systems: '(1) Gatekeepers mediate or control the flow of inputs and outputs with the natural and social environments through system gateways. (2) Channelers provide pathways or channels for the flow of influence and messages among system parts as they interact. (3) Switchers are located at vital decision points within the web of relationships among system parts and thus direct the flow of activities occurring within the system. (4) Storers provide storage places for whatever resources and information are not currently being used by the system but that may be needed in the future.'[16]

While closed mechanistic systems work only in accordance with predetermined internal programmes, open social systems are continually influenced by external and internal forces. The two basic types of processes displayed by social systems are morphostasis and morphogenesis. Morphostasis 'refers to all those processes that tend to preserve or maintain a system's present conditions or overall state, giving it suitability through time.'[17] Principal morphostatic processes are balancing, homeostasis and equilibrium maintenance, the concepts discussed earlier. Morphogenesis 'refers to those processes that tend to alter or elaborate a system's conditions or state, producing change or growth through time.'[18] This is the process of development, differentiation and adaptation which enables a system to deal more effectively with its environment and its own subsystems and to increase its ability to control its activities and attain its goals.

Models of System Analysis

There are three discernible modes of system analysis in sociology: the mechanistic, the organismic and the structural models.

The mechanistic model: Walter Buckley has eloquently summarized the origin and development of the mechanistic model as follows:

With the rapid advance of physics, mechanics, and mathematics in the seventeenth century men turned to an interpretation of man, his mind, and society in terms of the same methods, concepts and assumptions, partly in rejection of the less palatable teleology, vitalism, mysticism, and anthropomorphism of other views. Thus, the 'Social Physics' of the seventeenth century arose, whereby man was regarded as a physical object, a kind of elaborate machine, whose actions and psychic processes could be analysed in terms of the principles of mechanics. In 'social mechanics', society was seen as an 'astronomical system' whose elements were human beings bound together by mutual attraction or differentiated by repulsion; groups of societies or states were systems of balanced oppositions. Man, his groups, and their interrelations thus constituted an unbroken continuity with the rest of the mechanistically interpreted universe. All were based on the interplay of natural causes, to be studied as systems of relationships that could be measured and expressed in terms of laws of social mechanics.[19]

According to Sorokin, recent 'physicalistic and mechanistic' theories have made sociological language 'obtuse' and 'full of sham scientific slang'. 'Valence' is used instead of 'attractiveness', 'locomotion' instead of 'change' or 'transformation', 'social atom' instead of 'individual', 'dimension' instead of 'aspect', 'field' instead of 'class or category of phenomena', 'cohesion' instead of 'solidarity', and so on.[20] Other physical concepts include molecules, pressures and gravitation, centrifugal and centripetal forces, system of social coordinates, syntality and synergy, and moral and social space. Typical is Parsons' definition of 'the equilibrium of a social system in terms of "four-dimensional" space':

1. The Principle of Inertia. A given process of action will continue
   unchanged in rate and direction unless impeded or deflected by
   opposite motivational forces.
2. The Principle of Action and Reaction. If, in a system of action,
   there is a change in the direction of a process, it will be balanced
   by a complementary change which is equal in motivational force
   and opposite in direction.[21]

Other leading sociologists who have made use of the mechanistic
model include Homans and Znaniecki among others. Indeed,
Znaniecki's primary focus was not society but the abstracted and
generalized concept of system itself. At first he used the term
'closed system' but later, in response to criticism that the concept
implied 'a system isolated from external influence', he adopted the
term 'limited system to denote any combination of any particular
interdependent components with an inner order of its own'. Critical to his theory, however, was the concept of the plurality of
systems, that is, systems that are included in other systems and
themselves include others. Znaniecki thought it was possible to
establish a whole series of general laws regarding the interrelations between the elements of the system and changes in new
systems due to external factors.

Robert MacIver is one of those sociologists who have taken a
holistic view of social systems without taking a wholly mechanistic
view. He observes:

We postulate a social law roughly corresponding to the physical
law of inertia, to the effect that every social system tends to maintain itself, to preserve in its present state, until compelled by
some force to alter that state. Every social system is at every moment
and in every part sustained by codes and institutions, by traditions,
by interests. If a social order or any social situation within it suffers
significant change we think of some insurgent or invading force,
breaking as it were this 'inertia', the *status quo*. The simplest form
of the concept is that which we considered in the previous section,
where change is thought of as the disturbance of a persistent equilibrium. The defect of that concept was not its postulate of an equilibrium, but its unwarranted assumption that a single type of equilibrium, determined by relatively simple forces, was fundamental and
permanent so that any change affecting it was incidental, alien, or
extraneous. It is more in keeping with the historical record to think
in terms of a constant tendency towards equilibrium, beset always,
even in simple or primitive society and still more obviously in the
higher civilizations, by forces threatening to unbalance or disrupt it.
So the nature of the equilibrium is itself forever changing.[22]

In recent years the mechanistic model has come under sharp attack. With the emphasis on equilibrium, the mechanistic model has exaggerated the importance of shared expectations and reciprocity and failed to see that every society also has sets of alternative, deviant and counter norms and values. As Sorokin points out, vague conceptualizations of equilibrium have led to the neglect of 'two basic principles: the principle of immanent change of a system according to which any system or action, as a going concern, cannot avoid change from "within" even in the constant and unchangeable environment; and the principle of limit, according to which for any change in a certain direction there is always a limit.'[23] And Buckley contends that mechanical and sociocultural systems are very different types of systems with basically different organizing principles and dynamics and that continued reliance on the former to understand the latter only delays the development of other more appropriate and useful conceptualizations.

The organismic model: Organic analogizing in sociological thought is as old as Comte and Spencer. While the former utilized organic analogy in developing his *consensus universalis* without specifically identifying society with biological organism, the latter asserted the parallelism between the two as follows: 'So completely is society organized on the same system as an individual being that we may perceive something more than analogy between them; the same definition of life applies to both.'[24] Many followers of Spencer sought to identify the social analogue of the circulatory system, the sustaining system and the regulatory system. Like Spencer, they all chose the co-operative basis of biological organization as the model of society. As Spencer put it, 'All kinds of creatures are alike in so far as each exhibits co-operation among its components for the benefit of the whole; and this trait, common to them, is a trait common also to societies.'[25]

The organismic model of system analysis involves these assumptions: Like an organism, society is an integrated system. Its elements are functionally interrelated and mutually interdependent. The whole is prior to the part and the elements are to be understood within the context of the whole. Just as in biology it is impossible to explain an organ or a function apart from the living creature as a whole, here it is impossible to understand the state of a particular social phenomenon unless we restore it to its social context. Society is also viewed as a homogeneous system based on consensus and solidarity.

Probably the most important contribution to the organismic model of system analysis is Cannon's principle of homeostasis in terms of which the organism stabilizes itself. According to Cannon,

The constant conditions which are maintained in the body might be termed *equilibria*. That word, however, has come to have fairly exact meaning as applied to relatively simple physico-chemical states, enclosed systems, where known forces are balanced. The coordinated physiological processes which maintain most of the steady states in the organism are so complex and so peculiar to living beings . . . that I have suggested a special designation for these states, *homeostasis*. The word does not imply something set and immobile, a stagnation. It means a condition—a condition which may vary, but which is relatively constant.[26]

Cannon explained how the body, following any injury, prevents blood loss from too drastically upsetting its balance and brings into operation a series of mechanisms such as contraction of the blood vessels leading to the point of lesion, clotting, increased production of red blood cells and the like intended to restore equilibrium to the system. In a similar vein, structural-functionalists conceive of society as a system which seeks, by more or less automatic adjustments, to redress the balance of its equilibrium when it is upset by internal or external forces. For example, after a revolutionary movement has upset the order and stability of the social and political systems, a series of changes are introduced to bring about a steady state. Similarly if the rate of crime in a society assumes alarming proportions society is bound to take a closer look at its various institutions including the family, religion, the penal system and various social services in order to bring about the required changes.

Whereas Parsons and his followers have made extensive use of organismic analogies, this model is best represented by anthropological functionalism. However, the organismic model no longer enjoys a pivotal position in social thought. Its emphasis on integration, order and stability has often been carried to extremes. Moreover, the concept of the open system entertains notions like systemic-linkage, feedback and adaptation. Not only that, but the old view that the current state of a complex system is simply a function of its initial conditions is no longer tenable, for the complex, open system, though determinate, changes so that, as time goes on, its state is characterized more by the experiences that have come to it than by its state initially.'[27]

The structural model: The structural model of system analysis is not a single strain; it consists of a variety of approaches represented by Levi-Strauss, Nadel, Gerth and Mills, Parsons and Merton. According to Mullins,

> The distinctive aspect of structuralism is its practitioners' belief that all manifestations of social activity in any society constitute languages in a formal sense. Structuralism is a cognitive perspective, concerned with social system logic. Levi-Strauss talks of systems playing themselves out through people. Structuralists see human behaviour as ordered by a small number of simple systems that can be described in terms of boundaries, self-regulation, and transformation rules. *Boundaries* define a set. *Self-regulation* implies control of a set's activities by itself rather than by either historical or external systems; and *transformation* is the property of moving from one state to another in a regular, lawful manner . . . Structuralists thus give logical and analytic priority to a whole over its parts, emphasizing the complex web of relationships that link and unite those elements.[28]

Levi-Strauss conceived of social structure as a logic behind reality. He insisted that the 'term social structure has nothing to do with empirical reality but with models which are built up after it'. He took Radcliffe-Brown to task for not distinguishing between social structure and social relations. While social relations constitute the raw materials out of which the models making up the social structure are built, the structure itself cannot be reduced to an ensemble of social relations; rather such relations themselves result from some pre-existing structures. The structure exhibits the characteristics of a system and is made up of several elements, none of which can undergo change without effecting changes in all other elements.

Whereas Levi-Strauss regards social structure as a model behind reality, Nadel views it as reality itself. He regards the role system of any society, with its given coherence, as the matrix of the social structure. He outlines two specific advantages of structural analysis. These are: lending a higher degree of comparability to social data, and rendering such data more readily quantifiable. Nadel rejects the contention that structural analysis cannot cope with the time dimension. According to him structural analysis does not freeze an ongoing course of events at some arbitrary point, but tries to extract from it an orderliness assumed to be continuous and persistent. Thus he views structural analysis in quasi-static terms, as an attempt to capture the uniformities in the underlying processes.

Nadel contends that a particular social structure as described at a given moment is accurate only for a particular period of time. Structure and variance are not inherently contradictory; rather the former is defined or built up through taking account of the latter. If variance is unlimited, there would be absolute chaos, and no order in social life. Nadel's conception of structure is based on three criteria: repetitiveness of the social phenomena (that is, when some definable state of affairs can be said to reproduce itself), durability of the social phenomena (that is, when particular social phenomena last for a long time or run their full course), and moving equilibrium (when a regular state of affairs, on being upset by some identifiable disturbance, reasserts itself or returns to *Status quo*). Nadel cautions that stability in social process is not uniform and that the verification of repetitiveness of restoration after disturbance involves widely different time spans or scales.

Gerth and Mills defined social structure in terms of institutional orders and spheres. Although institutions are the basic building blocks, social structure is more than mere interrelations of institutions. The unit and composition of a social structure are determined by the precise weight which each institutional order and sphere has with reference to every other order and the ways in which they are related to one another. And an institution is an organization of roles, one or more of which is understood to serve the maintenance of the total set of roles. Gerth and Mills distinguish two fundamental traditions—character structure and social structure—and assert that the two are united by 'role' which links the 'person' in the former with 'institutions' in the latter, as illustrated in Fig. 1.

Character structure 'refers to the relatively stabilized integration of the organism's psychic structure linked with the social roles of the person. On the one hand, a character structure is anchored in the organism and its specialized organs through the psychic structure: on the other hand, it is formed by the particular combination of social roles which the person has incorporated from out of the total roles available to him in his society.'[29] And a social structure is made up of a certain combination or pattern of institutional orders. The role, which is the primary link between the character structure and the social structure, is what gives meaning to structure. For example,

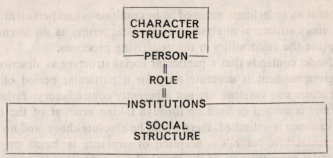

Figure 1. Adapted from Gerth & Mills, Character and Social
Structure, p. 32.

a family is not made up by a man and a woman but by man and
wife who assume institutionalized roles. Moreover, like Nadel,
Gerth and Mills also contend that 'Social structures are not frozen,
they may be static or dynamic, they have beginnings, duration,
varying degrees of unity, and they may disintegrate.'[30]

Parsons has undertaken the most elaborate treatment of structural analysis in modern sociology. He defined social structure as
'stable systems of social interaction'.[31] His structural model of
system analysis is an amalgam of mechanistic and organismic
models. In *The Social System*, Parsons has been primarily concerned
'with the categorization of the structure of social systems, the modes
of structural differentiation within such systems, and the ranges of
variability with reference to each structural category between
systems'.[32]

Boskoff observes: 'Structural analysis of social systems and their
components is an important methodological base for sociology. But
it is inherently descriptive and "formal"; it tends to reify or hypo-
stasize social phenomena and thereby disregards the teleological,
active, dynamic formalism . . . '.[33] And we will present a brief overview of Parsons' system theory,

Talcott Parsons' Social System Theory

Talcott Parsons is undoubtedly the most outstanding exponent of
the social system theory. In *The Structure of Social Action*, Parsons
focussed on unit act but, in *The Social System*, emphasis shifted
from unit act to institutional orders, and the system was the primary unit of analysis. However, it must be noted at the outset that

Parsons' 'social system' is a constructed type, an analytical conceptual framework, and not an empirical referent. It is an open system
in continuous balancing and its crucial elements are conditions,
'needs', and 'functions' which manifest themselves in total action
processes. The following definition of the social system offered by
Parsons and Shils seems to be the most comprehensive:

A social system is a system of action which has the following characteristics: (1) It involves a process of interaction between two or
more actors; the interaction process as such is a focus of the observer's attention. (2) The situation toward which the actors are oriented includes other actors. These other actors (alters) are objects of
cathexis. Alter's actions are taken cognitively into account as data.
Alter's various orientations may be either goals to be pursued or
means for the accomplishment of goals. Alter's orientation thus may
be objective for evaluative judgement. (3) There is (in a social
system) interdependent and, in part, concerted action in which the
concert is a function of collective goal orientation or common
values, and of a consensus of normative and cognitive expectations.[34]

Parsons takes 'action' as the building block of the system. He
prefers the term 'action' to 'behaviour' because he is 'interested not
in the physical events of behaviour for their own sake but in their
patterning, their patterned meaningful products (physical, cultural,
and other), ranging from implements to works of art, and the
mechanisms and processes that control such patterning. . . . Action
consists of the structures and processes by which human beings
form meaningful intentions and, more or less successfully, imple-
ment them in concrete situations'.[35] The social system is one of the
primary subsystems of human action systems; the other three are
the cultural, personality and biological systems. Because of the
interpenetrations, each of the other three action systems constitutes
a part of the environment of a social system.

The analytical sorters that delineate the system theory may be
summarized as follows: 1. The social system is made up of the
interaction of human individuals. 2. Each member is both actor
and object of orientation for both other actors and himself. 3. The
actor is seeking a goal or set of goals. 4. The actor is confronted
with a variety of situational conditions as societal environments
and ecological constraints. 5. The actor's orientation to the situation is both motivational and value-orientational.

The motivational orientation which supplies the energy, i.e., 'an urge to get something', is characteristically three-fold: (a) Cognitive. Corresponding to belief, cognitive meanings imply what *is* or what the actors perceive. (b) Cathectic. This corresponds to sentiments and involves the process through which an actor invests an object with affective significance or perceives what is pleasurable or painful. But the objects that an actor perceives to provide gratification are many and varied. Hunger may be satisfied with a variety of objects including the most exotic foods. Similarly, enjoyment of pleasures may take many forms. However, the actor may not indulge in any type of behaviour in order to maximize gratification. Some things are taboo, others are required, and some are judged appropriate. Hence cultural value patterns induce a third mode of motivation, namely (c) Evaluative, that is, judgement and interpretation of alternatives and selection of appropriate ones.

Value orientation, on the other hand, refers to the observance of social norms or standards. 'The value orientation supplies norms or standards of action. Internalized, they are need-dispositions within actors; institutionalized in the social system, they contribute to integration; abstracted from the concrete situation, they are cultural value-standards.'[36] The modes of value-orientation are three-fold: (a) Cognitive standard—those by which the validity of cognitive judgements is assessed. (b) Appreciative standards—those by which selections among the possibilities of cathectic significance can be made. (c) Moral standards or 'evaluative standards which are neither cognitive as such nor appreciative as such but involve a synthesis of both aspects' and 'constitute the standards in terms of which more particular evaluations are themselves evaluated'.[37]

Parsons identifies three types of action: 1. Instrumental action. This is oriented to the achievement of a goal which is an anticipated future state of affairs, and gives primacy to the cognitive mode of orientation. 2. Expressive action. 'Here the primary orientation is not to the attainment of a goal anticipated for the future, but the organization of the "flow" of gratifications';[38] action itself is a goal, and gives primacy to the cathectic mode of orientation. 3. Moral action. Here 'the focus is on the system of order itself, not on the goals transcendent to it nor on the gratification-interests of the actor. This may be called the "moral" aspect of the ordering of action and the cultural values which have primacy in relation to it, moral values ... the social system focus ... may be called the "relational" orientation of action while that to the integration of personality may be called the "ego-integrative".'[39]

The concept of institutionalization is crucial to Parsons' conceptualization of the system. Indeed, he regards institutionalization as the fundamental integrative mechanism of social systems. It is viewed both as a process and a structure. Institutionalization builds up and maintains social structure. It also refers to stabilized patterns of interaction which are normatively regulated by the cultural system. It involves both structuralization of value orientations in the social system and the internalization of value systems in the individual personality. The actor's internalization of the cultural values and beliefs is the primary basis of institutionalization. 'Put in personality terms this means that there is an element of superego organization correlative with every role-orientation pattern of the individual in question. In every case the internalization of a super-ego element means motivation to accept the priority of collective over personal interests, within the appropriate limits and on the appropriate occasions.'[40]

The types of institutions embodying value orientation patterns are: 1. Relational institutions: the most central institutions directly constitutive of the patterning of interactive relationships. 2. Regulative institutions: the class of institutions facilitating collectivity-integration through regulation of instrumental, expressive and ego-integrative interests. 3. Cultural institutions: beliefs, expressive symbols and patterns of moral value-orientations which provide general cultural orientation rather than commitment in action.

Relational institutions define reciprocal role-expectations and thus constitute the core of the social system. Regulative institutions define the legitimate means to be employed in the pursuit of interests. Cultural institutions, peripheral to the social relationship structure, define obligations and value orientations with regard to cultural patterns.

Parsons identifies two analytical concepts that delineate the structure of social action: 1. Dynamic modes of analysis—which refer to equilibrating processes, boundary exchanges and structural changes; 2. Hierarchy of relations of control—which refer to the cybernetic hierarchy that places the cultural system over the biological system. What links structural and dynamic modes of analysis is function, which explains the central place of this concept in Parsons' system analysis. Parsons outlines four fundamental functions which every functioning social system must perform:

1. The function of adaptation—to produce and allocate fluidly disposable resources.
2. The function of goal-attainment—to maximize the capacity of the society to attain collective goals.
3. The function of integration—to bring together motivational and cultural or symbolic elements in a certain kind of ordered system.
4. The function of pattern maintenance and tension-management—to maintain adequate motivation to conform with cultural values, to reward conformity and to check disruptive behaviour.

Bob Jessop has neatly summarized Parsons' framework as follows:

Every social system is confronted with four functional problems. These problems are those of pattern maintenance, integration, goal attainment, and adaptation. Pattern maintenance refers to the need to maintain and reinforce the basic values of the social system and to resolve tensions that emerge from continuing commitment to these values. Integration refers to the allocation of rights and obligations, rewards and facilities, to ensure the harmony of relations between members of the social system. Goal attainment involves the necessity of mobilizing actors and resources in organized ways for the attainment of specific goals. And adaptation refers to the need for the production or acquisition of generalized facilities or resources that can be employed in the attainment of various specific goals. Social systems tend to differentiate about these problems so as to increase the functional capabilities of the system. Such differentiation—whether through the temporal specialization of a structurally undifferentiated unit or through the emergence of two or more structurally distinct units from one undifferentiated unit—is held to constitute a major verification of the fourfold functionalist schema. It also provides the framework within which are examined the plural interchanges that occur between structurally differentiated units to provide them with the inputs they require in the performance of their functions and to enable them to dispose of the outputs they produce.[41]

In accordance with Parsons' schema, a factory as a social system may be analysed as under:

1. Adaptive functions: Proper lighting, air conditioning, suitable machinery, food services and other working conditions;
2. Goal-attainment functions: Processing, manufacturing, marketing, research activities;

3. Integrative function: Management-labour councils, clubs, publications and public relations, recreational and social events, insurance and labour welfare programmes.

4. Pattern-maintenance and tension-management functions: Training, orientation sessions, allocation of rank, salary structure, promotion, increments and bonuses, disciplinary control, mechanism for the redress of grievances.

As noted earlier, action involves an actor and an actor's orientation to the situation. Parsons' typology of action recognizes two more dichotomies:

1. External-internal dichotomy. This depends on whether the action is oriented toward external or internal situation of a social system.

2. Instrumental-consummatory dichotomy. The former indicates activity which represents the means to a goal and the latter an activity which is an end in itself.

The intersection of the two dichotomies together with the four primary functions described above point up several areas of action as illustrated by figure 2.

FIGURE 2

	Instrumental	Consummatory
A		G
External	Adaptive function	Goal-attainment function
Internal	Pattern-maintenance and tension management function	Integrative function
L		I

A: Adaptation; G: Goal-attainment; I: Integration; L: Originally called Latent and hence the 'L' but now revised as Pattern-maintenance and Tension management.

Pattern Variables

In delineating the structure of action Parsons initially followed the lead from Toennies' *Gemeinschaft* and *Gesellschaft*. However, soon he became convinced that a given structure might clearly exhibit attributes suggestive of both the polar types. The professional status-role of the physician is a case in point. In terms of the application of the general principles of medical science, the physician's relation to his patient is *Gesellschaft*-like but 'by virtue of the canon that the "welfare of the patient" should come ahead of the self-interest of the doctor, this was clearly one of *Gemeinschaft*'.[42] Therefore, Parsons sought to identify the choices between alternatives that an actor confronts in a given situation and the relative primacies assigned to such choices. Thus he proposed the five dichotomies of pattern variables listed below:

1. Affectivity vs. affective neutrality
   (The Gratification-Discipline dilemma):

The pattern is affective when an organized action system emphasizes gratification, that is when an actor tries to avoid pain and to maximize pleasure; the pattern is affectively neutral when it imposes discipline, and renouncement or deferment of some gratifications in favour of other interests. For example, soldiers are expected to ignore immediate gratification and be affectively neutral in their line of duty even if that involves risking their lives. Similarly, unbridled expression of emotions and impulse gratifications are negatively evaluated by cultural patterns.

2. Self-orientation vs. collectivity-orientation
   (The private vs. collective interest dilemma):

This dichotomy depends on social norms or shared expectations which define as legitimate the pursuit of the actor's private interests or obligate him to act in the interests of the group. Salesmen and shopkeepers are expected to glorify their products and give 'sales talk' in accordance with self-orientation but the doctor is expected to tell the patient what is best for him, even if he can make extra money from an expensive operation. This dichotomy has nothing to do with 'selfish' or 'altruistic' motives which are individual character traits but with shared expectations commonly held by a collectivity.

3. Particularism vs. universalism:
   (The choice between types of value-orientation standard)

The former refers to standards determined by an actor's particular relations with a particular object, the latter refers to value standards that are highly generalized. A teacher is supposed to give grades to all students 'impartially', that is, in accordance with the same abstract, general, *universal* principles. But if he favours his son or a friend who happens be in the same class, he is behaving particularistically, for he is treating people differently on the basis of their particular relationship to him. To give another example: a woman on the trial jury has to be universalistic, otherwise she will be dishonest; but as a wife she has to be particularistic, otherwise she will be unfaithful.

4. Quality vs. performance
   (Originally designated as Ascription vs. Achievement: The choice between 'modalities' of the social object)

This is the dilemma of according primary treatment to an object on the basis of what it *is* in itself, an inborn quality, or what it *does*, and the quality of its performance. The former involves defining people on the basis of certain attributes such as age, sex, colour, nationality, etc.; the latter defines people on the basis of their abilities. Compulsory retirement, racial discrimination and the notion of 'caste superiority' are based on considerations of quality. Recruitment of personnel in a modern bureaucracy based on technical qualifications and standard tests involves consideration of performance.

5. Diffuseness vs. specificity
   (The definition of scope of interest in the object)

This 'is the dilemma of defining the relation borne by object to actor as indefinitely wide in scope, infinitely broad in involvement, morally obligating, and significant in pluralistic situations (diffuseness); or specifically limited in scope and involvement (specificity).'[43] The relationship between the employer and the employees in a modern factory is specific since no obligation is assumed to exist beyond what is specified in the 'contract'. However, certain systems of land tenure such as the semi-feudal and zamindari types are supposed to involve the tenants in an infinite variety of obligations to their 'masters'. Similarly, patterns of friendship and husband-wife relationships are supposed to involve a 'limitless' number of obligations.

Systems and Subsystems

Parsons' general theory of system recognizes four different aspects of reality—social, cultural, personality and behavioural organism. Corresponding to these four realms of reality, there are four sub-systems of action: the social, the cultural, the personality and the biological systems which are analytically separable and mutually irreducible. The social system is analytically abstractable from the total interaction process; the other three systems are the environments of the social system but all four are at the same time sub-systems of action.

The social system: According to Parsons:

A social system consists in a plurality of individual actors interacting with each other in a situation which has at least a physical or environmental aspect, actors who are motivated in terms of a tendency to the "optimization of gratification" and whose relation to their situations, including each other, is defined and mediated in terms of a system of culturally structured and shared symbols.[44]

It is generated by the process of interaction among individual units. However, a social system is not made up of 'the *total* action of concrete persons and collectivities, but only their actions in specific roles'.

The core of a social system is the patterned normative order through which the life of a population is collectively organized. As an order, it contains values as well as differentiated and particularized norms and standards. As a collectivity, it displays a patterned conception of membership which distinguishes between those individuals who do and do not belong. And, the social system is an open system engaged in processes of interchange (or 'input-output' relations) with its environment, as well as consisting of interchanges among its internal units.

What are the units of social systems? In the most elementary sense the unit is the act. But for most purposes of the more macroscopic analysis of social systems, Parsons prefers a higher order unit than the act which he calls the status-role. 'Since a social system is a system of processes of interaction between actors, it is the structure of the *relations* between the actors as involved in the interactive process which is essentially the structure of the social system. The system is a network of such relationships.'[45]

Hence Parsons regards the *participation* of an actor in a patterned interactive relationship as the most significant unit of the social system. This participation has two principal aspects: the positional aspect or *status*—that of where the actor in question is 'located' in the social system in relation to other actors; the processual aspect or *role*—that of what the actor does in his relations with others seen in the context of its functional significance for the social system. Parsons emphasizes: 'It should be made quite clear that statuses and roles are not attributes of the actor, but *units* of the social system. Next, the actor himself, as a social actor or a composite bundle of statuses and roles, is a unit of the social system. Finally, the collectivity is also a unit of the social system.'

The structural components of social systems are delineated in terms of two analytical constructs:

(a) The normative order which involves norms and values. Norms are primarily social whereas values serve as the primary connecting link between the social and cultural systems.

(b) Collectively organized population which involves collectivity, the category of intra-social structure and the role, the category of boundary-structure.

A social system . . . may be analysed on four levels of generality so far as its units are concerned: (1) Individuals in roles are organized to form what we call (2) collectivities. Both roles and collectivities, however, are subject to ordering and control by (3) norms which are differentiated according to the functions of these units and to their situations, and by (4) values which define the desirable kind of system of relations.[46]

Collectivity is the organization of a series of institutions, 'a concrete system of interacting human individuals, of persons in roles. Values are defined as modes of normative orientation of action . . . which define the main directions of action.' Parsons writes:

These four structural categories—values, norms, collectivities, roles —may be related to our general functional paradigm. Values take primacy in the pattern maintenance functioning of a social system. Norms are primarily integrative; they regulate the great variety of processes that contribute to the implementation of patterned value commitments. The primary functioning of the collectivity concerns actual goal attainment on behalf of the social system. Where individuals perform *societally* important functions, it is in their capacity as collectivity members. Finally, the primary function of the role in the social system is adaptive. This is particularly clear for the category of service, as the capacity to fulfill valued role-performances is the most basic generalized adaptive resource of any society, though it must be coordinated with cultural, organic, and physical resources.[47]

If a system is to constitute a persistent order and to undergo an orderly process of developmental change, certain functional pre-requisites must be met (see ch. 4 for details): 1. A social system must provide for the minimum biological and psychological needs of a sufficient proportion of its component members. It is not the needs of any one, but only a sufficient proportion for a sufficient fraction of the population. 2. The system can only function if a sufficient proportion of its members perform the essential roles with an adequate degree of effectiveness. 3. It must avoid commitment to cultural patterns which either fail to define a minimum of order or which place impossible demands on people and thereby generate deviance and conflict. In other words, it must maintain a minimum of control over potentially disruptive behaviour. 4. There must be minimum social conditions necessary for the production, mainte-nance and development of cultural systems in general as well as of particular types of cultural systems.

The need to fulfill various functions of the social system gives rise to different structural arrangements. Thus, a total society, as a social system, tends to differentiate into subsystems (social struc-tures) and in terms of the four primary functions discussed earlier four sub-systems of society are identified by Parsons:

A. The adaptive sub-system. The economy is the primary spe-cialized subsystem in relation to the adaptive function of a society. It functions to produce generalized facilities, particularly commo-dities and resources, as means to numerous ends and, through the institutions of contract and property, the economic system regulates the processes of production and distribution.

B. The goal-attainment sub-system. The primary goal-attainment sub-system of society is the polity whose function is the mobiliza-tion of necessary pre-requisites for the attainment of given system goals of the society.

C. The integrative sub-system. All sub-systems that function to marshal agreement out of potenial or actual conflict and maintain the institutionalization of value patterns are integrative subsystems of society. They include political parties, interest groups, health agencies, courts, etc.

D. The pattern-maintenance and tension-management sub-systems. These focus on the institutionalized culture which, in turn, centres on patterns of value-orientations. These sub-systems of the social system articulate most closely with the cultural systems. They include familial institutions, churches, schools, the arts, research activities, etc.

The cultural system: Parsons defines the cultural system as

'the aspect of action organized about the specific characteristics of symbols and the exigencies of forming stable systems of them. It is structured in terms of patternings of meaning which, when stable, imply in turn generalized complexes of constitutive symbolisms that give the action system its primary 'sense of direction', and which must be treated as independent of any particular system of social interaction. Thus, although there are many ramifications into such areas as language and communication, the prototypical cultural systems are those of beliefs and ideas. The possibilities of their preservation over time, and of their diffusion from one personality and/or social system into another, are perhaps the most important hallmarks of the independent structure of cultural systems.[48]

Cultural institutions consist of cognitive beliefs, systems of expressive symbols and private moral obligations. The main function of the cultural system is the legitimation of the society's normative order. Cultural value patterns provide the most direct link between the social and cultural systems in legitimizing the normative order of society. They define what is appropriate and what is not, not necessarily in a moral sense but in accordance with the institutionalized order. As Parsons puts it:

The cultural (or pattern-maintenance) system centers on the instituionalization of cultural value patterns, which, at the general cultural level, may be regarded as moral. Institutionalized societal values, and their specifications to societal subsystems, comprise only part of the relevance of moral values of action; moral values are also involved, through internalization, in structures of the personality and behavioural organism; and, more generally, they articulate with religion, science, and the arts within the cultural system.[49]

Parsons points out that cultural patterns have a dual relation to action; they may be the object of the situation or they may be internalized to become components of the actor's orientation pattern. This peculiarity of culture, Parsons claims, is the main basis for treating it as a special category. Some culture patterns function primarily as symbolic forms for the organization of the actor's cognitive orientation; others serve a similar function in relation to the cathectic aspect of this orientation and finally there are those which mediate or structure his evaluative orientations. Accordingly, Parsons proposes a typology of culture patterns which includes: systems of cognitive ideas or beliefs; systems of adjustive patterns or expressive symbols; systems of integrative patterns or value-orientation standards.

The personality system: Parsons views personality as 'the aspect of the living individual, as "actor", which *must* be understood in terms of the cultural and social content of the learned patternings that make up his behavioural system.'[50] Personality is autonomous as a distinct sub-system of action. It 'forms a distinct system articulated with social systems through their political sub-systems, not simply in the sense of government but of any collective ordering. This is to say that *the* primary goal output of social systems is to the personalities of their members.' Parsons also claims that the 'Personality system is the *primary meeting ground* of the cultural system, the behavioural organism and, secondarily, the physical world'.

The main function of the personality system involves learning, developing, and maintaining through the life cycle an adequate level of motivation so that individuals will participate in socially valued and controlled activities. In turn, society must also adequately satisfy and reward its members if it is to maintain the level of motivation and of performance. This relationship constitutes socialization, the process by which individuals become social beings. Since personality is the *learned organization* of the behaving individual, an effective process of socialization is crucial. And successful socialization requires that social and cultural learning be strongly motivated through the engagement of the pleasure mechanisms of the organism. Whereas the maintenance of adequate levels of motivation involves mainly the social structures concerned with socialization, the individual's value-commitments link primarily with the cultural system. Consensus and intermeshing of interests are not always enough. In addition to rewarding conformity and punishing deviance, motivation must be furnished at different levels. Parsons observes:

Thus a society's *primary* exigency *vis-a-vis* the personalities of its members is the motivation of their participation, including their compliance with the demands of its normative order. This exigency may be divided into three levels. First is the highly generalized commitment to the central value patterns that relate directly to the religious orientations. Second is the "sub-stratum" of the personality which, stemming from early socialization, links with the erotic complex and the motivational significance of kinship and other intimate relations. Third is the level more directly involved with services and the instrumental activities which vary with particular goal situations. These levels of the personality correspond roughly to the superego, id, and ego in Freud's classification.'[51]

Parsons makes it absolutely clear that it is not the relevance of interaction that distinguishes the social system from the personality system, for interaction is equally constitutive of both systems.

It is rather the functional focus of organization and integration which is the basis of the difference between personalities and social systems. Personality is the relational system of a living organism interacting with a situation . . . . The relation of personality to a uniform role structure is one of interdependence and interpenetration but not one of 'inclusion' where the properties of the personality system are constituted by the roles of which it is allegedly 'made up'.[52]

Parsons also identifies[6] 'four categories of outputs from the personality to the organism [which] act as both controls and facilities'. These are:

1. Motive force to increase instrumental performance.
2. Directional output or the control of organic facilities by the motivational structures of the psychological system.
3. Expectation component or attitudinal set, the 'expectation' that organic interests will be served by 'going along' with the psychological system.
4. 'Organic security', or the stability of the whole relationship between organic and psychological systems.[53]

The Biological system According to Parsons, 'all relations between the social system and the *physical* environment are mediated through the behavioural organism.' The perceptual processes of the organism are the source of information about the physical environment, which gains cultural organization from its conceptual and theoretical components. The organism is also the source of the 'instinctual' components of the motivation of individuals' personalities.[54]

Parsons lists two fundamental properties of biological 'human nature': the 1. 'plasticity' of the human organism, its capacity to learn any one of a large number of alternative patterns of behaviour instead of being bound by its genetic constitution to a very limited range of alternatives. It is, of course, within the limits of this plasticity that the independent determinant significance of cultural and social factors in action must be sought; the 2. 'sensitivity', or 'the accessibility of the human individual to influence by the attitudes of others in the social interaction process, and the resulting dependence on receiving relatively particular and specific reactions.'[55] This provides the motivational basis for accessibility to influence in the learning process.

The organism is to be analysed in terms of its relation to the physical world. Primordial problems concern the provision of food and shelter. Parsons considers technological organization as the boundary-structure between society as a system and the organic physical environment because technology is the socially organized capacity for actively controlling and altering objects of the physical environment in the interest of human needs. Parsons defines the organism 'as a fourfold set of "facilities", which, conceived functionally, can be thought of as inputs to the psychological (personality) system. These consist of (1) motivational energy; (2) the perceptual or cognitive capacity; (3) "performance" or "response" capacity, or the capacity to utilize the structures of the organism, notably the skeletal-muscular structures; and (4) the mechanisms that integrate these facilities with each other and the needs of psychological system, especially the pleasure mechanism.'[56]

Now a word about the interpenetration between the four sub-systems (social, cultural, personality, and biological) of action. The social system is the integrative sub-system of action in general. The other three principal systems constitute the environments of the social system. The four primary sub-systems of society (adaptive, goal-attainment, integrative, and pattern-maintenance and tension-management) are functionally specialized around their inter-relations with the three other sub-systems of action (or the environments of a social system), each relating most directly to one of these environments. Each of the four societal sub-systems may also be considered a distinct environment of the sub-system which is the society's integrative core. Loomis has effectively summarized the relationship between the systems and sub-systems as follows:

Organization and control are exhibited by one ordering of levels of the four systems. The psychological system organizes and controls the organism (in its behavioural aspects); the social system organizes and controls the psychological system and the cultural system performs similarly in respect to the social system. By an opposite ordering of the levels, sets of conditions are provided. Social systems provide a set of conditions basic to the cultural systems, psychological systems a set of conditions on which the social systems depend, and the organism provides the conditions underlying the psychological system. There are characteristic interchanges among the four systems. The organism, for example, provides the personality system with inputs of motivational energy part of which is fed back to the organism in the form of control that increases the performance potential of the organism. Between the psychological and cultural systems a mutually integrative interchange takes place in which the psychological system is provided with legitimation by cultural components by which its functioning is made subject to normative patterns. Culture is provided with a 'motivational commitment' by the psychological system which transcends an understanding of the norm to become a total internalization of it, so that the norm becomes a part of an internal regulatory mechanism which is part of the personality system itself.[57]

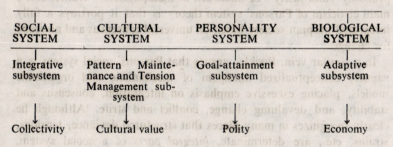

SUBSYSTEMS OF ACTION

SOCIAL SYSTEM	CULTURAL SYSTEM	PERSONALITY SYSTEM	BIOLOGICAL SYSTEM
Integrative subsystem	Pattern Maintenance and Tension Management subsystem	Goal-attainment subsystem	Adaptive subsystem
Collectivity	Cultural value	Polity	Economy

Figure 3

The overall action system and each of the subsystems fulfilling one of the four system requisites—A, G, I, L—are described by Turner as follows:

The organism is considered to be the subsystem having the most consequences for resolving adaptive problems, since it is ultimately through this system the environmental resources are made available to the other action subsystems. As the goal-seeking and decision-making system, personality is considered to have primary consequences for resolving goal-attainment problems. As an organized network of status-norms integrating the patterns of the cultural system and the needs of personality systems, the social system is viewed as the major integrative subsystem of the general action system. As the repository of symbolic content of interaction, the cultural system is considered to have primary consequences for managing tensions of actors and assuring that the proper symbolic resources are available to assure the maintenance of institutional patterns [latency].[58]

Critics have charged that Parsons' system of concepts does not correspond to events in the 'real' world. Dahrendorf compares Parsons' social system with utopia. The absence of change and the existence of universal consensus on prevailing values characterize all utopias. Contemporary system theorists in sociology view society as a system that is 'self-sufficient, internally consistent, and closed to the outside'.[59] Dahrendorf does not see anything logically wrong with the term 'system' but when it is applied to total societies and is made the ultimate frame of reference of analysis, 'all kinds of undesirable consequences' follow. 'It is certainly true that sociology deals with society. But it is equally true that physics deals with nature, and yet physicists would hardly see an advance in calling nature a system and trying to analyse it as such. In fact, the attempt to do so would probably—and justly—be discarded as metaphysics.'[60] Dahrendorf's main criticism of Parsons' system theory is that it portrays a fully integrated utopian society based on universal consensus and no scope for change.

In a similar vein, Buckley argues that Parsons' social system is a vaguely conceptualized amalgam of mechanistic and organismic models, placing excessive emphasis on integration, consensus and stability, and devaluing change, conflict and strife. 'Although he clearly recognizes in many places that structured deviance, tensions, strains, etc., are determinate, *integral parts* of a social system, nevertheless somewhere along his line of exposition the "system" comes to be identified . . . with the dominant, legitimized, institutionalized structure, or at least with those characteristic structures that *do not include* patterned strains or structured deviance and disorder. And the concept of "institutionalized deviance" now widely recognized in one form or another by many sociologists, could be a contradiction in terms for Parsons.'[61] Buckley also claims that the fundamental components of Parsonian system model are only 'those determinate relations making up an "institutionalized" dominant structure of conformity to role expectations'. And since this dominant structure is taken as the fixed point of reference against which other structures or latent consequences are seen as potentially 'disruptive', deviance and strains of various kinds are residual in the model.

Buckley also insists that the 'Parsonian model is rife with anthropo-morphism and teleology. The system "seeks" equilibrium, it has "problems" and "imperatives" of control, it has "systemic needs". Parsons is always careful to enclose such terms in quotes, and expli-citly pays lip service to the dangers involved. But unfortunately, as the history of science shows, this is not enough to cover the full price that we may eventually have to pay for using such notions for their presumably heuristic value.'[62]

Some of these criticisms are valid. But it must be borne in mind that Parsons has been primarily concerned with developing an analytical tool for the study of total societies, not with describing empirical realities. In this endeavour he has developed the most com-prehensive conceptual framework for the analysis of social systems and their structural components. Parsons' critics have often failed to see that his scheme for the analysis of the systematic aspects of social relationships is essentially an ideal-typical construct, not a general descriptive replica of the organization of concrete collectivi-ties. Indeed, Parsons' social systems are not concrete; they are conceptual constructs. They are not made up of individuals but social actions and status-role bundles. As Theodore Abel points out, 'since Parsons' intention was to forge an analytical tool for the compara-tive study of any organized group from the viewpoint of the order manifested in its stability, the abstract character of his conceptual scheme is an asset, not a liability.'[63]

NOTES

1. Anatol Rapoport, 'General Systems Analysis', in David Sills (ed.), *International Encyclopedia of the Social Sciences*, vol. 15 (New York, Macmillan Company, 1968), p. 453.
2. Bernard Barber (ed.), 'L. J. Henderson on the Social System: Selected Writings' (Chicago, University of Chicago Press, 1970), p. 28.
3. Ludwig von Bertalanffy, 'General System Theory: Foundations Develop-ment Applications' (New York, Braziller, 1968, p. 188).
4. As quoted by Robert Lilienfeld, *The Rise of Systems Theory* (New York, John Wiley and Son, 1978), p. 18.
5. Bertalanffy, 'General System Theory', in N. J. Demerath and Richard Peterson (eds.), *System, Change, and Conflict* (New York, Free Press, 1967), p. 117.
6. Lilienfeld, op. cit., pp. 23-4.
7. Ibid., p. 25.

8. Bertalanffy, in Demerath and Peterson, op. cit., p. 118.
9. Rapoport, op. cit., p. 457.
10. Talcott Parsons, 'Social Systems', in Sills (ed.), *International Encyclopedia of the Social Sciences*, op. cit., p. 458.
11. Don Martindale, *The Nature and Types of Sociological Theory* (Boston, Houghton Mifflin Company, 1960), pp. 466-7.
12. Walter Buckley, *Sociology and Modern Systems Theory* (Englewood Cliffs, Prentice-Hall, 1967), p. 2.
13. Ibid., p. 39.
14. Marvin E. Olsen, *The Process of Social Organization* (New York, Holt, Rinehart and Winston, 1978), p. 22.
15. Ibid., p. 24.
16. Ibid., pp. 25-6.
17. Ibid., p. 26.
18. Ibid.
19. Buckley, op. cit., p. 8.
20. Pitirim A. Sorokin, *Sociological Theories of Today* (New York, Harper and Row, 1966), pp. 45-6.
21. Talcott Parsons, Robert Bales, and Edward Shils, *Working Papers in the Theory of Action* (Glencoe, Free Press, 1953), p. 102.
22. Robert M. MacIver, *Social Causation* (New York, Harper Torchbook, 1964), pp. 172-3.
23. Sorokin, op. cit., p. 55.
24. Quoted by Nicholas Timasheff and George Theodorson, *Sociological Theory* (New York, Random House, 1976), p. 37.
25. Quoted by Buckley, op. cit., p. 13.
26. Quoted by Buckley, ibid., p. 14.
27. Ibid., p. 39.
28. Nicholas Mullins, *Theories and Theory Groups in Contemporary Sociology* (New York, Harper and Row, 1973), pp. 258-9.
29. Hans Gerth and C. Wright Mills, *Character and Social Structure* (New York, Harcourt, Brace and World, 1953), p. 22.
30. Ibid., p. 31.
31. Talcott Parsons, *The Social System* (New York, Free Press, 1951), p. 36.
32. Ibid., p. 21.
33. Alvin Boskoff, *Theory in American Sociology* (New York, Thomas Y. Crowell Company, 1969), p. 190.
34. Talcott Parsons and Edward Shils (eds.), *Toward a General Theory of Action* (Cambridge, Harvard University Press, 1951), p. 55.
35. Talcott Parsons, *Societies: Evolutionary and Comparative Perspectives* (Englewood Cliffs, Prentice-Hall, 1966), p. 5.
36. Charles Loomis and Zona K. Loomis, *Modern Social Theories* (Princeton, D. Van Nostrand Company, 1965), p. 331.
37. Parsons, *Social System*, pp. 13-14.
38. Ibid., p. 49.
39. Ibid., p. 50.
40. Parsons and Shils, op. cit., p. 150.

41. Bob Jessop, *Social Order, Reform, and Revolution* (London, Macmillan Company, 1972), pp. 16–18.
42. As quoted by Loomis, op. cit., p. 341.
43. Ibid., p. 342.
44. Parsons, *Social System*, pp. 5–6.
45. Ibid., p. 25.
46. As quoted by Loomis, op. cit., p. 333.
47. Parsons, *Societies*, p. 19.
48. Talcott Parsons, 'Social Systems', in David Sills (ed.), *International Encyclopedia of the Social Sciences*, op. cit., p. 459.
49. Ibid., p. 463.
50. Ibid., pp. 459–469.
51. Parsons, *Societies*, pp. 14–15.
52. Parsons, *Social System*, pp. 17–18.
53. Quoted in Daniel Rossides, *The History and Nature of Sociological Theory* (Boston, Houghton Mifflin Company, 1978), p. 488.
54. Parsons, *International Encyclopedia*, op. cit., p. 466.
55. Parsons, *Social System*, pp. 32–3.
56. From Rossides, op. cit., p. 488.
57. Loomis, pp. 332–3.
58. Jonathan Turner, *The Structure of Sociological Theory* (Homewood, Dorsey Press, 1974), p. 41.
59. Ralf Dahrendorf, 'Out of Utopia: Toward a Reorientation of Sociological Analysis', in N. J. Demerath and Richard Peterson, *System, Change, and Conflict* (New York, Free Press, 1967), p. 472.
60. Ibid., p. 462.
61. Buckley, op. cit., p. 25.
62. Ibid., p. 29.
63. Theodore Abel, *The Foundation of Sociological Theory* (New York, Random House, 1970), p. 165.

41. Bob Jessop, *Social Order, Reform, and Revolution* (London, Macmillan
Company, 1972), pp. 16-18.

CHAPTER 4

Functionalism

Modern sociological theory has been profoundly influenced by functional analysis which became enormously popular at the turn of the century. During the last two generations, functional analysis has become the principal, if not the only reigning, paradigm of contemporary sociology with more adherents than any other mode of sociological analysis or school of thought. It emerged and established itself at the most opportune time when sociologists had just abandoned the numerous partial explanations and deterministic theories and were looking for a more comprehensive theoretical and methodological tool for the analysis of various social phenomena and their inter-relatedness. It emerged in the tradition of great sociological theories 'consciously orienting itself to them and continually developing them'[1] and gave sociology a new and powerful explicative paradigm of society unmatched, yet, by any competing mode of sociological thinking.

Functional analysis is not new; it has a long history in both the natural and the social sciences. It borrowed heavily from biological sciences, especially the extension of the many analogies between society and organism. Although the early organicism with its emphasis on almost total integration of parts with the whole is now abandoned, its theoretical consequences persist in such central concepts as structure and inter-relatedness of elements. Thus, functionalism is simply a view of society as a self-regulating system of interrelated elements with structured social relationships and observed regularities. It is a sociological perspective which seeks to explain a social element or cultural pattern in terms of its consequences for different elements as well as for the system as a whole. Although functionalism manifests itself in a great variety of approaches, there is one common element: 'an interest in relating one part of a society or social system to another part or to some aspect of the whole'.[2]

Intellectual background

The history of functional analysis may be traced to Comte's *consensus universalis*, Spencer's organic analogy, Pareto's conception of society as a system in equilibrium and Durkheim's causal-functional analysis. Comte viewed society as a functionally organized system, its components in harmony. To him *consensus universalis*, the necessary correlation between the elements of society, was the very foundation of social structure. Spencer presented an organic biological model and contended: 'If organization consists in such a construction of the whole that its parts can carry on mutually-dependent actions, then in proportion as organization is high there must go a dependence of each part upon the rest so great that separation is fatal; and conversely. This truth is equally well shown in the individual organism and in the social organism.'[3] However, he attributed social structures and processes to individual needs such as desire for happiness, a contention rejected outright by Durkheim.

Durkheim insisted on the primacy of the system over elements and maintained that social facts, the proper subject matter of sociology, are independent of the individual will and imposed upon him from without. He cautioned against confusing the consequences with the causes of a social phenomenon: 'To show how a fact is useful is not to explain how it originated or why it is what it is. The uses which it serves presuppose the specific properties characterizing it but do not create them.'[4] A fact can exist without being useful, it may outlive its purpose or it may change its function over time. The role of Christianity is not the same today as it was in the Middle Ages but its religious dogmas have not changed for centuries. Therefore, Durkheim insisted on a separation of the two methods of explanation—the causal and the functional—but maintained both were necessary. 'When, then, the explanation of a social phenomenon is undertaken, we must seek separately the efficient cause which produces it and the function it fulfils.'[5] Thus did Durkheim elaborate the logic of functionalism by systematically explaining the causes and consequences of social facts and establish functionalism as a viable methodological and theoretical tool for sociological analysis. And the two British anthropologists, Radcliffe-Brown and Malinowski, elaborated and codified functionalism as the basis of anthropological—and sociological—thinking.

Malinowski's functionalism is often termed as individualistic functionalism because of its treatment of social and cultural systems as collective responses to fundamental biological needs of individuals modified by cultural values. Social structures and processes, institutions and values, are all regarded as functional responses to individual physiological needs such as hunger and sex which prompt cultural usages and social institutions which, in turn, shape the way these basic drives express themselves. He also viewed culture as a totally integrated way of life, an organic whole, homogeneous and harmonious. He tried to show the inter-relatedness of various cultural structures but rejected the rough approach to functionalism that reduces it to the almost useless proposition that everything is related to everything else. Rather, he viewed culture as an instrumental reality that existed and functioned in response to a variety of individual needs whose fulfilment led to the development of numerous cultural patterns and social usages.

Radcliffe-Brown rejected Malinowski's individualistic functionalism and, following the Durkheimian tradition, emphasized structured social relationships. But he substituted Durkheim's term 'needs' by 'necessary condition of existence' to avoid teleological interpretations. Having rejected Malinowski's emphasis on stated motives of individual participants, Radcliffe-Brown chose social structure as the unit of analysis and sought to explain numerous interpersonal relationships and socially patterned ways minimizing built-in strains inherent in such relationships. Radcliffe-Brown focussed primarily on the function of each element in the maintenance and development of a *total* structure, and largely overlooked functional consequences of specific elements for differentiated parts of the whole and for the individual components. In the words of Radcliffe-Brown:

By the definition here offered 'function' is the contribution which a partial activity makes to the total activity of which it is a part. The function of a particular social usage is the contribution it makes to the total social life as the functioning of the total social system. Such a view implies that a social system (the total social structure of a society together with the totality of social usages in which that structure appears and on which it depends for its continued existence) has a certain kind of unity, which we may speak of as a functional unity. We may define it as a condition in which all parts of the social system work together with a sufficient degree of harmony or internal consistency, i.e., without producing persistent conflicts which can neither be resolved nor regulated.[6]

What is Functionalism ?

According to Marion Levy, 'structural-functionalism is simply a synonym for explicit scientific analysis in general.'[7] It is nothing more complicated than asking one of the following empirical questions: (1) What structures are involved? That is, what observable uniformities can be discovered or alleged to exist in the phenomena studied?; (2) What functions have resulted? That is, what conditions resultant from previous operations can be discovered or alleged to exist in the phenomena studied?; and (3) What functions take place in terms of a given structure? that is, when process can be discovered to take place in terms of observable uniformities, what resultant conditions can be identified?

Bredemeir summarized functionalism as follows:

The functional approach to sociology consists basically of an attempt to understand social phenomena in terms of their relationship to some system. At least two distinct kinds of procedures, however, seem to be covered by that statement.

One is an attempt to assess that part played by an observed pattern of behaviour in the maintenance of some larger system in which it is included . . . . A second type of functional analysis should be clearly distinguished from the foregoing. This is an attempt to *explain the persistence* of an observed pattern of behaviour, that is, to approach an observed phenomenon with the question of its causes in mind.[8]

The term 'function' has at least four different connotations:

1. As an activity, reflected in popular speech, the term 'function' refers to social gatherings, public ceremonies, meetings, rallies, etc.

2. In a mathematical sense, 'function' is a variable whose value is determined by those of two or more other variables. An example would be the statement that population growth is a function of fertility and mortality rates.

3. As an occupational role, the term 'function' may refer to a specialized activity, duties, work or a set of official roles assigned to a public functionary. Examples would be the function of a tax assessor or of the Mayor of a town.

4. The term 'function' may mean an appropriate and sustaining activity or part played by a unit within the context of a larger whole. Labelled by Martindale as 'system-determined and system-sustaining activity', the term 'function' in this sense refers to positive and negative consequences of social institutions and processes. Although in earlier

times, function was commonly defined in a positive sense meaning contributions made by a part for the adaptation or adjustment of a given structure or its component parts, today the term 'function' is used in the more general and neutral sense of 'consequences' which may or may not be intended or recognized. Levy defines functions as 'a condition, or state of affairs, resultant from the operation of a structure through time.[9] He uses the term 'eufunction' to refer to positive or favourable consequences which contribute to the maintenance and survival of the social system, and the term 'dysfunction' to mean negative or unfavourable consequences that contribute to the system's disintegration and change.

Functions are not to be confused with subjective feelings. The social functions have, Merton insists, 'observable objective consequences'. Functional analysis seeks to describe the consequences of a given cultural usage or social elements; explain the persistence of an observed pattern of behaviour; and analyse specific contribution of a part of some whole to other parts and to the whole. Bredemeier summarized the methodology of functionalism as follows:

1. Productive analysis begins with a statement of the kind of action necessary to maintain some system of inter-relationships, namely, the system of which the observed uniformity is a part.
2. It states the motivational conditions which are necessary to produce that action (the normative criteria of gratification which will yield the relevant action).
3. It describes the motivational patterns actually operating so as to produce the uniformity under analysis.
4. It seeks to find the source of those patterns (to isolate the normative criteria responsible for the observed actions).
5. It compares the consequences of the operating motivation with the motivations described as necessary, including the deviant modes of adjusting to frustration of efforts to meet the criteria in question.
6. It finally assesses the role played by the uniformity in question in contributing to the system of which it is a part.[10]

Premises and propositions

1. Functional analysis involves the prior conceptualization of a system and a definite emphasis on the primacy of the system over elements. In the words of Abrahamson, 'Functionalism ... requires the prior conceptualization of a system before its "explanatory imagery" makes any sense.'[11] Martindale considers the organic system

to be the fundamental explanatory model of functionalism. According to him:

The distinctive property of functional analysis is the utilization of some concept of system as primary for sociological analysis. The first requirement of a comprehensible analysis is the clear definition of the system presumed. Nothing will render a functional analysis ambiguous more quickly or completely than uncertainty as to just what, in the particular case, constitutes the system. Once one has isolated the system, the next task is to identify its components. And once the components have been identified, the relation between these components becomes primary.[12]

To the functionalists, a system is more than the sum of its parts, it is also the relationships among its parts; their primary interest is in the contribution of the elements to the maintenance of the system (or its disintegration).

2. The elements of the system are functionally inter-related. Society, like an organism, is perceived as a system of functionally interrelated components each of which, like an organ, performs a function essential for the survival of the system. The normal operation of one element, then, requires the normal operation of other elements. Referring to the 'structural-functional system', Parsons writes:

On the one hand, it includes a system of structural categories which must be logically adequate to give a determinate description of an empirically possible, complete empirical system of the relevant class. One of the prime functions of *system* on this level is to insure completeness, to make it methodologically impossible to overlook anything important, and thus explicitly to describe *all* essential structural elements and relations of the system . . . .

On the other hand, such a system must also include a set of dynamic functional categories. These must articulate directly with the structural categories—they must describe processes by which these particular structures are maintained or upset, the relations of the system to its environment are mediated.[13]

3. Every element of the system has a function which contributes positively to the continued operation of that system or, negatively, toward its disintegration and change. The central focus of functionalism is the analysis of such contributions which are called eufunctions (positive), dysfunctions (negative) or 'survival' that is, an element which makes no contribution at all or has outlived its purpose. Thus religion is supposed to relieve the tension in a social group, incest taboo is supposed to regulate sexual access and avoid jealousy and

confusion of status, and the prison system is to enforce social control.

4. Every system is a well integrated configuration of elements that constitute an organic whole. In the words of Parsons, 'functionally specialized or differentiated sectors of living systems stand in some kind of an order of cybernetically hierarchical control relative to each other. This is quite a fundamental principle of ordering such systems and, as such, is an enormous aid to the solution of a wide variety of theoretical problems.'[14] For example, conventional wisdom in early anthropological analysis has portrayed traditional societies as coherent, harmoniously interwoven cultural systems with greater internal consistency, uniformity and homogeneity. Although modern societies are complex, rather than homogeneous, and characterized by greater structural differentiation, they are still regarded as systems with interdependent parts.

5. Every society is a relatively persistent structure of elements with built-in mechanisms for self-regulation. Using the principle of homeostasis, Parsons and his associates view society as a self-regulating system, attempting by more or less automatic adjustments to redress the balance of its equilibrium when it is upset by internal or external forces. 'The maintenance of relative stability, including stability of certain processes of change like the growth of an organism, in the face of substantially greater environmental variability, means that ... there must be "mechanisms" that adjust the state of the system relative to changes in its environment.'[15] The development of this strain of thought has proceeded through three distinct stages. First, functionalists regarded society as a stable system of patterned interaction or structured social relationships. In this view, basic relationships among system components change little over time, and emphasis was on such concepts as order, stability, structure, integration and persistence. In the second stage, functionalists sought to overcome the difficulties of 'normative' interpretations and problems of invariance by shifting from a more teleological type of explanation fashioned after the biological model to a more mechanistic or causal type of analysis following the lead of the physical science model. Thus, functionalists introduced the principle of homeostasis which postulates that society maintains a state of equilibrium which may be temporarily disturbed by crisis but will be automatically restored. Thirdly, faced with the criticism that equilibrium meant maintenance of status quo with no scope for fundamental changes, functionalists introduced the concept of dynamic equili-

brium meaning 'a minimum of integration' of 'a net balance of an aggregate of consequences'. According to this view change is possible, *status quo* is not necessarily restored, and the new balance simply maintains the new order and the new equilibrium. As van den Berghe points out, 'Although integration is never perfect, social systems are fundamentally in a state of dynamic equilibrium, i.e., adjustive responses to outside changes tend to minimize the final amount of change within the system. The dominant tendency is thus towards stability and inertia, as maintained through built-in mechanisms of adjustment and social control.'[16]

6. The functioning of a social system depends on consensus of its members on common goals and values related to the basic needs of the society. Parsons views the entire social system as resting heavily upon shared values. Indeed, the consensual requirements of a social system are central to Parsonian functionalism. Parsons observes:

This integration of a set of common value patterns with the internalized need-disposition structure of the constituent personalities is the core phenomenon of the dynamics of social systems. That the stability of any social system except the most evanescent interaction process is dependent on a degree of such integration may be said to be the fundamental dynamic theorem of sociology. It is the major point of reference for all analysis which may claim to be a dynamic analysis of social process.[17]

According to this view, order and stability are made possible because individuals internalize the norms of society and conform to this. van den Berghe adds:

The most important and basic factor making for social integration is value consensus, i.e., underlying the whole social and cultural structure, there are broad aims or principles which most members of a given social system consider desirable and agree on. Not only is the value system (or ethos) the deepest and most important source of integration, but it is also the stablest element of socio-cultural systems.[18]

7. As a logical corollary of propositions 5 and 6, it may be reiterated that the dominant condition of society is order reinforced by stability and consensus, and not conflict based on coercion and dissensus. To quote van den Berghe again,

Dysfunctions, tensions and 'deviance' do exist and can persist for a long time, but they tend to resolve themselves or to be 'institutionalized' in the long run. In other words, while perfect equilibrium or integration is never reached, it is the limit towards which social systems tend . . . . Change generally occurs in a gradual, adjustive fashion, and not in a sudden, revolutionary way. Changes which appear to be drastic, in fact affect mostly the social superstructure while leaving the core elements of the social and cultural structure largely unchanged.[19]

8. There are certain functional requisites that must be met if a system is to survive. The functional requisite may be defined as a generalized condition necessary for the maintenance of a system or a specific unit thereof. The best-known attempt to formulate the functional pre-requisites is by Aberle and his associates[20] who have presented a long list of positive and negative conditions. The four negative conditions any one of which is sufficient to bring a collapse of social systems are:

1. The biological extinction or dispersion of members;
2. Apathy of the members, i.e. the cessation of individual motivation;
3. The war of all against all; and
4. The absorption of the society into another society.

The functional pre-requisites that must be met to ensure the survival of society are:

1. Provision for an adequate relationship to the environment and for sexual recruitment
2. Role differentiation and role assignment
3. Communication
4. Shared cognitive orientations
5. A shared, articulated set of goals
6. The normative regulation of means
7. The regulation of affective expression
8. Socialization
9. The effective control of disruptive forms of behaviour.

According to Parsons, the functional requirements of a social system are adaptation to external situation, instrumental goal-attainment, integration among units of the system and pattern maintenance and tension-management. He emphasizes the problem of order and the adequacy of motivation. The system can sustain itself only if a sufficient proportion of its members perform the essential social roles with an adequate degree of effectiveness. Parsons insists that the system must 'have a sufficient proportion of its component actors adequately motivated to act in accordance with the requirements of its role system, positively in the fulfilment of expectations and negatively in abstention from too much disruptive, i.e., deviant, behaviour.'[21] He classifies the minimum conditions for the stability of a system into three categories: (1) Functional pre-requisites with respect to the individual. The minimum needs of the majority of the actors must be met and individuals must be motivated to participate in socially valued and rewarding activities. (2) Functional pre-requisites with respect to society. There must be a minimum of control over potentially disruptive behaviour and adequate mechanisms of social control. (3) Functional pre-requisites with respect to culture. There must be sufficient cultural resources to internalize a level of personality adequate for a social system; minimum conditions necessary for the production, maintenance and development of cultural systems in general and of particular types of cultural systems including language, symbols and communication, must be met.

It is true that every social system must fulfil certain fundamental structural and functional requirements for its survival. For example, sexual reproduction and assured food supply will be critical. However, the heuristic value of such formulations is not significant. It is easy to produce a long list of requisites some of which are too broad (communication, for example), too vague (shared cognitive orientations) and too obvious (sexual recruitment). Since it is only a list, you can always add to it. Moreover, it is difficult to test the empirical validity of the so-called functional pre-requisites. That is why Homans asks how many societies have actually failed to survive? However, we can and must distinguish between a particular social system and society as a generalized grouping. European society has survived but the feudal system has perished. Hindu society survived but Aryan society disappeared long ago. Thus, it may be too vague to ask 'What are the functional requisites for the survival of the society?' Rather, we should ask 'What conditions must be met if a given social system is to be maintained in its present setting?' Thus we may speak of the functional pre-requisites of any society but more accurately of Japanese society or Hindu society. While the generalized conditions for the survival of human society are approximately the same for Western society and Chinese society, the functional requisites for the survival of the Chinese communes, caste system or Hopi Indians are rather specific and unique. In short, functional requirements or pre-requisites are to be determined for different levels of generality.

Moreover, Sjoberg suggests that while societies do have functional pre-requisites, several of them may conflict to produce 'contradictory functional requisites which inhere within social systems or impinge upon them from without'. He suggests

That all social systems are, at one time or another, plagued by contra-dictory functional requirements (or imperatives) and that these are associated with the formation of mutually antagonistic structural arrangements that function to meet these requirements. Implied in this is the notion that some of these mutually contradictory structures may actually be essential to the 'operation' or 'maintenance' of the system.[22]

Sjoberg identifies three sources of contradictory demands: the needs of the internal system alone, the disjunctiveness between internal needs and external constraints, and the conflict among the external constraints themselves.

Robert Merton's Codification of Functional Analysis

More than any other sociologist Robert Merton has contributed to the codification and systematization of functional analysis. He re-viewed the essential postulates in functional analysis and critiqued and modified them as follows:[23]

1. Postulate of the functional unity of society. Based on biological analogy, this postulate views society as a well integrated and consis-tent whole the elements of which contribute to the maintenance of the total system. Radcliffe-Brown speaks of the contribution of parti-cular social usages 'to the total social life as the functioning of the total social system', and Malinowski, going one step further, even argues that usages are functional 'for culture as a whole—indirectly therefore for the biological and mental welfare of each individual member'. The underlying assumption is that standard social institu-tions or commonly shared beliefs and practices are functional for every member of the society. Merton questions the assumption and contends that cultural items do not function uniformly for the society and for all of its members. Anthropologists have exaggerated the social solidarity, homogeneity and integration of primitive societies. Even if such a conception has merits as a working hypothesis for anthropologists doing field work in fairly static and 'homogeneous' little communities, its application to modern complex societies characterized by functional specialization, structural differentiation and rational bureaucracy, is of doubtful value. Moreover, social integration, or even society for that matter, is no longer given but a

problem to be investigated. Therefore functional analysis must bring out both positive and negative consequences and specify which elements contribute to what and how.

2. Postulate of universal functionalism. This postulate assumes that 'all standardized social or cultural forms have positive functions.' Nineteenth century anthropologists, for instance, assumed that every continuing social pattern or custom must have positive functions contributing to the maintenance of the system and dubbed as 'survivals' any patterns whose functions could not be readily identified. Typical is Malinowski's contention that 'in every type of civilization, every custom, material object, idea and belief fulfils some vital function.' This assertion is certainly open to debate. What is good for the individual is not necessarily good for the society. A social custom that has positive consequences for the elite may have negative consequences for the masses. Even social institutions which are deliberately created for the betterment of society as a whole may have disastrous consequences at times and under certain circumstances for segments of the society. For example, universities and technical schools in developing countries that turn out educated people faster than the economy can absorb them into gainful employment may be sowing the seeds of frustration leading to greater violence and political instability.

3. Postulate of indispensability. The assumption is that if a social pattern is well established, it must be meeting some basic needs of the system, and hence it must be indispensable. It is a double-barrelled assumption—certain functions are indispensable for the survival of the social system; and certain social or cultural forms are indispensable for fulfilling these functions. Merton rejects the postulate as formulated and suggests that the same cultural item may perform multiple functions and alternative items may fulfil the same function. The need for government may be met by a ruthless dictator, a liberal democrat or a traditional monarch. If social integration is the function of religion, this function could be served by a strong, centralized government. If salvation is the function served by religion, a simple system of faith would do, and the complexity of numerous religious forms is hard to explain. Therefore Merton introduces such complementary concepts as 'functional alternatives', functional equivalents' or 'functional substitutes'.

Merton has codified functional analysis as follows:
1. Functional analysis begins with the selection of a standardized

(i.e., patterned or repetitive) social or cultural item whose functions are supposed to be studied.

2. Functional analysis generally involves reference to subjective dispositions such as motives and purposes of individuals involved in a social system which are not to be confused with the concepts of objective consequences of attitude, belief and behaviour.

3. In an attempt to eliminate some of the prevailing types of confusion, Merton sets out to redefine current conceptions of 'function'.

Functions are those observed consequences which make for the adaptation or adjustment of a given system; and *dysfunctions*, those observed consequences which lessen the adaptation or adjustment of the system. There is also the empirical possibility of *non-functional* consequences, which are simply irrelevant to the system under consideration.

In any given instance, an item may have both functional and dysfunctional consequences, giving rise to the difficult and important problem of evolving canons for assessing the net balance of the aggregate of consequences.

The second problem (arising from the easy confusion of motives and functions) requires us to introduce a conceptual distinction between the cases in which the subjective aim-in-view coincides with the objective consequence, and the cases in which they diverge.

Manifest functions are those objective consequences contributing to the adjustment or adaptation of the system which are intended and recognized by participants in the system.

Latent functions, correlatively, being those which are neither intended nor recognized.[24]

4. Seeking to identify functions being fulfilled for the society as a whole can be misleading since items may be functional for some individuals and some groups and dysfunctional for others. We must therefore consider a range of units for which the item has designated consequences.

5. The assumption of functional requirements which involves fulfilling 'conditions of survival' or meeting 'biological needs' must be re-examined. We must seek to establish types of functional requirements (universal *vs.* specific) as well as procedures for validating the assumption of these requirements.

6. Functional analysis must seek to identify and analyse the social mechanisms through which functions are fulfilled.

7. Having abandoned the gratuitous assumption of the functional

indispensability of particular cultural items, we must focus attention on the range of possible variation in the items which can serve as functional alternatives, equivalents or substitutes.

8. Functional analysis must recognize the inter-dependence of the elements of the social system as well as the limited range of variation in the items which can fulfil designated functions in the system. It is useless to say that everything is related to everything else. Nor can it be assumed that certain elements of a social system can be eliminated without affecting the rest of that system.

9. Functionalists generally tend to focus on the statics of social structure and to reject the study of structural change. However, the concept of dysfunction, which implies strain, stress and tension on the structural level, provides an analytical approach to the study of dynamics and change.

10. Merton calls for greater attention to the problem of the validation of various functional assumptions and postulates. 'This requires, above all, a rigorous statement of the sociological procedures of analysis which most nearly approximate the *logic* of experimentation.'[25]

11. Functional analysis itself has no intrinsic commitment to any ideological position; however, specific functional formulations advanced by particular sociologists may have an identifiable ideological note. The two are not to be confused.

Two of Merton's most significant contributions to functional analysis are subsumed under his discussion of the distinction between manifest and latent functions and between function and dysfunction. Manifest functions are those consequences that are intended and recognized by the participants in the system of action concerned, and latent functions are those consequences neither intended nor recognized by participants. Function (or eufunction in the words of Levy) is any activity or usage that contributes to the adaptation or adjustment of the unit to the unit's setting, and dysfunction is any activity that lessens the adaptation or adjustment of the unit to its setting. These distinctions and Merton's clarification of them have made functional analysis of cultural patterns and social institutions both more meaningful and scientific.

The same social arrangement can have, or may be perceived to have, both positive and negative consequences. Religion is perceived as means of salvation by the faithful but it is characterized as the opiate of the people by Marxists. What is functional for some may be dysfunctional for others. The rain that saves a crop spoils a picnic. What is in the best interest of the individual may be detrimental to the solidarity of the collectivity. The Chinese custom of accumulating and burning large sums of paper money to propitiate the spirit of the ancestors may be 'functional' for the ancestors and the progeny from the point of view of the 'faithful' but not necessarily so for the economy or population in general. What is functional for a particular group under certain circumstances may be dysfunctional for the same group under other circumstances. Maintenance of a rigidly stratified ascriptive society may be functional for the aristocracy but not for ever. The disgruntled poor and the oppressed may rise in rebellion and overthrow the oligarchy for whom the system has been functional. Thus what was functional for the elite in the short run works toward their destruction in the long run. Conversely, the socio-economic arrangement that is dysfunctional for the proletariat leads to revolutionary movements and new structural arrangements with positive consequences for the proletariat.

The typology of manifest and latent functions is equally illuminating. Merton gives the example of Hopi Indians who, in times of drought, gather to perform a ritual dance with the professed intention of magically causing rain. Whether the ritual brings rain or not, it does promote a general feeling of social solidarity, and even provides possibly relaxation and entertainment, and the custom continues. The Muslim who undertakes the traditional pilgrimage to Mecca and the Hindu who organizes an elaborate ritualistic ceremony to write the name of his favourite deity a million times are both trying to acquire spiritual merits, the intended function of the activity, but the latent function may be a substantial enhancement of the status and prestige of the actor. Furthermore, latent functions of certain activities are recognized by interested groups although not intended by the sponsors of those activities. For example, the intended function of establishing a new university in a town is to serve the needs of higher education. But the latent function—a significant boost to the local economy—is certainly recognized by the business community. What is latent to some is manifest to others. Also the very process of reporting the latent functions by the observer makes them manifest. Sometimes the intended consequences manifest themselves in myriad ways and even overshadow the professed intentions as in the case of many ritualistic ceremonies in old societies which assume significance as great social events. This explains why the Hopi rain dance and similar religious ceremonies persist regardless of whether they fulfil their manifest magical functions or not, for they have important social consequences like promoting social solidarity or enhancing the social status of the participants.

Varieties of Functionalism

Functionalism is not a single strain of thought; it represents a variety of approaches, systems of definitions and philosophical orientations. If Malinowski proposed an individualistic functionalism, Durkheim's was necessarily societal functionalism. Radcliffe-Brown established structural-functionalism and Talcott Parsons sought to provide a synthesis of social-structural and individualistic types of functionalism. Abrahamson observes:

An individualistic emphasis, associated with Malinowski, poses as its central question: How do social institutions function to satisfy individual need? A societal emphasis, by contrast, treats the social organism as a *sui generis*, viewing individual needs as socially determined. Its central issue involves the way in which social institutions function to meet the needs of the social system, or of the nonreducible collectivity. Parsons' synthesis merged the two, emphasizing the interpenetration of the social and the personality, as well as the cultural, systems.[25]

And Robert Merton codified and systematized functional analysis in terms of contemporary sociological theory.

Functionalism as Theory

Kingsley Davis[26] equates functional analysis with sociological analysis. He wants the debate about functional analysis to be abandoned, for there is no special method or body of theory called functional analysis which can be distinguished from other methods or theories within sociology. The assumption of a 'homogeneous' mode of analysis distinct from other sociological modes of analysis is false and has become a source of widespread confusion. Functional analysis is sociological analysis itself, and 'the lack of agreement on functionalism reflects the lack of agreement on the issues of sociological analysis itself'. According to Davis functional analysis may be said to do two things: to relate the parts of a society to the whole, and to relate one part to another. Indeed, this is what every science does: to 'explain phenomena from the standpoint of a *system* of reasoning which presumably bears a relation to a corresponding *system* in nature. In the case of sociology, what is distinctive is the subject, not the method; for it deals with human societies whereas other disciplines deal with other kinds of systems.'[28]

The main source of misunderstanding about functionalism is the language used in describing relationships. For example, phrases like 'has the function of', 'meets the need of', etc., borrowed from common discourse are thought to imply 'moral imperatives or volitional intent' rather than sheer causal relationships. Davis feels that if such terms were used in the natural sciences there would be no quarrel over their meanings. In response to criticism that functionalism 'abounds in principles and categories' but offers little by way of verification, Davis says that 'it is because functionalism is pre-eminently social theory. The broader and more general a theory, the less is the chance of proving or disproving it in its entirety. Social theory, in particular, tends to be broad and complex, because the observer reared in a society himself, comes equipped with knowledge and opinion about social matters including abstractions of great generality.'[29]

According to Davis, non-functionalism falls into one or the other of two classes: 'either they constitute some sort of reductionism and are therefore non-sociological in character, or they constitute some form of raw empiricism or sheer data manipulation and are therefore non-theoretical. In other words, whatever falls outside the domain of sociological theory falls outside the realm of functionalism'.[30] Davis claims that functionalism emerged as a revolt against reductionism, biologism, psychologism, evolutionism and varieties of determinism; it also represents a rebellion against trait-distributionism, empiricism and crude historicism. And, functionalism became popular because of the absence of a sociological point of view. Sociology was characterized by conflicting views and partial and deterministic theories and was in need of a term to represent sociological analysis, and functionalism fulfilled that need efficiently.

Functionalism as a Method

George Homans, although commonly regarded as one of the leading functionalists, insists that functional analysis is a method, not a theory. To have a theory one should have properties, propositions stating the relations between them, and the propositions must form a deductive system. Functionalists simply state that institutions are inter-related but do not explain what the inter-relations are. If a theory is an explanation, the functionalists have not yet produced a theory. It is not that their theory was wrong, but that it was not a theory. However, Homans claims that he is empirically a functionalist.

One carries out functional analysis when, starting from the existence of a particular institution, one tries to find out what difference the institution makes to the other aspects of social structure. That is, one carries out the empirical programme of functionalism. Since we have all learned to carry out functional analysis, we are in this sense all functionalists now. But functional analysis, as a method, is not the same thing as functional theory. And if we are all functional analysts, we are certainly not all functional theorists.[31]

Functionalism as a Perspective

Alex Inkeles treats functionalism as a perspective which 'stops the motions of the system at a fixed point in time, in order to understand how, at that moment, it works as a system.' According to him,

The basic perspective of the structural-functional point of view emerges in its prime emphasis on society, and on the interrelations of its institutions, rather than on the individual or groups such as the family. The main question to which it addresses itself is this: 'How is social life maintained and carried forward in time despite the complete turnover in the membership of society with every new generation?' The basic answer it gives is: 'Social life persists because societies find means (structures) whereby they fulfill the needs (functions) which are either pre-conditions or consequences of organized social life.'[32]

The structural-functional perspective also seeks to delineate the way in which the different structures are coordinated and integrated to preserve the unity of society as a complete system. This approach has contributed significantly to our understanding of many features and customs of society which otherwise are puzzling and seem to have no reason for existence. Inkeles, for instance, points out how the functional perspective has effectively treated certain violent, and even individually harmful, *rites de passage* in primitive societies as useful training in the sort of publicly sanctioned bravery and endurance which is required in societies that rely on hunting scarce and dangerous game. Similarly, 'the romantic love complex in our society may be seen as serving the function of providing the "push" required to free young people from the dependence encouraged by our family system, thus getting them to accept the responsibilities of marriage.'[33] Inkeles insists that every sociologist is to a degree something of a functionalist, for there are very few who would deny the existence of order or system in social life.

Formal Functionalism

Formal functionalism consists in rigorously formulated models which describe how units of a system are inter-related so as to maintain each other as well as the entity itself. Nagel has proposed the best-known formalization of functionalism which is brilliantly summarized by Cancian as follows:

A functional system, according to Nagel's definition, is made up of two types of variables: G's and state coordinates. G is the property of the system that is maintained or is stable. State coordinates determine the presence or absence of G and may include parts of the system's environment. The values of the state coordinates vary to such an extent that the maintenance of G is threatened, but when one exceeds the 'safe' limits for G, the other(s) compensates and G is maintained. Such a system of G and state coordinates may be called functional with respect to G, and state coordinates may be described as having the function of maintaining G.[34]

The model describes how G or the property of the system is maintained by one or more cultural usages, or social activity.

For example, a small task-oriented group could be treated as a functional system. Let G be the solution of the group's task or problem. Let the state coordinates be task-oriented activity and emotionally supportive activity. If these three variables can be usefully treated as a functional system, then: (1) problem solution is dependent on task-oriented activity and emotionally supportive activity; (2) at certain times, there will be such a preponderance of task-oriented activity that problem solution will be threatened because of decreased motivation or resentment over following others' suggestions—at these times emotionally supportive activity will increase, and problem solution will no longer be threatened; (3) at certain times, there will be such a preponderance of emotionally supportive activity that problem solution will be threatened. At these times task-oriented activity will increase to maintain problem solution or G.[35]

Formalization does not provide precise definition of concepts and specification of entities; it also avoids problematic concepts such as integration, survival, etc. But it does not offer substantive propositions and hence cannot explain much.

Alternative Approaches

Functionalism is certainly not a single theoretical stance; it is a multi-faceted approach with diverse perspectives and varying systems of definition. To view functionalism monotonically is to disregard the complexity of sociological phenomena. Structural-functionalism involves strands of Pareto, Marshall, Marx, Durkheim, Weber, Radcliffe-Brown, Malinowski, Parsons, Merton, Homans and others. Demerath suggests that much of the heterogeneity within structural functionalism revolves about the part-whole distinction:

On the one hand, it is possible to concentrate on the 'part', using the 'whole' as a kind of backboard off which to bounce effects and consequences. On the other hand, one can concentrate on the whole itself. Here the various parts are constituent elements and only really interesting as they contribute to the entirety. Put into more rococo terms, one can focus on a particular structure, using its contributions to the system as a source of information about the structure itself. *Or* one can stress the system and the relationships which compose it and make or break its equilibrium. Here individual structures are means to the end but not analytic ends in themselves. Here the level of analysis is shifted to a higher, but not necessarily more valid or significant plane. Using Hoult's language, the first option can be termed 'structuralism', and the second may be called 'functionalism', thus giving new life to a once moribund hyphen.[36]

Some of the alternative approaches may be summarized as follows:

1. One approach is the consideration of smaller units or micro systems rather than total societies in general. Although Martindale makes a distinction between macro functionalism which presumes the existence of large-scale systems and micro-functionalism which takes small scale systems as units of analysis, traditionally functionallism has been oriented primarily to the macrosociological approach. With the rise of exchange theory, theories of the middle range and the popularity of group dynamics, structural-functionalism has to orient itself to the reality of small scale systems as units of analysis.

2. Structural functionalism must abandon focus on notions of adaptation, integration and survival, and instead, analyse causes, conditions, effects and inter-relationships of social phenomena.

3. Structural functionalism must give up attempts to document functional pre-requisites of total societies; rather it should look for conditions of existence and persistence of particular social systems; similarly in describing the functions of particular social forms or

culture traits, every effort must be made to identify functional equivalents and alternatives.

4. Functionalism must substitute the notion of 'dynamic equilibrium' for 'static equilibrium' and balance its emphasis on structure, stability and invariance with concern for change, deviance and conflict.

5. The functional approach may be effectively combined with other paradigms and theories in sociology. Indeed, functionalism is the only broad, multifaceted approach that can meaningfully integrate the procedures and perspectives of other paradigms in sociology, both old and new. In the words of Eisenstadt:

First, it provided continuity with former 'master theories' and paradigms of social order. Second, it served as a focus for bringing together various areas of investigation into common analytic frameworks. Third, it revived the macro-sociological orientation by opening up its problems to empirical research through the provision of broad orienting frameworks and—despite the claims of critics—powerful explanatory concepts which covered a wide range of fields and areas of social life.[37]

6. Functionalism must be concerned with causes as well as consequences of social phenomena. However, to attribute the existence of a certain cultural item to the function it serves is a logical fallacy. Generally functionalists have been concerned primarily with the explanation of the part played by a social or cultural item in a given setting. Cancian remarks:

One frequently used alternative is to turn functional explanations around, that is, to reverse the explicans and the explicandum in the paradigm of explanation so that phenomena are explained by their causes, not by their effects or functions. Instead of explaining a social pattern by deducing it from the assumption that the society has survived, one explains the survival of society by the patterns whose effect is to ensure survival.[38]

7. An appropriate alternative functional approach may be enumerated as follows:

(a) First of all, identify the system to be investigated or the unit of analysis;

(b) Document its properties sytematically;

(c) Identify the various elements of the system;

(d) Determine the functions of the various elements;

(e) Explain the nature of the inter-relationship in terms of both functional integration and functional autonomy of elements;

(f) Examine the conditions under which the system operates; and

(g) In providing the functional interpretations of the findings of the investigation, keep in mind the 'bearings' of other theories or paradigms on the phenomena.

Critical Evaluation

An oft-repeated criticism of functionalism is that it is teleological. Function is often equated with purpose and the existence of any social form or cultural usage is readily attributed to its function. Typical is Davis' explanation of the existence of incest taboo. According to him: 'The incest taboo confines sexual relations and sentiments to the married pair alone, excluding such things from the relation of parent and child, brother and sister. In this way confusion is prevented and family organization maintained. The incest taboos therefore exist because they are essential to and form part of the family structure.'[39] In this case the contribution of a custom is confused with its cause. Apart from the fact that such an assumption is beyond empirical test, the reasoning is logically fallacious. The existence of incest taboo is explained (rather, explained away) by Davis in terms of the present-day role relationship between parent and child and between brother and sister. His line of reasoning cannot explain how the structure of parent-child and brother-sister relationship was so patterned as to require the establishment of a custom like incest taboo. On the other hand, if, as Davis says, the incest taboo is caused by its consequences namely preventing sexual jealousy and confusion of status, how do we explain the fact that several societies have institutionalized polygamy and polyandry which inhere the same types of potential conflicts?

The common assumption in functional analysis that the contribution an element makes to society is the society's maintenance or self-preservation is, as Spencer observes, 'frankly teleological. It argues that the purpose of society is its own preservation.'[40] To equate function with purpose or cause leads to other misleading assumptions as well. Levy declares:

Thus, it is not permissible to say that a given process of allocation of duties in a business firm exists because it is a functional requisite of that firm in its setting—that is teleology, pure and simple, little if at all different from the statement 'legs were created to wear pants and noses to wear spectacles'. It is permissible to say that, if there is to be such a firm in such a setting, there must be (or even in some cases that people planned it so in order to have such a firm) a definite allocation of duties, that in its absence the firm would cease to function.[41]

If children in India are polite and submissive to elders, it is certainly a function of child-rearing and socialization. But can we then say that child-rearing and socialization were created to make children polite and submissive? Although the custom of untouchability may 'function' to keep caste Hindus from pollution, it will be absurd to argue that untouchability was created to prevent pollution of the 'superior' castes, for if untouchability were not created, there would have been no pollution in the first place. This line of reasoning is no different from the argument that prisons were created to keep people out of prisons. Bredemeier in his brilliant essay on *The Methodology of Functionalism* has effectively exposed the efforts of functionalists to explain the causes of certain behaviour patterns in terms of their consequences. 'This is the failure systematically to realize that certain needs of individuals, which must be satisfied if they are to play certain roles necessary to the operation of a system, may themselves be generated by other aspects of the system. That is to say, a functional analysis which concentrates only on locating the function (need-satisfaction) of a given culture pattern is very likely to be seriously incomplete and therefore misleading. A complete understanding of the pattern in question would require asking not only 'what need does it satisfy?' but also 'what is the source of the need, i.e. what culture patterns give rise to that need'.[42]

Critics have charged that functionalism is speculative as a theory and untestable as a deductive system. They argue that it is only a conceptual frame of reference built around numerous principles and assumptions with a regretable lack of any data base. This argument is quite refutable. Functionalists have produced an abundant crop of literature, and much of it is made up of significant empirical studies. No one can deny the importance of Malinowski, Radcliffe-Brown, Robin Williams, Robert and Helen Lynd, Warner, Robert Merton, Marion Levy, Goode and Davis whose empirical works have profoundly influenced contemporary sociology. However, the language used by some of the leading functionalists is often so vague and imprecise as to be a mere exercise in phraseology or verbal tapestry. Yet, others have contributed significantly to the clarification, elaboration and operationalization of numerous sociological concepts such as role, status, social structure and institutionalization. Moreover, functionalists do not claim to have developed an exact science of human society but only a systematic theory of social phenomena. Davis is right when he observes:

From the standpoint of scientific discovery, the interesting part of theory is not the verified but the unverified propositions. A theory proved is no longer theory; it is fact. What is still unproved is speculation; it is, as commonly said, 'theoretical'. If the broadest theory in sociology is thrown out on the ground that it is 'functionalism', and if what is recommended in its stead are neat single propositions whose validity is proved but whose significance is not, the result will be scientific ritualism.[43]

A major difficulty associated with functional analysis is the ambiguity of the concepts like function, consensus and integration which are used inconsistently and often without clear definition. The use of a single term to cover several distinctly different referents has caused confusion and disagreement even among outstanding functionalists. Although Merton has done much to clarify the most important concepts, the terminological confusion still persists.

Functional analysis has exaggerated the homogeneity, stability and integration of the social systems. This view is derived from anthropological studies of simple societies on remote islands or remote quarters of the globe. Although its application to modern complex societies with considerable structural differentiation and functional specialization is extremely limited, many functionalists continue to overstress the integrative function of values giving credibility to the criticism that functionalism resembled a closed system model with emphasis on systemic needs, boundaries, boundary maintaining mechanisms and functional requisites. Parsons, for example, has generally overplayed consensus on values and ideas and the almost complete internalization of norms by social actors. Parsons views society as a well integrated system held together by value consensus and shared expectations. Actors in Parsons' scheme of system always comply with each other's expectations because of what Gouldner calls 'norm of reciprocity', 'institutionalization' or 'complementarity'. Denis Wrong's essay on the *Over-socialized Conception of Man* represents the sharpest attack on internalization theories. He notes that socialization provides man with a social identity but the individual is creative and has the ability to evaluate critically the social reality and take an autonomous stand toward concrete social roles. He feels that 'when our sociological theory over-stresses the stability and integration of society we will end up imagining that man is the disembodied, conscience-driven, status-seeking phantom of current theory.'[44]

Consensus is an important but insufficient basis for integration. Societies fall far short of complete consensus and often exhibit considerable dissensus. Moreover, consensus may have disintegrative consequences in the long run. Also there are alternative bases of integration such as economic interdependence and political coercion. Dahrendorf, for instance, attacks functionalists for minimizing the role of power, authority and coercion in enforcing consensus and integration.

This takes us to the next criticism of functional analysis, namely, that it has consistently underplayed conflict and structural strain. Abrahamson notes that 'functional theories conventionally view system needs as inherent rather than intended; and deliberate, or enacted, change is seen as problematic, both in terms of frequency of occurence and probability of success.'[45] Thus, having overstressed integration and consensus, functionalists overlook conflicts especially contradictions inherent in social structure. Even when they refer to conflicts, they treat them as 'deviance', 'abnormalities' or 'alteration of the dominant pattern'. This sort of 'shortcoming results from looking at social structure as the static "backbone" of society and considering structural analysis in social science as analogous to anatomy or morphology in biology.'[46]

Critics have, thus, charged that functional analysis is incapable of dealing with social change because of its reliance on 'a "static" or "circular" explanatory theory, based on the conception of social phenomena as being functionally adjusted to one another through their contribution to societal needs, and on the assumption of the existence of equilibrating mechanisms in the social system which counteracted any tendencies to functional maladjustment or inconsistency.'[47] C. Wright Mills has especially drawn attention to functionalists' inability to explain the great range of historical institutional variability of social systems. And Dahrendorf has observed that the concept of equilibrium is a static notion primarily concerned with maintaining a stable, integrated and harmonious equilibrium; with the notion of equilibrium change does not matter because even if there is change, it occurs within the framework of eventual re-equilibrium.

These criticisms are not entirely justified. In the first place, with the concept of dysfunction, structural conflicts and negative consequences of cultural items are recognized. Secondly, most of the leading functionalists have adopted a neo-evolutionary perspective which views change as a continuous process of increasing structural differentiation and functional specialization. Thirdly, the concept of dynamic equilibrium has change built into it and views society as a system in imperfect balance and open to adjustive changes. Fourthly, 'sensitivity to the interrelations of the component elements of a social system has increased our understanding of social change'[48] by reminding us that changes in one part of society have important implications for other parts of the system. Above all, Davis insists that the best analyses of social change have come from the so-called functionalists and that these works do not differ in any significant way from many studies of social change by persons opposing functionalism.

However, van den Berghe contends that:

a dynamic equilibrium model cannot account for the irreducible facts that:

1. Reaction to extra-systemic change is not always adjustive.
2. Social systems can, for long periods, go through a vicious circle of ever deepening malintegration.
3. Change can be revolutionary, i.e. both sudden and profound.
4. The social structure itself generates change through internal conflicts and contradictions.[49]

van den Berghe also points out that a society may resist exogenous change, fail to adapt by remaining static or inducing reactionary change. 'In this case, a cycle of cumulative dysfunction and increasing malintegration is initiated which, beyond a certain point, becomes irreversible, and makes drastic revolutionary change inevitable.'[50] Yet van den Berghe suggests we must modify the equilibrium model rather than abandon it.

Some critics attribute an inherent ideological bias to functionalism. Dahrendorf insists that functional analysis is utopian. As a functionally integrated, self-regulating system in equilibrium, society is perceived to be in an ideal state of adjustment both in terms of individual happiness and common welfare. Therefore, *status quo* is viewed as good—and not to be disturbed. Others have charged that functionalism is a politically and ideologically conservative theory which tends to support the establishment. For instance, Myrdal states:

If a thing has a 'function' it is good or at least essential. The term 'function' can have a meaning only in terms of an assumed purpose; if that purpose is left undefined or implied to be the 'interest of society' which is not further defined, a considerable leeway for arbitrariness in practical implication is allowed but the main direction is given; a description of social institutions in terms of their functions must lead to a conservative teleology.'[51]

van den Berghe argues that both Marxists and functionalists utilize part-whole relations and the concept of system equilibrium. But their emphases vary: while Maxists stress particular segments of society, functionalists focus on the whole. Analysis of function does not necessarily preclude consideration of change; nor does conflict mean change, for it may be regulated, resolved or suppressed. Conflict theorists and functionalists seem to view the function of religion curiously in the same light—maintenance of social control. To conflict theorists, religion functions as an opiate, maintains *status quo*, legitimizes the privileges of the oligarchy and establishes order to the detriment of the oppressed, but maintains order. Functionalists see religion as an integrative force, maintaining *status quo*, legitimizing the normative order and enforcing social control through value consensus. Thus, while conflict theorists see the role of religion in terms of its consequences for various parts of the whole and emphasizes the dysfunctional consequences, functionalists generally analyse the role of religion in terms of its consequences for the system as a whole, and underplay the dysfunctional consequences for the various parts. If some functionalists have overlooked the dysfunctional consequences of religion and its long-term disintegrative potential, it is not a shortcoming inherent in functionalism itself. It only means either functionalism has not been pursued to the fullest extent or that the observer shares certain strong ideological orientation. However, it is conceivable that functionalism and conflict theory converge on the same line of analysis. Neither functionalism nor the conflict theory is conservative or liberal; they are both conservative and liberal depending on the subject matter of particular inquiry and the analytical framework employed to describe short-term versus long-term functions of particular elements.

Merton has gone to great lengths to defend functional analysis against the charge of ideological bias which, according to him, is not at all inherent in it. If some have accused functionalism of conservative bias, others have accused it of radical bias. Merton insists 'functional analysis is neutral to the major ideological systems' and it is the particular functionalists who inject implicit valuations into their modes of inquiry. To this Davis adds: 'similarly, the view of functionalism as disguised ideology is most often advanced by those who are themselves ideologically oriented—as shown by the selectivity of the evidence adduced and by the purport of the theories proposed as substitutes. Strictly speaking, a theory's support of a moral or political bias is independent of its scientific validity.'[52]

And according to Abrahamson, although 'functional theories have rarely provided support for radical movements, while they have frequently supported establishments' it is merely an accurate conceptual picture of the society which represents strong and pervasive conservative forces. Thus those who are attacking functionalism's conservativeness are in fact often attacking society's conservativeness. Perhaps, Harold Fallding has put the whole debate in proper perspective in the following statements:

1. Functional analysis involves evaluation.
2. The evaluation involved in functional analysis is objective and needs no apology.
3. Evaluating social arrangements as functional or dysfunctional is equivalent to classifying them as normal or pathological; this is a necessary preliminary to the search for causal explanation.
4. It is because the demand for need-satisfaction through them is unrelenting, that social arrangements must achieve stability, adaptive change and integration. For this reason, making judgments of function or dysfunction, normality or pathology, presupposes a whole catalogue of assumptions about human needs.[53]

The methodology of functionalism tends to be weak, for it rests on intuition or the ability of the observer to see or detect functions performed by particular elements. Sometimes the function of a particular social form or cultural item seems to be an invention of the observer, especially if it is a latent function which is neither intended nor recognized by the actor. Does the ritual of rain dance really function to enhance group solidarity among the Hopi Indians? Does religion really promote social integration and relieve tension? Is it not also possible to argue the obverse with reference to its various dysfunctions? Thus the recognition of functions often depends on the perception and even imagination of the observer, and not on scientific testimony. A closely related criticism is that functional analysis provides no adequate basis for deductive or inductive prediction and that it cannot predict or explain what forces push a society toward the adjustive or maladjustive alternative.

However, prediction may not be all that crucial; but functional analysis does explain the interrelationship between social phenomena and thus enhance the predictive power of theory. Functionalism has contributed substantially to both sociological theory and research; developed and refined numerous sociological concepts; elaborated and strengthened different paradigms in contemporary sociology; enhanced the heuristic value of other theoretical orientations; classified social, cultural and personality systems and furnished an effective conceptual apparatus to deal with them; refined and operationalized many basic sociological concepts like social structure, role, status, rank, institution and prestige; developed and articulated several analytical frameworks and led to the systematization of disparate empirical generalizations. Eisenstadt writes:

the impact of the broad structural-functional paradigm and its analytic concepts and orientations impinged on many areas of research. Hardly an area of research remained unaffected by these developments. In almost all fields of sociology, the structural-functional approach not only provided a general view, image, or map of the social system, but gave hints about more analytic specifications that could become foci of research. In such areas of research as stratification, political organization, educational sociology, and the study of deviance, many specific paradigms and research programs were related to or derived from the structural-functional framework. In other substantive fields, as in studies of public opinion and voting behavior, which had developed strong concentrations on middle-range theories, not only were the concepts those that had been developed in the structural-functional model. This model also provided the basis for a broader analytic orientation.[54]

Finally functionalism is accused of neglecting the individual and of inadequate treatment of the relationship between the individual and society. Functionalists regard the individual as a trained role player, an empty receptacle into which culture is poured from the overflowing cup of society. The individual is thought to make no responses but is conceived as an uncritical receiver who acquires socially prescribed values by moving from role to role. Homans thought the functionalists acted as if there were no men around and hence spoke of 'Bringing Men Back In'. Emmet cautions:

The elements of a social system may be institutionalized roles, but the members of a society are individuals with wills of their own. They may

67072

therefore be deemed to have purposes which cannot simply be reduced to their function, where 'function' is defined as the contribution each makes to maintaining the equilibrium of the social system. Their purposes may sometimes have a negative effect on this, or be simply indifferent.[55]

However, Parsons' formulation of the personality system with the motivation, gratification-deprivation complex and other psychological variables and Inkeles' theory of personality and social structure have given the individual his due place in sociological analysis.

Some of these criticisms are justified, and functionalism has effectively responded to them by revising and codifying many of its original premises and propositions. Indeed, it has also been pointed out functionalists have been too sensitive and too quick to respond to criticism. Abrahamson claims that 'much of the criticism has been directed at a straw man, an exaggerated version of functionalism that nobody advocated in the first place.'[56] Moreover because of the historic centrality of functionalism in sociological theory, 'sociologists are unsure about what would be left of sociological theory if it were expurgated of all functionalist content.'[57]

In the final analysis the question whether functionalism is a theory or method is difficult to answer. While Homans insists that functionalism is not a theory because it lacks a set of propositions that form a deductive system, Landau argues that with all its deficiencies, 'the essential premises of this model offer some working rules of inquiry' and it is possible to 'essay and assess its use as an ordering and explaining mechanism for studies that are empirically grounded.' Kaplan says functionalism need not be regarded as a theory in the strict sense. 'It may be viewed as a program of inquiry, a set of methodological prescriptions: to find an explanation for a given pattern of behaviour look first to the purposes it might be serving.'[58] And refering to Kuhn's point of view that any science at any point in its history tends to be dominated by a paradigm—a conception of what constitutes the appropriate subject matter of the discipline, how it ought to be studied, and what an investigator is likely to find—Abrahamson contends that functionalism is neither a theory nor a method but a paradigm which includes both.

Thus the adherents of this model, by virtue of combining the analytic transformation of concepts with broad, albeit vague, conceptions of the working of the social system, provided both an important framework for a macrosocietal approach and, perhaps paradoxically, some

Lincoln Christian College

of the most important analytic starting points and concepts around which middle range theories of different levels could converge.[59]

Functionalism has been a very effective counter to many partial and deterministic theories. 'In anthropology, functionalism successfully opposed the diffusionists and the empiricists, who tended to ignore general patterns, and the evolutionists and the rigid monocausalists, who tended to ignore the necessity of careful description.'[60] In sociology functionalism continues to fight neopositivists who would reduce sociology to measurement and nominalists who would reduce sociological phenomena to psychological phenomena. 'Like the classic paradigmatic models, structural-functionalism combined a certain vision of the nature of society with the formulation of an analytic conception of social order.'[61] We may conclude with Timasheff: 'Functionalism is perhaps more promise than achievement. But it is an important promise.'[62]

NOTES

1. S. N. Eisenstadt, *The Form of Sociology: Paradigms and Crises* (New York, John Wiley and Sons, 1976), p. 181.
2. Francesca M. Cancian, 'Varieties of Functional Analysis', in David Sills (ed.), *International Encyclopedia of the Social Sciences*, vol. 6 (New York, Macmillan Company, 1968), p. 29.
3. Herbert Spencer, 'Social Structure and Social Function', Lewis Coser and Bernard Rosenberg (eds.), *Sociological Theory* (New York, Macmillan Company, 1971), pp. 615–16.
4. Emile Durkheim, 'Causal and Functional Analysis', in Coser and Rosenberg, Ibid., p. 618.
5. Ibid., p. 622.
6. Radcliffe-Brown, 'Structure and Function in Primitive Society', in Coser and Rosenberg, Ibid., p. 626.
7. Marion Levy, 'Structural-Functional Analysis', *International Encyclopedia of the Social Sciences*, op. cit., p. 22.
8. Harry C. Bredemeier, 'The Methodology of Functionalism', *American Sociological Review*, 20 (April, 1955), 173.
9. Marion Levy, *The Structure of Society* (Princeton, Princeton University Press, 1952), p. 56.
10. Bredemeier, op. cit., p. 180.
11. Mark Abrahamson, *Functionalism* (Englewood Cliffs, Prentice-Hall, 1978), p. 6.
12. Don Martindale, *The Nature and Types of Sociological Theory* (Boston, Houghton Mifflin Company, 1960), p. 477.

13. Talcott Parsons, *Essays in Sociological Theory: Pure and Applied* (Glencoe, Free Press, 1949), p. 23.

14. See Lewis Coser (ed.), *The Idea of Social Structure, Papers in Honor of Robert Merton* (New York, Harcourt, Brace Jovanovich, 1975), p. 77.

15. Ibid., p. 68.

16. Pierre L. van den Berghe, 'Dialectic and Functionalism', in R. Serge Denisoff et al. (ed.), *Theories and Paradigms in Contemporary Sociology* (Itasca, F. E. Peacock Publishers, 1974), p. 281.

17. Talcott Parsons, *The Social System* (New York, Free Press, 1951), p. 42.

18. van den Berghe, op. cit., p. 281.

19. Ibid., p. 281.

20. D. F. Aberle et al., 'The Functional Prerequisites of a Society', *Ethics*, **60** (January, 1950), 100–11. Also reprinted in N. J. Demerath and Richard Peterson, *System, Change, and Conflict* (New York, Free Press, 1967), pp. 317–37.

21. Parsons, Social System, op. cit., p. 27.

22. Gideon Sjoberg, 'Contradictory Functional Requirements and Social Systems', in N. J. Demerath and Peterson, op. cit., p. 340.

23. Robert K. Merton, *Social Theory and Social Structure* (Glencoe, Free Press, 1957), summarized from pp. 25–37.

24. Ibid., p. 51.

25. Ibid., p. 54.

26. Abrahamson, op. cit., p. 35.

27. Kingsley Davis, 'The Myth of Functional Analysis as a Special Method in Sociology and Anthropology', *American Sociological Review*, **24** (December, 1959), 757–73. Also reprinted in Demerath and Peterson, op. cit., pp. 379–402.

28. Ibid., Demerath, p. 381.

29. Ibid., pp. 387–88.

30. Ibid., pp. 383–84.

31. George C. Homans, 'Bringing Men Back In', *American Sociological Review*, **29** (December, 1964): 809–18. Also reprinted in R. Serge Denisoff, op. cit., 357–71. Quoted from p. 359.

32. Alex Inkeles, *What is Sociology?* (Englewood Cliffs, Prentice-Hall, 1964), pp. 34–5.

33. Ibid., p. 35.

34. Cancian, op. cit., p. 38.

35. Ibid., p. 38.

36. N. J. Demerath: 'Synecdoche and Structural-Functionalism', in Demerath and Peterson, op. cit., p. 506.

37. S. N. Eisenstadt, op. cit., p. 186.

38. Cancian, op. cit., p. 37.

39. Kingsley Davis, *Human Society* (New York, Macmillan Company, 1949), p. 402.

40. See Abrahamson, op. cit., p. 39.

41. Levy, *The Structure of Society*, p. 54.

42. Bredemeir, op. cit., p. 176.

43. Davis, *The Myth*, op. cit., 396.

44. Dennis H. Wrong, 'The Oversocialized Conception of Man in Modern Sociology', *American Sociological Review*, **26** (April, 1961), 183–93. Also reprinted in Milton L. Barron (ed.), *Contemporary Sociology* (New York, Dodd, Mead and Company, 1972), p. 559.

45. Abrahamson, op. cit., p. 9.

46. van den Berghe, op. cit., p. 283.

47. Eisenstadt, op. cit., p. 197.

48. Inkeles, op. cit., p. 36.

49. van den Berghe, op. cit., p. 283.

50. Ibid., p. 284.

51. As quoted by Merton, op. cit., p. 37.

52. Davis, The Myth, op. cit., p. 393.

53. Harold Fallding, 'Functional Analysis in Sociology', *American Sociological Review*, **28** (February, 1963), 5–13.

54. Eisenstadt, op. cit. p. 185.

55. Dorothy Emmet, 'Function and Purpose', in Demerath and Peterson, op. cit., p. 423.

56. Abrahamson, p. 37.

57. Ibid.

58. Abraham Kaplan, 'Purpose, Function, and Motivation', in Demerath and Peterson, op. cit., p. 428.

59. Eisenstadt, op. cit., p. 184.

60. Cancian, op. cit., p. 29.

61. Eisenstadt, op. cit., p. 181.

62. Nicholas Timasheff, *Sociological Theory* (New York, Random House, 1967), p. 228.

CHAPTER 5

Conflict Theory

Whereas structural-functionalism has established itself as a dominant mode of sociological analysis, conflict theory is still in its infantile stage. As a matter of fact, there is no such thing as *the* conflict theory of sociology; rather, there are several conflict theories which seek to explain specific aspects of social phenomena. However, there are many attempts in contemporary sociology to develop a unified conflict mode of sociological analysis to match the theory of structural-functionalism. Although the sociological conflict theory is of recent origin, the foundations of conflict theory *per se* were laid by ancient philosophers and statesmen. Martindale has provided a comprehensive historical account of conflict theory beginning with Kautilya's *Arthasastra* written in the third century B.C. We can do no better than quote him here:

Once conflict was accepted as a central fact of society, a rich intellectual tradition was available for its interpretation. Every society has its conflicts; every society has persons who face up to them. In classical Greece a series of thinkers from Heraclitus to the Sophists treated conflict as *a* primary, perhaps *the*, primary social fact. The best developed conflict theory of antiquity was that of Polybius, for whom it was the fundamental fact in the evolution of political institutions. In fact, he visualized the state as a kind of stabilized system of power. In the medieval Arabic world, Ibn Khaldun developed a conflict theory of society based on the assumption that the struggles between the nomad and the tiller were fundamental to the evolution of civilization.

While Ibn Khaldun's ideas did not affect Western thought until the nineteenth century, Polybius' conceptions were transmitted directly to Niccolo Machiavelli, who found the origin of the state and its key institutions in the same place. These ideas were expanded by Jean Bodin, who became a harbinger of the modern theories of sovereignty. They were also transmitted to Thomas Hobbes, who developed them into a materialistic rationalism.

Modern conflict theory was pulled out of its rationalistic context and turned into an empirical investigation by David Hume and Adam Ferguson. In treating conflict as an empirical fact, Hume laid the foundations for the contemporary theory of the political party. Ferguson turned these ideas into a general account of political institutions and government, conceived as arising out of struggle. Parallel theories appeared in France in the works of Turgot.

The idea of universal competition taken from modern conflict theory became central to classical economics. Competition, in turn, was transformed from the central law of economic behaviour by Thomas Malthus into a general competition to survive. It became the basis of his population theories. Conflict theory was now ready to migrate to biology, where, in the works of Darwin, it became the foundation for a reconstruction of biological science.

The theory of social conflict has had a richly colorful career in the West. At one time it had been turned into a very particular explanation of special events: at another it had been turned into a general examination of human affairs. A treasure of experience and insight was available to the new school of theory.[1]

There are two distinct traditions of conflict theory in the classical works:

1. The power relations tradition of political philosophy. Machiavelli, Bodin, Hobbes, and Mosca have analysed conflicts in the polity in terms of power relationships and have treated the 'state' as the central object of analysis.

2. The tradition of competitive struggle in classical economics. Adam Smith, Robert Malthus and generations of economists following them placed economic competition at the centre of their inquiry.

Sociological conflict theory is largely a synthesis of these two traditions with primary focus on the unequal distribution of rewards in society. Karl Marx is its leading architect. C. Wright Mills, Ralf Dahrendorf, Irving Louis Horowitz, Lewis Coser, Herbert Marcuse, Randall Collins and André Gunder Frank are among the noted conflict theorists of contemporary sociology.

Generally speaking, conflict theories tend to be specific, restricted to the interrelationship between two or more units within society. Racial tension, class war, religious conflicts, strikes, protests, student power movements, revolutions, peasant uprisings and the like often become subjects of analysis. Although conflict sociology abounds in partial theories, there are also a few noteworthy attempts at comprehensive theories of conflict which seek to explain social change in total societies. Karl Marx and Ralf Dahrendorf represent macro-level conflict theories; C. Wright Mills' theory of the power elite is also a general theory but its frame of reference is limited to American society.

Marx is undoubtedly the master theoretician of conflict sociology. According to him, the existence of different social classes is the continuous source of inevitable conflict, and changes in the social structure occur through violent upheavals affecting class composition. Weber, Simmel, Mosca and Michels are identified as other pioneers of conflict tradition. Weber's political writings, especially his emphasis on power, authority, and social change, have contributed substantially to the development of a conflict theory of society. Mosca's theory of conflict centres around power struggle in the polity. He argues that there is a ruling class in every society which constantly tries to monopolize political power at the expense of the lower class and that 'this conflict produces an unending ferment of endosmosis and exosmosis between the upper classes and certain portions of the lower.' According to him,

In all societies—from societies that are very meagerly developed and have barely attained the dawnings of civilization, down to the most advanced and powerful societies—two classes of people appear—a class that rules and a class that is ruled. The first class, always the less numerous, performs all political functions, monopolizes power and enjoys the advantages that power brings, whereas the second, the more numerous class, is directed and controlled by the first, in a manner that is now more or less legal, now more or less arbitrary and violent, and supplies the first, in appearance at least, with material means of subsistence and with the instrumentalities that are essential to the vitality of the political organism.[2]

It is the monopoly on the use of force that sustains the ruling class in power and hence it can be overthrown only by the force of a revolution. Mosca asserts that even in a democratic form of government, in spite of all protestations to the contrary, 'an organized minority imposes its will on the disorganized majority'. Similarly, Michels' 'Iron Law of Oligarchy' is clearly in the conflict perspective. The 'technical and administrative' imperatives of a large organization lead to the formation of a ruling elite who exercise oligarchical influence over the average members of the group. Democracy is 'inconceivable without organization' and hence subject to the law of oligarchy.

Class, however, is only one of the many areas of conflict in society. Social Darwinists spoke of the 'struggle for existence' and the 'survival of the fittest' while physiocrats concentrated on competition for the necessities of life; political philosophers addressed themselves to questions of power and authority. And whereas psychologists dealt with inner conflicts and the dynamics of attitudinal change, anthropologists studied conflicts rooted in primitive customs that had integrative functions. Amidst this disjointed perusal of conflict in society, sociologists have identified two broad categories of conflict:

1. Endogeneous conflict. These are sources of change from within a society and indicate the most common areas of conflict which may be analytically distinguished as follows:

(a) Inherent predilections to change. Comte's concept of social dynamics, Sorokin's principle of immanent self-directing change, or the functionalists' concept of structural strain all in effect refer to inherent possibilities of change. However, to functionalists, change is often a deviation from the normal whereas conflict theorists treat change as the essential condition of social order at all times.

(b) Conflict over the distribution of desirables. One of the primary sources of societal conflict is the differential distribution of rewards such as wealth, power and prestige within a given society. Many conflict theories, notably Marx, Mosca, and Mills, have kept this at the centre of their theoretical schema.

(c) Conflict of values. The cumulative effects of innovation, techno-logical revolution, environmental crisis, generation gap, automation, sexual revolution, new value-orientations and the 'break-up' of the normative structure have been a series of conflicts which manifested themselves in a variety of social movements and individual identity crises.

(d) Conflict of authority. To some sociologists, particularly Dahrendorf, the authority structure is the primary source of conflict. No organization exists without a system of authority; and a system of authority necessarily involves conflict between those who give orders and those who take them.

(e) Conflict between the individual and society. What is good for society is not necessarily good for the individual, for often there is a basic conflict between the interests of the two. Societies flourish at the expense of some individuals and vice versa. W. I. Thomas has argued that the evolution of the individual personality is the result of a continuous struggle between society and the individual; the in-dividual fights for unbridled self-expression while society seeks to suppress it and mould him into ready-made pigeonholes of conven-tional status roles.

2. Exogenous conflicts, or those from without or between systems, normally fall into three categories:

(a) Wars. Today's wars are often waged between systems unlike those in the past which were conquests for loot and booty. The study of the rise of Nazism, Hungary, Vietnam, the Banana Republics, the Bay of Pigs, and Bangladesh have produced a number of political and intellectual treatises that have used the conflict frame of reference. However, a comprehensive conflict theory is yet to be developed as a tool for the analysis of war as a social phenomenon.

(b) Cultural invasion. Intercultural transactions are a perpetual source of conflict between societal orders. Variously interpreted as boundary exchanges, cultural frontiers, westernization, modernization and the like, cultural invasion operates in a myriad of ways—technological innovation, mass media and the revolution of rising expectations, disruption of traditions and new political movements. Several developmental sociologists have used conflict perspectives in their analysis of social change in the developing societies.

(c) Conflict of ideology. Repercussions of ideological conflicts overflow the boundaries of the nation-state or society. Capitalism, communism, democracy, fundamentalism, egalitarianism, racial determinism, and other similar persuasions account for periodic conflicts on the international scene. Throughout the history of man, ideological conflicts have been at the root of revolution, warfare, and international strife.

Simmel considered conflict, a form of sociation, endemic in any interaction. The 'instinct of opposition' and the element of hostility are thought of as being essential ingredients of group relationships. Nevertheless, more often than not, conflict establishes unity and strengthens the group. To quote Simmel:

Conflict is admitted to cause or modify interest groups, unifications, organizations . . . . If every interaction among men is a sociation, conflict—after all one of the most vivid interactions, which, furthermore, cannot possibly be carried on by one individual alone—must certainly be considered as sociation. And in fact, dissociating factors—hate, envy, need, desire —are the causes of the conflict; it breaks out because of them. Conflict is thus designed to resolve divergent dualisms; it is a way of achieving some kind of unity, even if it be through the annihilation of one of the conflicting parties . . . . Conflict itself resolves the tension between contrasts. The fact that it aims at peace is only one, an especially obvious, expression of its nature: the synthesis of elements that work both against and for one another.[3]

Simmel, thus, rejected the notion that conflict is a disruptive temporary phase. He considered peace and conflict to be equivalent faces of social reality; neither is inherently constructive or destructive. 'In contrast to such pure negativity, conflict contains something positive. Its positive and negative aspects, however, are integrated; they can be separated conceptually, but not empirically.'[4]

Lewis Coser distinguishes between two types of conflict—realistic and nonrealistic.

Conflicts which arise from frustration of specific demands within the relationship and from estimates of gains of the participants, and which are directed at the presumed frustrating object, can be called *realistic conflicts*, in so far as they are means toward a specific result. *Nonrealistic conflicts*, on the other hand, although still involving interaction between two or more persons, are not occasioned by the rival ends of the antagonists, but by the need for tension release of at least one of them. In this case the choice of antagonists depends on determinants not directly related to a contentious issue and is not oriented toward the attainment of specific results.[5]

Realistic conflict entails *functional alternatives as to means* wherein the participant has the option of employing means other than conflict. Since realistic conflicts revolve around specific goals, the attainment of those goals is more important than the destruction of the enemy. For instance, workers demanding higher wages may elect to cooperate with the management and reach accommodation, rather than strike, if cooperation is perceived to be more effective in goal attainment. On the other hand, when negative attitudes toward the capitalist system and the 'oppressive bourgeoisie' builds up aggressive tension in the workers, non-realistic conflict manifests itself in a variety of ways. And precisely because it invoves only *functional alternatives as to objects*, not means, nonrealistic conflicts are often less 'stable' and more disruptive. Realistic conflicts, which emanate from conflicting values and inequitable allocations of scarce resources, are directed toward the achievement of realistic ends. Nonrealistic conflicts which arise from deprivations and frustrations manifest themselves in varieties of antagonistic behaviour 'since satisfaction is derived from the aggressive act itself'.

Dahrendorf distinguishes between two theories of society in contemporary sociology: the integration theory of society and the coercion theory of society. Whereas the former is equated with structural-functionalism, the latter corresponds to conflict theory. According to Dahrendorf, coercion theory 'views social structure as a form of organization held together by force and constraint and reaching continuously beyond itself in the sense of producing within itself the forces that maintain it in an unending process of change.'[6] And unlike structural-functionalism, conflict theory is anti-systemic in character. Functionalists deal with society as a social system, whereas conflict theorists often concentrate on specific units within societies such as classes, parties, factions, interest groups, etc. Whereas functionalists consider their units of analysis, namely social systems, to be voluntary associations of people held together by value-consensus, conflict theorists perceive associations to be imperatively coordinated by the forces of constraint and domination.

Horowitz decries the

mechanical notion of the relation of consensus and conflict as structured and unstructured modes of behaviour respectively. Consensus involves objectification of position, group cohesion, collective representations, common traditions, and rules for inducting and indoctrinating new members; while conflict is seen as external to social structure, as spontaneity, impulsive action, lack of organization, intuitive response to immediate situations. In short, consensus differs from conflict as organization differs from deviance. Thus to discuss social structure is by definition not to examine conflict situations, and of course, the pernicious *vice versa*, to examine conflict situations is to discuss something extraneous to social structure.[7]

According to Horowitz, the tendency to treat conflict as alien to social structure or as destructive of the social organism has led to the erroneous assumption that changes can be brought about only by apocalyptic or spontaneous methods. Moreover, consensus does not necessarily imply social equilibrium; nor does conflict invariably entail disequilibrium. Using an analogy from game theory, he argues that there are conflicts which are part of the normative structure, especially 'conflicts programmed for continuation of the game (such as parliamentary debates), and there are those programmed to end the game through a change of the rules as such (such as *coup d'etats*).'[8] The existence of a perfect constitution as well as the prolonged absence of a formal constitution are equally disruptive. 'In short, both consensus and conflict are phenomena which may promote or retard social cooperation or political cohesion.'

The underlying assumptions of conflict theory may be summarized as follows:

1. Dahrendorf argues that 'In the sense of strict sociological analysis, conflicts can be considered explained if they can be shown to arise from the structure of social positions, independently of the orientation

of populations and of historical *deiex machina*.'[9] In other words, from the point of view of general sociological analysis, it is not enough to explain unique group conflicts in specific societies (blacks *v.* whites in the United States, Protestants *v.* Catholics in Ireland or Christians *v.* Moslems in Lebanon); rather a comprehensive conflict formulation should demonstrate how conflicts emanate from the very nature of social stucture, the fundamental assumption being that there are seeds of conflict embedded in every social structure.

2. The social universe and its component elements are in a state of flux. 'Moreover, change is ubiquitous not only in time but also in space, that is to say, every part of society is constantly changing.'[10] Hence, conflict theory focusses on factors interfering with the processes of change. Since functionalists consider order and stability to be the dominant conditions of society, to them change is a deviation from the normal, equilibrated system, whereas conflict theorists, believing in incessant change, will be 'perturbed' only if social structure fails to produce change.

3. Although conflict is inherent in the social structure, it is not always violent or manifest. Social conflict can be latent, regulated or momentarily constrained (controlled). The inherent predilections to change within the social structure may be rated on a continuum ranging from perfect harmony, an ideal situation, to bloody revolution, an infrequent occurrence. In any given social structure, there is a continuum ranging from violent upheavals like wars and revolutions to parliamentary debates and more subtle, hidden conflicts or competition between interest groups.

4. Dahrendorf stresses 'the underlying assumption that conflict can be temporarily suppressed, regulated, channeled, and controlled but that neither a philosopher-king nor a modern dictator can abolish it once and for all.' He rejects the notion of conflict resolution on the ground that it deals with causes rather than expressions of social conflict. Since social conflicts are inherent in the very nature of social organization, they cannot be eliminated altogether, only their expressions in specific contexts can be resolved as in the case of a labour strike or lock-out.

5. There is a third notion which, together with change and conflict, constitutes the instrumentarium of the conflict model of society: the notion of constraint. From the point of view of this model, societies and social organizations are held together not by consensus but by constraint, not by universal agreement but by the coercion of some

by others. It may be useful for some purposes to speak of the 'value system' of a society, but in the conflict model such characteristic values are ruling rather than common, enforced rather than accepted, at any given point of time. And as conflict generates change, so constraint may be thought of as generating conflict. We assume that conflict is ubiquitous, since constraint is ubiquitous wherever human beings set up social organizations. In a highly formal sense, it is always the basis of constraint that is at issue in social conflict.

6. In attempting a theoretical synthesis of dialectic and functionalism, van den Berghe identifies the following facts which cannot be accounted for by a dynamic equilibrium model, the implication being that only conflict theory can deal with them:

'(i) Reaction to extra-systemic change is not always adjustive.

(ii) Social systems can, for long periods, go through a vicious circle of ever deepening malintegration.

(iii) Change can be revolutionary, i.e., both sudden and profound.

(iv) The social structure itself generates change through internal conflicts and contradictions.'[11]

To the extent that the existence of these phenomena is presumed by dialectic, a comprehensive conflict formulation incorporates them as underlying assumptions.

Major Propositions

The essential postulates of conflict theory are enumerated below:

1. Society is not a system in equilibrium but a nebulous structure of imperfectly coordinated elements which are held together by the coercion of some elements and the subjection of others.

2. Society and its elements are in the process of incessant change although at varying degrees; change and conflict are continuous and normal features of human society.

3. Society is a stage populated with living, struggling and competing actors; the social universe is the setting within which the conflicts of life are acted out.

4. Social conflicts are inherent in the very nature of social structure, the distinction between exogenous and endogenous conflicts is valid only in the analytical sense.

5. The inherent predilections to change in society vary in scope, nature, intensity and degree of velocity; they may be latent or manifest, gradual or destructive.

6. Endogenous conflicts arise out of malintegration or differential articulation of structural concomitants, incompatibility of the interests of groups and individuals, differential distribution of rewards, and the imperatives of super-orientation and subordination and the lack of value-consensus.

Dahrendorf has summarized the essential elements of conflict theory as follows:

1. Every society is subjected at every moment to change; social change is ubiquitous.
2. Every society experiences at every moment social conflict; social conflict is ubiquitous.
3. Every element in a society contributes to its change.
4. Every society rests on constraint of some of its members by others.[12]

Karl Marx: The Theory of Class Struggle

In spite of all the Marxists, genuine and self-styled, the conflict theory of Marx is plain and simple. Class struggle constitutes the central theme of Marx's theoretical scheme which is based on the following premises:

1. The history of all hitherto existing society is the history of class struggles.

Free man and slave, patrician and plebeian, lord and serf, guildmaster and journeyman, in a word, oppressor and oppressed, stood in constant opposition to one another, carried on an uninterrupted, now hidden, now open fight, a fight that each time ended either in a revolutionary reconstitution of society at large or in the common ruin of the contending classes.[13]

2. It is not the consciousness of men that determines their being, but, on the contrary, their social being that determines their consciousness.[14]
3. The ideas of the ruling class are, in every age, the ruling ideas; i.e., the class which is the dominant *material* force in society is at the same time its dominant *intellectual* force.

Marx was a great student of history. His mastery of the historical processes gave him valuable insights into the future of human society. He saw the emergence of a new socioeconomic system known as capitalism built upon the ruins of feudalism. He believed that human society passed through different stages of development and that each stage contained the seeds of its own destruction. However, Marx did not see history as a monotonous succession of struggles between the rich and the poor. Although the class war has always been between the oppressor and the oppressed, the leading contenders in the social drama of conflict differed markedly in different historical periods. 'The fact that modern workers are formally "free" to sell their labour while being existentially constrained to do so makes their condition historically specific and functionally distinct from that of earlier exploited classes.'[15]

Marx's analysis of social conflict in the capitalist society may be summarized as follows:

1. The importance of property.   To Marx, the most distinguishing characteristic of any society is its form of property, and the crucial determinant of an individual's behaviour is his relation to property. Classes are determined on the basis of the individual's relation to the means of production. It is not a man's occupation but his position relative to the instruments of production that determines his class. Property divisions are the crucial breaking lines in the class structure. Development of class consciousness and conflict over the distribution of economic rewards fortified the class barriers. Since work was the basic form of man's self-realization, economic conditions of the particular historic era determined the social, political and legal arrangements and set in motion the processes of evolution and societal transformation.

2. Economic determinism.   The capitalist society is based on the concentration of the means of production and distribution in the hands of a few. The capitalists who hold the monopoly of effective private property take control of the political machinery, and their interests converge in the political and ideological spheres. 'Political power, properly so called, is merely the organized power of one class for oppressing another.'[16] The bourgeoisie use the state as an instrument of economic exploitation and consolidation of self interests. 'The State is the form in which the individuals of a ruling class assert their common interests.'[17] The economic power of the bourgeoisie is transformed into political power, and the entire political processes and institutions including the courts, the police and the military and the ruling elites become subservient to the interest of the capitalists.

3. Polarization of classes.   Inherent in capitalist society is a tendency toward the radical polarization of classes. 'The whole society breaks up more and more into two great hostile camps, two great,

directly antagonistic classes: bourgeoisie and proletariat',[18] the capitalists who own the means of production and distribution, and the working classes who own nothing but their own labour. This is not to deny the existence of other classes; indeed, Marx repeatedly referred to the small capitalists, the petty bourgeoisie, and the lumpenproletariat. But on maturation of class consciousness and at the height of the conflict, the petty bourgeoisie and small capitalists will be deprived of their property and drawn into the ranks of the proleteriat.

4. The theory of surplus value. Capitalists accumulate profit through the exploitation of labour. The value of any commodity is determined by the amount of labour it takes to produce it. 'The labour time necessary for the worker to produce a value equal to the one he receives in the form of wages is less than the actual duration of his work. Let us say that the worker produces in five hours a value equal to the one contained in his wage, and that he works ten hours. Thus he works half of his time for himself and the other half for the entrepreneur. Let us use the term 'surplus value' to refer to the quantity of value produced by the worker beyond the necessary labour time, meaning by the latter the working time required to produce a value equal to the one he has received in the form of wages.[19] Since employers have the monopoly of the instruments of production, they can force workers to do extra hours of work, and profits tend to accumulate with increasing exploitation of labour.

5. Pauperization. The poverty of the proletariat grows with increasing exploitation of labour. One capitalist kills many others and the wealth of the bourgeoisie is swelled by large profits with corresponding increase in 'the mass of poverty, of pressure, of slavery, of perversion, of exploitation', of the proletariat.

It follows that in every mode of production which involves the exploitation of man by man, the social product is so distributed that the majority of people, the people who labour, are condemned to toil for no more than the barest necessities of life. Sometimes favourable circumstances arise when they can win more, but more often they get the barest minimum—and at times not even that. On the other hand, a minority, the owners of means of production, the property owners, enjoy leisure and luxury. Society is divided into rich and poor.[20]

Thus, to Marx poverty is the result of exploitation, not of scarcity.

6. Alienation. The economic exploitation and inhuman working conditions lead to the increasing alienation of man. (See Chapter 7 for

a detailed discussion.) Work is no longer an expression of man himself, only a degraded instrument of livelihood. It is external to the worker and imposed upon him; there is no fulfillment in work. The product of work becomes an instrument of alien purpose. Man becomes more and more enslaved as he sinks to the level of a commodity. And indeed, the worker becomes the most wretched of commodities. He becomes estranged from himself, from the process as well as product of his labour, from his fellow men and from the human community itself. 'The more the worker expends himself in work the more powerful becomes the world of objects which he creates in face of himself, the poorer he becomes in his inner life, and the less he belongs to himself.'[21] Thus economic alienation results in the 'devaluation of the world of men', self-estrangement and powerlessness. Man can liberate or realize himself only by communist revolution.

7. Class solidarity and antagonism. With the growth of class consciousness, the crystallization of social relations into two groups becomes streamlined and the classes tend to become internally homogeneous, and the class struggle more intensified. In the words of Marx:

... with the development of industry, the proletariat not only increases in number; it becomes concentrated in greater masses, its strength grows, and it feels that strength more. The various interests and conditions of life within the ranks of the proletariat are more and more equalized, in proportion as machinery obliterates all distinctions of labour and nearly everywhere reduces wages to the same low level. The growing competition among the bourgeois and the resulting commercial crises make the wages of the workers ever more fluctuating. The unceasing improvement of machinery, ever more rapidly developing, makes their livelihood more and more precarious; the collisions between individual workmen and individual bourgeois take more and more the character of collisions between two classes. Thereupon the workers begin to form combinations (trade unions) against the bourgeoisie; they club together in order to keep up the rate of wages; they found permanent associations in order to make provisions beforehand for these occasional revolts. Here and there the contest breaks out into riots.[22]

8. Revolution. At the height of the class war a violent revolution breaks out which destroys the structure of capitalist society. This revolution is most likely to occur at the peak of an economic crisis which is part of the recurring booms and repressions characteristic of capitalism. To quote Marx:

Finally, in times when the class struggle nears the decisive hour, the process of dissolution going on within the ruling class, in fact within the whole range of old society, assumes such a violent, glaring character, that a small section of the ruling class cuts itself adrift and joins the revolutionary class, the class that holds the future in its hands. Just as, therefore, at an earlier period, a section of the nobility went over to the bourgeoisie, so now a portion of the bourgeoisie goes over to the proletariat and, in particular, a portion of the bourgeois ideologists who have raised themselves to the level of comprehending theoretically the historical movement as a whole.[23]

9. The dictatorship of the proletariat. The bloody revolution terminates capitalist society and leads to the social dictatorship of the proletariat. The revolution is violent but does not necessarily involve mass killings of the bourgeoisie; since property is wrested from them, the bourgeoisie will cease to have power and will be transformed into the ranks of the proletariat. Thus the inevitable historical process destroys the bourgeoisie and the proletariat establishes a social dictatorship, merely a transitional phase, to consolidate the gains of the revolution. The political expression of the social dictatorship was conceived by Marx as a form of workers' democracy which later became 'a fateful bone of contention' among Marxists. Irving Howe observes:

By now, almost all socialists have abandoned the treacherous phrase 'dictatorship of the proletariat', both because it is open to obvious misconstruction and because it has acquired, in the Stalinist and post-Stalinist dictatorships, abhorrent connotations. Marx himself had written that he differentiated himself from 'those communists who were out to destroy personal liberty and who wish to turn the world into one large barracks or into a gigantic warehouse.'[24]

10. Inauguration of the communist society. Socialization of effective private property will eliminate class and thereby the causes of social conflict. The state will eventually wither away as it becomes obsolete in a classless society in which nobody owns anything but everybody owns everything and each individual contributes according to his ability and receives according to his need.

This, in a nutshell, is Karl Marx' theory of social conflict.

Marx had almost no influence on the development of early sociology which was dominated by evolutionists, particularly social Darwinists. The mid-twentieth century witnessed the rebirth of Marxist sociology which remains today at the centre of dialectic and conflict analysis. The ideas of Marx constitute the gospel of revolution, and the *Communist Manifesto* is the handbook of revolutionaries around the world. Marxism has become the state dogma and the creed of political orthodoxy in many countries. However, the theory of Marx is plagued by several methodological and conceptual problems. His theory about capitalist society's inevitable tendency toward radical polarization and self-destruction is too simplistic and in error. The most distinct characteristic of modern capitalism has been the emergence of a large, 'contented and conservative' middle class consisting of managerial, professional, supervisory, and technical personnel. Modern corporations entail a separation between ownership and control; the capitalists who own the instruments of production are not necessarily the 'effective' decision-makers. Today's capitalism does not justify Marx's belief that class conflict is essentially revolutionary in character and that structure changes are always the product of violent upheavals; organized labour has been able to sway the balance of power and effect profound structural changes without violent revolution. Marx's theory of labour and the deductive reasoning which flows directly from it, namely the pauperization of the masses, are wrong. If the value of surplus labour is the only basis of profit, there is no way to eliminate exploitation and profit accumulation. In fact, most socialist countries have a higher percentage of accumulation than do capitalist countries.

Marx misjudged the extent of alienation among the average worker. The great depth of alienation and frustration which Marx 'witnessed' among the workers of his day is not 'typical' of today's capitalism or its worker who tends to identify increasingly with a number of 'meaningful' groups—religious, ethnic, occupational and locality. This is not to deny the existence of alienation but to point out that alienation results more from the structure of bureaucracy and of mass society than from economic exploitation. Marx also overemphasized the economic base of political power and ignored other important sources of power. Moreover, Marx's predictions about the downfall of capitalism have not come true. Contrary to his belief, socialism has triumphed in predominantly peasant societies whereas capitalist societies show no signs of destructive class war. And Marx's classless and stateless society is an utopia; there can be no society without an authority structure or a regulatory mechanism which inevitably leads to a crystallization of social relations between the rulers and the ruled, with inherent possibilities of internal contradiction and conflict.

Today's Marxists, however, are striking back. They blame imperialism for the failure of Marx's prophecy. They argue that advanced

industrialized nations have been able to fortify their capitalist economy by exploiting the rest of the world through colonialism and the
'sovereign' multi-national corporations. Conflict sociologists make
effective use of Marxian theoretical schema to explain the processes
of class conflict and revolutionary movements around the world:
conflicts between landless peasantry and landed aristocracy, between
political and military elites, between incongruent status groups in
newly emerging industrial societies, populist movements and conservative counter-revolutions, colonialism and imperialism, international
conspiracies and ideological warfares, and between socialism and
democracy. Contemporary Marxist sociology has accumulated a
considerable amount of evidence to substantiate the Marxian postulates that economic position is the major determinant of one's life-
style, attitudes, and behaviour, and that a strategic position in the
economic structure along with access to effective means of production
and distribution hold the key to political power. The modern theory
of power elite is only a variation of the Marxian theme of economic
determinism.

Above all, Marx's theory of class is not a theory of stratification
but a comprehensive theory of social change—a tool for the explanation of change in total societies. This, T. B. Bottomore, a leading
expert on Marxist sociology, considers to be a major contribution
of Marx to sociological analysis: '. . . the view of societies as inherently
mutable systems, in which changes are produced largely by internal
contradictions and conflicts, and the assumption that such changes, if
observed in a large number of instances, will show a sufficient degree
of regularity to allow the formulation of general statements about
their causes and consequences.'[25]

Bottomore accounts for the recent growth of Marxist sociology as
follows:

One important reason for the present revival of interest is the fact that
Marx's theory stands in direct opposition on every major point to the
functionalist theory which has dominated sociology and anthropology
for the past twenty or thirty years, but which has been found increasingly unsatisfactory. Where functionalism emphasizes social harmony, Marxism emphasizes social conflict; where functionalism
directs attention to the stability and persistence of social forms,
Marxism is radically historical in its outlook and emphasizes the
changing structure of society; where functionalism concentrates upon
the regulation of social life by general values and norms, Marxism
stresses the divergence of interests and values within each society and

the role of force in maintaining, over a longer or shorter period of time, a given social order. The contrast between 'equilibrium' and 'conflict' models of society, which was stated forcefully by Dahrendorf in 1958, has now become a commonplace; and Marx's theories are regularly invoked in opposition to those of Durkheim, Pareto and Malinowski, the principal architects of the functionalist theory.[26]

Herbert Marcuse's *Re-examination of the Concept of Revolution* is a significant contribution to Marxist sociology. According to him:

the *Marxian concept of a revolution* carried by the majority of the exploited masses, culminating in the "seizure of power" and in the setting up of a proletarian dictatorship which initiates socialization, is *"over-taken" by the historical development*: it pertains to a stage of capitalist productivity and organization which has been overtaken; it does not project the higher stage of capitalist productivity, including the productivity of destruction, and the terrifying concentration of the instruments of annihilation and of indoctrination in the hands of the powers that be.[27]

Although the Marxian prophecy of the downfall of capitalism has not come true, Marx's concept of revolution which is at once a historical concept and a dialectical concept is relevant in two different contexts:

(a) In the capitalist countries, there is a standing opposition between those members who are drawn from the ghetto population and the middle-class intelligentsia, especially when represented among students.

These groups are vocal; they reject the 'system', form counter-cultures and profess adherence to radical political beliefs and new lifestyles. Yet, they cannot become agents of revolutionary change unless actively supported by a politically articulate working-class freed from the shackles of bureaucratic trade unions and establishment-oriented party machinery.

(b) In the predominantly agrarian countries of the Third World, there are peasant revolutions and national liberation movements.

Marcuse also perceives a 'fateful link' between the two revolutionary movements. In the first place, the national liberation movements in the developing countries 'are expressive of the *internal contradictions* of the global capitalist system'—the colonialism and economic exploitation perpetrated by the corporate capitalism. This position is actively endorsed by André Gunder Frank[28] whose extensive research in Latin America has led him to conclude that the underdevelopment of the Third World countries is initiated and aggravated by the capitalist system of the developed countries which have satellized and exploited developing countries. Marcuse identifies specifically certain objective factors which 'announce themselves in the strains and stresses of the corporate economy'. These are:

1. The necessity of competition, and the threat of progressive automation, with the ensuing unemployment, demand over enlarged absorption of labour by non-productive, parasitarian jobs and services.
2. The costs of neo-colonial wars, or controls over corrupt dictatorships, increase more and more.
3. As a result of the increasing reduction of human labour power in the process of production, the margin of profit declines.
4. Society requires the creation of needs, the satisfaction of which tends to conflict with the morale and discipline necessary for work under capitalism. The realm of necessity is invaded by the non-necessary, gadgets and luxury devices exist side by side with continuing proverty and misery, 'luxuries' become necessities in the competitive struggle for existence.[29]

Thus the radical protests in capitalist countries and the revolutionary tendencies in the developing nations are closely related—in their orientation to the imperatives of a global revolution.

The Marxian concept of revolution must comprehend the changes in the scope and social structure of advanced capitalism, and the new forms of the contradictions characteristic of the latest stage of capitalism in its global framework. The modifications of the Marxian concept then appear, not as extraneous additions or adjustments, but rather as the elaboration of Marxian theory itself.

C. Wright Mills: *The power elite*

The central thesis of Mills' theory is that economic, social and political power in American society is manipulated by three interlocking hierarchies—the military, the industrial, and the political. Mills writes:

At the pinnacle of each of the three enlarged and centralized domains there have arisen those higher circles which make up the economic, the political, and the military elites. At the top of the economy, among the corporate rich, there are the chief executives; at the top of the political order, the members of the political directorate; at the top of the military establishment, the elite of soldier-statesmen clustered in and around the Joint Chiefs of Staff and the upper echelon. As each of these domains has coincided with the others, as decisions tend to become total in their consequence, the leading men in each of the three domains of power—the warlords, the corporation chieftains, the political directorate—tend to come together, to form the power elite of America.[30]

The theory descriptive of the 'military-industrial complex' expounds the principle of a monolithic power structure in American society. That is, all major decisions are made by a fairly autonomous few whose interests are cohesive. These elite hail from the same kinds of families, have superior education at prestigeous schools, enjoy important connections, and have direct access to strategic power centres. 'As the institutional means of power and the means of communications that tie them together have become steadily more efficient, those now in command of them have come into command of instruments of rule quite unsurpassed in the history of mankind.'[31] According to Mills, the Marxian view, which makes the economic dominants the real power-wielders, and the liberal view, which treats the political leaders as the captains of power, and the folk assumption of warlords as virtual dictators, are oversimplifications. That is why he uses the term 'power elite' to indicate the reality of a triumvirate consisting of the top men in economic, political, and military positions who coalesce to form a unified hierarchy.

The main criticism of the power elite theory has come from pluralists who reject the notion that power is concentrated in the hands of a small stratum of elites but contend rather that there are many veto groups who compete with one another for power and who seek to influence decisions in specific contexts with varying degrees of success. The pluralists also point out that the elitist approach invariably overlooks factional disputes and conflicts of interests within leadership groups. They denounce notions like 'monolithic political machines' and 'ruling elite' but emphasize concepts like 'multiple decision centres' and 'balance wheels'. Moreover, the ruling elite model frequently involves the imputation of motives to covert leadership without any empirical backing. The critics argue that the history of federal legislation during the past three decades has been consistently on the side of labour and those 'left behind'. However, it must be emphasized that the distinction between elitist and pluralist systems is a matter of degree, rather than of mutually exclusive contrasts. As Presthus contends, the two perspectives uncover two facets of social reality. In his judgement,

'To some extent, where the sociologists found monopoly and called it elitism, political scientists found oligopoly but defined it in more honorific terms as pluralism.'[32]

The theory of power elite is only one of Mills' several contributions to conflict sociology. His analysis of the managerial demiurge among American middle-classes is a classic essay in conflict perspective. He identifies rationalization of higher functions, development of the enterprise and the bureau into fetishes and the growing tendency on the part of power-wielders to use manipulation rather than authority as the major trends in modern bureaucracy. Impersonal manipulation and organized irresponsibility are leading characteristics of contemporary industrial societies. Coercion is pervasive but the powerful are anonymous and operate the hidden string of control from behind the scene. Mills contends: 'Impersonal manipulation is more insidious than coercion precisely because it is hidden; one cannot locate the enemy and declare war upon him. Targets for aggression are unavailable and certainty is taken from men.'[33] Mills continues:

Under the system of explicit authority, in the round, solid nineteenth century, the victim knew he was being victimized, the misery and discontent of the powerless were explicit. In the amorphous twentieth-century world, where manipulation replaces authority, the victim does not recognize his status. The formal aim, implemented by the latest psychological equipment, is to have men internalize what the managerial cadres would have them do, without their knowing their own motives, but nevertheless having them. Many whips are inside men, who do not know how they got there, or indeed that they are there. In the movement from authority to manipulation, power shifts from the visible to the invisible, from the known to the anonymous. And with rising material standards, exploitation becomes less material and more psychological.[34]

These trends are reinforced and perpetuated by the bureaucratic tendencies of the modern democratic state, the means of mass communication, and the monstrosity of seemingly remote organizations which make the individuals feel 'dwarfed and helpless before the managerial cadres and their manipulated and manipulative minions'.

Class struggle is at the centre of the theoretical schema of Marx, Mills and Dahrendorf. Where Marx saw effective private property, Dahrendorf saw authority as the basis of class structure. For Mills, class struggle revolves around the graded hierarchy of modern bureaucracy. According to him, 'Bureaucracies not only rest upon classes, they organize the power struggle of classes.'[35] Whereas Marx saw that coercion is necessarily manifest in the economic arrangement of capitalist society leading to open revolution, Dahrendorf preceives degrees of coercion arising out of the dichotomy of super-ordination and subordination characteristic of authority structure, while according to Mills, modern bureaucracies exercise coercion not so much through authority as through impersonal manipulation.

Ralf Dahrendorf: The rulers and the ruled

The conflict theory of Dahrendorf is based exclusively on the relations of authority. To him, social organizations are imperatively coordinated associations rather than social systems. Authority structure, which is an integral part of every social organization, leads inevitably to the crystallization of interest groups and inherent possibilities of conflict.

Changes in the social structure are brought about by conflict between classes. According to Dahrendorf, 'different modes of structure change co-vary with different modes of class conflict. The more intense class conflict is, more radical are the changes likely to be which it brings about; the more violent class conflict is, the more sudden are structure changes resulting from it likely to be.'[36]

Authority structure always involves relations of super-ordination and subordination. It defines rights and obligations, prescribes sanctions and enforces conformity. 'Where there are authority relations, the superordinate element is socially expected to control, by orders and demands, warnings and prohibitions, the behaviour of the subordinate element.'

In every imperatively co-ordinated association there is a differential distribution of authority creating a dichotomy of positions of domination and subjection. Some are entrusted with the legitimate right to exercise control over others who are subordinate to the former. This distribution of authority leads to the formation of two conflict groups corresponding to the two positions of control and subjection—those who give orders and those who take orders. Every association, even the smallest office consisting only of the boss and the secretary, involves two classes—the rulers and the ruled, and inherent possibilities of conflict arising out of incompatible interests.

Dahrendorf summarizes his theory in the following propositions:

1. In every imperatively coordinated group, the carriers of positive and negative dominance roles determine two quasigroups with opposite latent interests.
2. The bearers of positive and negative dominance roles, that is, the members of the opposing quasi-groups, organize themselves into groups with manifest interests, unless certain empirically variable conditions . . . intervene.
3. Interest groups which originate in this manner are in constant conflict over the preservation or change of the status quo.
4. The conflict among interest groups in the sense of this model leads to changes in the structure of their social relations, through changes in the dominance relations.

Since every social organization is an imperatively co-ordinated association and the structure of authority the sole basis of conflict, it is impossible to eliminate conflict altogether. Latent or manifest, conflict makes up one of the essential ingredients of social structure. Conflicts may be regulated and their specific expressions temporarily contained but until the authority structure is done away with—an impossibility—conflicts cannot be permanently resolved.

Since differential distribution of authority is the fundamental source of conflict, changes resulting from class conflict are essentially changes in the authority system. Structural changes may be brought about by total or near-total exchange of personnel in dominant positions as in the case of revolutionary overthrow of governments, or partial exchange of personnel as in the case of coalition and class alliances in politics; changes may also be brought about without exchange of personnel if an accommodative ruling group is willing to incorporate the proposals and interests of the opposition as in the case of a parliamentary system of democracy.

Dahrendorf, after calling attention to the ubiquity of conflict and change in society, has developed a general theory of social conflict of his own. By so doing, he has made a significant contribution to dialectic sociology through his reformulations of class conflict. However, Dahrendorf is guilty of the fallacy of the binary model which we have discussed later in the chapter. To attempt to trace all conflicts to dichotomous authority relations involves straining the facts. Dahrendorf's theory involves a special case of class conflict. Class is defined in terms of authority and class conflict revolves around the struggle for authority. Authority, however, is an effective but not the only determinant of class; income, status, prestige, life-style and material possessions are also significant ingredients of class structure. Nor is authority the only—or even primary source of social conflict. Intercaste and inter-religious conflicts were seldom based on authority relations. Throughout human history, ideology, values, lifestyles, customs and belief-systems have provided ammunition for social unrest.

Although Dahrendorf claims his formulation to be a general theory of social conflict, its frame of reference is narrow and limited. It is a variant of a theory of class which cannot analyse social change in total societies. Dahrendorf's position that social change is necessarily the result of changes in the authority structure is untenable. Profound changes have come about in societies without corresponding changes in the authority structure; sometimes these changes were initiated by the power-wielders themselves. Dahrendorf rejects the Marxian emphasis on property as the determinant of class and substitutes it with authority. Indeed, he has reversed the Marxian chain of causation by postulating the primacy of the differential distribution of authority and in that process substituted his own brand of political determinism for Marx's economic determinism. 'But he neither demonstrates why authority is prior to the relation to the means of production, nor convincingly shows how "classes" are different from other conflict groups, and, hence, why they should constitute a special analytical category.'[37] Moreover, this reformulation suffers from the same shortcomings that plague any deterministic theory. To quote van den Berghe:

In short, authority, while an important dimension of conflict, is not necessarily an overriding one, nor is it logically or empirically prior to other sources of conflict. As to polarization, it is an empirical tendency rather than a necessary condition of conflict. A pluralistic model thus seems to impose itself.

Marx, Mills and Dahrendorf viewed social conflicts as being structurally induced. And they kept power at the centre of their theoretical schema. In terms of power relations, they saw a structural tendency toward polarization into a two-class model—the rulers and the ruled. Dahrendorf rejects Marx's 'overemphasis' on the primacy of class conflicts and their revolutionary character. Where Marx saw class antagonism manifest in violent and abrupt changes, Dahrendorf and Mills concede the possibilities of gradual and peaceful changes as well. The following excerpts from Dahrendorf run parallel to the propositions from Mills' power elite theory:

Managerial or capitalist elites may be extremely powerful groups in society, they may even exert partial control over governments and parliaments, but these very facts underline the significance of governmental elites: whatever decisions are made are made either by or through them; whatever changes are introduced or prevented, governmental elites are their immediate object or agent; whatever conflicts occur in the political arena, the heads of the three branches of government are the exponents of the *status quo*. It is admittedly not sufficient to identify a ruling class solely in terms of a governmental elite, but it is necessary to think of this elite in the first place and never to lose sight of its paramount position in the authority structure of the state.[38]

The tendency to treat functionalism as a theory of stability and conflict theory as a theory of social change is a futile exercise. In historical as well as empirical reality, stability and change are so inextricably intertwined that it is difficult to distinguish one from the other. Hence both theories deal with both aspects of the social reality but with varying emphasis and 'background assumptions'.

Varieties of Conflict Theory

It is unfortunate that conflict theory has become identified with Marxist revolutionary ideology. To equate conflict with disruptive behaviour or negative forces is equally unfortunate. Many social philosophers before Marx and many non-Maxist social scientists after him have furnished some of the deepest insights concerning society through conflict perspectives which dwell on the constructive aspects of conflict. In the contemporary sociological tradition, there appear to be six different variants of conflict theory. They are:

1. The Frankfurt school and critical theory
2. The new or radical sociology
3. Dialectic sociology
4. Conflict functionalism
5. Analytic conflict theory
6. Formal conflict theory

The Frankfurt School and Critical Theory

The controversial theoretical system of the Frankfurt school is so-called because of its association with the Institute for Social Research in Frankfurt, Germany, which was established in 1923 by a group of young neo-Marxists to undertake an independent study of Marxism. The most outstanding members of the Institute were Theodore Adorno, Max Horkheimer, Herbert Marcuse, Eric Fromm, Leo Lowenthal and Franz Neumann. In the 1930's, with the rise of Hitler, the group went into exile, and later on continued their work in the United States until 1950 when the Institute was reopened as part of the University of Frankfurt, and Adorno and Horkheimer returned to Germany.

The theoretical system of the Frankfurt school is essentially conflict-oriented and owes a great deal to Marx. However, its proponents are by no means orthodox Marxists. They draw heavily on the theories of Hegel and the early and more Hegelian work of Marx. They also employ 'conventional' sociological analysis of Max Weber and Karl Mannheim. Above all, they attempt to tie together psychoanalysis and Marxism by synthesizing the Marxist theory of social structure and change and the Freudian theory of individual motivation and personality. In the process of developing their 'critical theory' the leaders of the Frankfurt school conducted extensive studies of authoritarianism, alienation, mass culture, and various social movements. In Europe, T. B. Bottomore, Alaine Touraine, Svetozar Stojanovic and Jurgen Habermas continue to expand the dimensions of critical theory and neo-Marxism.

Habermas, one of the most articulate spokesmen of the school, attempts to develop a new 'humanistic tradition' with greater emphasis on the works of Hegel and the young Marx. Convinced that the orthodox Marxist theory of capitalism can no longer account for the basic contradictions of the advanced industrial society, Habermas has developed his own model of critical theory with particular attention to the recent developments in the capitalist system. Unlike Marx, Habermas sees three different types of capitalist societies: (1) Liberal capitalism—the nineteenth-century capitalism that Marx theorized about; (2) Organized capitalism that characterizes western industrialized societies; and (3) Post-capitalism of the 'state-socialist societies' with 'political-elitist disposition of the means of production'. Like Marx, Habermas sees contradictions inherent in each of the systems which will ultimately lead to its disintegration and change, and also emphasizes the role of ideas and consciousness in bringing about such changes. But in Habermas' reconstruction of Marxism, Schroyer points out, 'the materialist model of society is now reconceptualized as societal systems of action', that is,

1. Instead of talking about the substructure, we refer to the systems of purposive rational action.
2. Instead of talking about the superstructure, we refer to the systems of symbolic interaction.
3. Instead of talking about the forms of social consciousness we can speak about the reflexive recognition of legitimate authority which is internal to societal modes of self-reflection.[39]

According to Habermas, the rise of huge, oligopolic firms and the disappearance of competitive capitalism characterize the transition from liberal to organized capitalism. Also the self-regulated market commerce of liberal capitalism is gradually replaced by the expanding role of the state which intervenes in almost every realm of economic and social enterprises by regulating economic cycles, guaranteed employment, social welfare functions and the like. The 'recoupling' of the economic and political enterprises requires a new system of legitimacy that is formal and explicit. The system of 'formal democracy' attempts to fill the need. But increased social participation in the process of decision-making only makes more people aware of the inherent contradictions of the system and the crisis of capitalism continues to grow.

Critical theory has become an influential school of thought within conflict sociology. Schroyer defines critical theory 'as that kind of inquiry which is capable of analysing the supposed and actual necessity of historical modes of authority and which presupposes the interest of the emancipation of men from law-like patterns of nature and history.'[40] He contends:

A critical theory of society derives from the philosophical tradition of the critique of appearances. Such a totalizing theory cannot emerge from a compilation of empirical facts. It is by now clear to all that the methodological rationales of established social science predefine the reality investigated. In nailing down the facts about society, the activity of men is reified into a thing-like facticity. A critical theory, on the other hand, transcends its facts, rendering them meaningful, but at the same time placing them in the context of the tension between the given and the possible. Construction of a critical theory follows the principle of an immanent critique. By first expressing what a social totality holds itself to be, and then confronting it with what it is, a critical theory is able to break down the rigidity of the object. Hence, Marx's identification of the ideology of 'equivalence exchange' as the self-image of capitalist society is contradicted by the formulation of the 'developmental laws of capitalism'. The phenomenal appearance of capitalism is negated by its own internal dynamics. Marx's critical theory is, in his mentor's terms, a 'determinate negation' of capitalism, and has remained till our time the foundation for critical research.

Let us try to enumerate a few of the most outstanding features of critical theory. First, its proponents believe that intellectuals should assume an active role and develop a critical attitude to society; in the name of objectivity and value-free sociology, they should not hesitate to make value-judgments when necessary. Second, critical theory holds that people's ideas are a product of the social system in which they live and, therefore, it is impossible to be entirely objective and to eliminate completely the biases that are culture-bound and time-bound. Third, critical analysts emphasize the importance of society's economic organization, especially 'the class-related form of work', property and profit, and its impact on culture, personality and polity. Fourth, unlike orthodox Marxists, critical theorists reject pure economic determinism and assign culture and ideology an independent role in society. Fifth, critical theory also includes the study of the inner dynamics of psychic structure within the purview of its analysis of social phenomena. Sixth, critical theory emphasizes the 'rational constitution of society' and seeks to judge the present social order in terms of Hegelian humanism and reason. Finally, it has concentrated to a great extent on a critique of mass culture, the causes and consequences of alienation and the interaction between personality and social structure.

Horowitz and radical sociology

Although C. Wright Mills has been primarily responsible for the development of radical sociology in the United States, in recent years a number of young sociologists have come to identify themselves with a conflict perspective known as 'the New Sociology'. Irving Louis Horowitz has emerged as one of the most articulate spokesmen of the new or radical sociology. Horowitz believes that classical American liberalism has now been replaced by the new radicalism, which 'is tied to the future of the world rather than to the present of the United States'. Radicalism supports the weak against the strong, the oppressed against the oppressor, 'the rights of the masses against the claims of classes'. According to Horowitz, to be radical is to deny the canons of self-interest. A white fighting for blacks, an Arab defending the Jew, a Catholic condemning a papal injunction or a landlord advocating land reforms are examples of radical behaviour; to defend self-interests, as in the case of the exploited fighting the exploiter, is only natural behaviour, not radical. To Horowitz, radicalism is primarily an individual trait. To equate radicalism with cheap political movements is to debase the concept and 'castrate its meaning for individuals' who alone can behave radically. 'Individualism has remained an exclusive preserve of the conservatives because Left-wing *politicos* have failed to face the fact that governmental bigness is evil, and that solutions based on radical principles rather than radical people is a disease, and not a cure.'[41]

Generally speaking, radical sociology focuses on negative aspects of social structure—poverty, racism, exploitation, powerlessness, and military-industrial establishment. Radical sociology treats them as defects of the 'system'. 'Radical sociology asks whether the problems generated by social structure are inherent within it (a consequence of "internal contradictions", if one will) or simply "mistakes" or unintended consequences.'[42] Social problems are attributed to the 'establishment' and a total transformation of the 'system' is called for. Radical sociologists become fully involved in current controversies and do not hesitate to 'take sides' on issues and policies. They emerge as champions of great 'causes' and become involved in building the 'good society'. Thus, 'radical sociology is a sociology of *engagement*',[43] and often is instrumental in the formulation of public policy. As reformers and critics, radical sociologists have contributed substantially to the understanding of contemporary social problems; however, their contribution to the development of conflict theory in sociology is regrettably rather limited.

The 1960s witnessed an abrupt resurgence of radicalism in the United States. The new radicalism was triggered by the growing militancy of the civil rights movement, followed by the awakening of other minorities and women, the 'free speech' movement, student power and antiwar movements and an ideology and counter culture in contradistinction to the norms of the 'establishment'. The radical movement, in need of an ideology, invoked conflict theories of all sorts—Marxist, power elite, anti-establishment and so on. The opposition manifested itself in fights against poverty, racial discrimination, war, sex discrimination, colonialism, conventional morality and political hypocrisy. This movement had its reverberating repercussions in the academic world as well. Departments of socio-

logy across the land became involved in the hottest debate between
the Parsonian school of functionalism and contemporary conflict
theorists. For a while it looked as though a 'civil war' had broken
out between old-guard functionalists and young radical sociologists.
The conservatives held an objective and scientific view of society
and sociology; they abstained from value-judgements and largely
ignored issues of social policy. Radical sociologists, disenchanted by
problems of poverty, discrimination and other social ills and inspired by new ideologies, felt that social sciences must be 'relevant';
they used the conflict theory as an instrument of social change and
involved themselves actively in social policy matters. However, in
recent years a more rational orientation has replaced the utopianism
of the sixties. As the pessimism and paranoia of the late sixties
subsided, a reconciliation of the two sides has taken place. The
'pure' structural-functionalism of the Parsonian school has been
substantially modified to take into account the processes of conflict
and change. And the radical ideological conflict perspective has
become mellowed, realistic and rational.

Collins and the analytic conflict theory

Randall Collins has undertaken one of the most thoroughgoing
analyses of modern complex organizations and other social arrangements such as state and stratification in a conflict perspective.
Collins believes that sociology does have 'a solid core of explanatory
principles' but it is contained primarily within the conflict tradition
which incorporates 'a network of causal, testable explanatory
generalizations', and a 'fair amount of sociological research, on
both contemporary and historical materials'. He argues that conflict
theory is 'a scientific tradition, both in that the ideal of social
science was developed within it, and in that we may draw from it a
consistent network of casual generalizations of considerable empirical power.'[44]

Collins' is not a dialectical conflict theory in the conventional
sense; he does not even propose a generalized conflict theory applicable to total societies. Rather, he analyses a wide range of social
phenomena on the basis of a general assumption of conflicting
interests of the parties involved, their social location, available
resources and options. Collins does not rely exclusively on any one
of the several pioneers of conflict theory. He draws heavily from

Marx, Max Weber and even Durkheim as well as from Mead, Schutz, and Goffman. He has also incorporated the perspectives of symbolic interactionism, phenomenology and ethnomethodology in an attempt to develop an integrated theory of social conflict. As Collins acknowledges, his aim has been:

> to take up the universal side of Machiavelli, rather than his schemes for the Florentine state; the leading insights of Nietzsche and Freud, without their biologism and their sexism. Conflict theory is Machiavelli without the Prince; Marx without Hegel; Darwin without Spencer; Weber without idealism; Freud without Victorianism—better yet, Freud restored to his Nietzschean historical premises. With sufficient detachment, the main line of explanatory accomplishment in sociology should come into view.[45]

We will attempt a capsule summary of Collins' conflict theory. According to Collins, 'human beings are sociable but conflict-prone animals'. The primary basis of conflict is violent coercion which is always a potential resource and a zero-sum sort. In every society there is a differential distribution of desirables such as wealth, power, prestige and other valued goods. The system of inequality divides society into rank hierarchies—graded levels of individuals with more or less resources available to them. There is a continuing competition between groups or social strata for a greater share of the desirables. Every individual seeks to maximize his subjective status according to the resources available to him and to his rivals. Collins observes:

> ... each individual is basically pursuing his own interests and that there are many situations, notably ones where power is involved, in which those interests are inherently antagonistic. The basic argument, then, has three strands: that men live in self-constructed subjective worlds; that others pull many of the strings that control one's subjective experience; and that there are frequent conflicts over control. Life is basically a struggle for status in which no one can afford to be oblivious to the power of others around him. If we assume that everyone uses what resources are available to have others aid him in putting on the best possible face under the circumstances, we have a guiding principle to make sense out of the myriad variations of stratification.[46]

In summary, conflict inevitably arises from the unequal distribution of desirables such as wealth, power, prestige and other goods. Individuals strive to maximize their share of the scarce commodities. Those who possess a greater share of the goods, try to consolidate their position, maximize their interests and dominate the structural arrangements by various means, especially coercion. But men dislike intensely being ordered around and resist subjection. In constructing his conflict model, Collins introduces a number of other variables: the resources people bring to their struggle, their social position, the groups to which they belong and their numerical strength and the intensity of interpersonal attraction. He then applies his model to organizations which 'are best understood as arenas for conflicting interests', to state where 'violence is organized', and to social stratification which is characterized as a system of 'dominance relationships'. Collins concludes: 'The basic premises of the conflict approach are that everyone pursues his own best line of advantage according to resources available to him and to his competitors; and that social structures—whether formal organizations or informal acquaintances—are empirically nothing more than men meeting and communicating in certain ways.'

Coser and Conflict Functionalism

Coser, in the tradition of Simmel, is concerned primarily with how 'conflict prevents the ossification of the social system by exerting pressure for innovation and creativity'.[47] He has written extensively on the positive functions of social conflict. Conflict allows expression of hostility and the mending of strained relationships. It leads to the elimination of specific sources of conflict between parties and enables redress of grievances through the establishment of new norms or the affirmation of old ones. Hostility toward the outgroup unifies the ingroup. When the need for greater solidarity is felt, members of the ingroup tend to exaggerate conflicts with other groups, and where such conflicts exist any deviation from the group norms is severely condemned. Social conflicts not only generate new norms and institutions but also new coalitions and alliances; they bring about technological improvements, revitalize the economy, and lubricate the social system; they facilitate the release of tension and frustration and enable the social system to adjust itself.

Conflict within and between groups in a society can prevent accommodations and habitual relations from progressively impoverishing creativity. The clash of values and interests, the tension between what is and what some groups feel ought to be, the conflict between vested niterests and new strata and groups demanding their share of power, wealth and status, have been productive of vitality; note for example the contrast between the 'frozen world' of the Middle Ages and the burst of creativity that accompanied the thaw that set in with Renaissance civilization.[48]

Coser has also suggested a number of propositions concerning the intensity and impact of conflict. Listed below are some of the key propositions from his book entitled *The Functions of Social Conflict*:[49]

1. Internal social conflicts which concern goals, values or interests that do not contradict the basic assumptions upon which the relationship is founded tend to be positively functional for the social structure.

2. Internal conflicts in which the contending parties no longer share the basic values upon which the legitimacy of the social system rests threaten to disrupt the structure.

3. . . . the closer the group, the more intense the conflict. Where members participate with their total personality and conflicts are suppressed, the conflict, if it breaks out nevertheless, is likely to threaten the very root of the relationship.

4. In groups comprising individuals who participate only segmentally, conflict is less likely to be disruptive. Such groups are likely to experience a multiplicity of conflicts.

5. In flexible social structures, multiple conflicts crisscross each other and thereby prevent basic cleavages along one axis . . . . Thus segmental participation in a multiplicity of conflicts constitutes a balancing mechanism within the structure.

6. In loosely structured groups and open societies, conflict, which aims at a resolution of tension between antagonists, is likely to have stabilizing and integrative functions for the relationship.

7. Social systems tolerate or institutionalize conflict to different degrees. . . . Societies dispose of mechanism to channel discontent and hostility while keeping intact the relationship within which antagonism arises. Such mechanisms frequently operate through 'safety-valve' institutions which provide substitute objects upon which to displace hostile sentiments as well as means of abreaction of aggressive tendencies.

8. . . . the need for safety-valve institutions increases with the rigidity of the social structure, i.e., with the degree to which it disallows direct expression of antagonistic claims.

Caplow and the Formal Conflict Theory

Some sociologists include the coalition theory and the game theory in the conflict perspective. Theodore Caplow expanded Simmel's theory of the tendency of the triad to form a coalition of two against one and identified eight possible types of triads ranging from the one extreme of all parties being equal to the other extreme of all parties being unequal. Caplow distinguished between revolutionary coalitions and conservative coalitions, the former being an alliance of the weak against the strong and the latter being the coalition of the powerful in support of the *status quo*. Peasant uprisings and populist movements in developing countries illustrate the revolutionary coalitions whereas the power elite is representative of the conservative coalition.

The game theory, sometimes called a 'science of conflict' is a formalized theory of competitive struggle intended to maximize one's own values. In the words of James Duke,

Game theory is based on the assumption that individuals are generally oriented to the pursuit and achievement of their own interests even at the expense of the interests of others. In a game situation, where generally there is a winner and one or more losers, each party usually will be oriented to winning and will commit his energies and resources to the achievement of victory . . . . Parties to such games are thus pitted against each other in a competitive struggle and each seeks to gain the victory over the other. The result is almost inevitably an unequal distribution of rewards such that winners gain ascendency in some ways over the losers.[50]

Dahrendorf and dialectic sociology

Dialectic sociology is the systematic study of social conflict which involves a conceptualization of opposing forces with conflicting interests. The dialectical model begins with a dichotomy of opposites such as the individual and society, lord and serf, rich and poor, elites and the masses, majority and minority or conservatives and liberals. Dahrendorf's conceptualization, which we discussed earlier, is a dialectical model because he saw conflict as inherent in the dichotomous division of all social organizations into contending categories of roles—those who have authority and those who are subjected to authority. Since conflict is conceived as an inexorable process arising out of opposing forces within the authority structure, innovations and revolutions do not eliminate conflicts; they only introduce new authority structures which perpetuate the dichotomous division of associations into superordinates and subordinates, and the endless dialectical process goes on.

Unlike radical sociology, dialectic sociology does not begin with a specific social problem; rather it begins with society as a whole and seeks to demonstrate how conflicts emanate from structural arrangements and inherent inconsistencies. Dialectic sociology is at once holistic and argumentative. Karl Marx and Ralph Dahrendorf have substantially aided the development of a scientific theory of social conflict which attempts to explain the inherent possibilities of change in society, the structural origin of dissension as well as the multiplicity of forms of conflict and their degrees of intensity. In a sense, the roots of conflict theory may be traced back to the debate between Thrasymachus and Socrates in *The Republic*: 'the evil is all that destroys and corrupts, and the good is what preserves the benefits . . . each thing has its evil and good . . . the natural evil of each thing destroys it.'[51] This dialectic is at the root of contemporary conflict theories whose central concern is internal contradictions and inherent predilections to change characteristic of any social structure. G. W. F. Hegel expanded the theme of the dialogue in Plato and laid the foundation of modern dialectics which served as the starting point for Marx who, in turn, laid the foundation of modern dialectic sociology. From Hobbes to Mosca and from Marx to Simmel, social scientists have held the position 'that social organization does not flow from the consensus of *vox populi*, but from the contradictory yet interrelated needs and designs of men,'[52] and that coercion, not consensus, is the dominant form of social relationship. Simmel's 'tendency of domination by means of levelling' appears in the contemporary conflict theories of Mills and Dahrendorf in the concepts of superordination and manipulation by means of coercion.

Critical Evaluation

The attempt to reduce the multiplicity of social conflicts to a common principle (what may be termed the fallacy of the binary model) is one of the most fundamental drawbacks of conflict analysis. Most conflict theorists have a dualistic view of social reality in relation to a single principle, for instance, property for Marx, power for Mills, and authority for Dahrendorf. Such analyses portray the multifarious conflicts and contradictions in the social universe as polarizing into pairs of opposites—bourgeois and proletariat, the elite and the masses, the rulers and the ruled. However, reality is quite different. Social conflicts manifest themselves in a variety of ways and numerous interest groups and any attempt to reduce them to a common principle or a dualistic conception is inevitably sterile.

Just as functionalists consider stability and equilibrium the dominant order of society, conflict theorists assume that human society is in a continuous and unending process of change. This assumption, termed as the fallacy of incessant flux, is the negation of an historical reality exemplified for thousands of years by many traditional societies and tribal states which have changed very little. To equate change with traumatic conditions is one thing, but to assume that every element of every society is in the process of change at all times is quite another thing. Empirical reality lies somewhere between the two extremes; change is a normal feature of society, for no human society is entirely static. But so is stability a natural characteristic of society, and at any point in time it is analytically possible to separate the structure and its invariance from the social system.

A third fallacy is the conflict analysts' tendency to equate conflict with change. They tend to assume that change flows necessarily from conflict, of classes, of interests, of values, or whatever; and if there is no conflict, latent or manifest, there is no change. This, again, is the negation of empirical reality. Substantial changes in society, even a total transformation of socio-economic systems, have occurred without significant conflicts, as in the case of many new nation-states where silent revolutions have been initiated and legitimized by enlightened political elites. Whereas conflict may necessarily lead to change, the obverse is not always true.

Related, too, is the conflict theorists' failure to distinguish between positive and negative conflicts, or forms of conflict and their varied repercussions for different elements of society. Whereas functionalists equate conflict with structural strain and disruption, conflict analysts tend to believe that social conflict is inevitable and, therefore, ought to be good. It does not make sense to ask if conflict is good or bad, rather we should ask which conflict, with what consequences, and for whom. Conflict can contribute as much to social integration and stability as to disintegration and change; it may disrupt or restore equilibrium. Moreover, there are safety valves in society which facilitate legitimate expressions of social conflict as well as built-in mechanisms which institutionalize social conflicts. Similarly, there are occasions when conflicts have irreparably damaged the fabric of societies and led to their total disintegration. Therefore, a scientific theory of conflict should employ a broader and more refined frame of reference and transcend the realm of analysis to a higher level of abstraction.

Another general criticism against the conflict theory is the inadequacy of empirically verifiable data that have been incorporated into the theoretical schema. Most conflict theorists have relied primarily on illustrative materials rather than empirically verifiable data. Duke complains: 'No less than functionalism before it, contemporary statements of conflict theory contain few empirical illustrations and fewer crucial tests of their statements. The theoretical debate is still being carried on as a test of mind and a clash of reason, rather than reflecting a careful scrutiny of available data.'[53] Duke argues that there is no dearth of conflict data; in fact, there is an abundance of scientifically gathered data on role conflicts, political and economic conflicts, value conflicts and from studies of deviant behavior, decision-making, leadership and influence; what is needed, according to him, is an attempt to 'codify and synthesize' them in order to formulate a comprehensive theory of social conflict. And in his judgement, 'any methodology may be adopted for use by conflict theorists and no methodology is unusable.'

Although a general, comprehensive conflict theory of society will be primarily a structural theory, every conflict theory need not be structural in character. Subjectivist orientations, value references, and ideological differences which manifest themselves in open conflict may be analysed with only peripheral reference to structural properties.

In spite of the limitations mentioned above, conflict theory is a significant and, in many ways, an essential mode of sociological analysis. Although it is more a promise than an accomplishment, its untapped potential could be an invaluable aid in the process of sociological inquiry. Structural-functionalism deals with abstract social systems in equilibrium; conflict theory points to the dynamic aspects of society and the empirical realities of conflict and change. Actually, conflict and consensus, harmony and constraint, are two faces of the same social reality. Social phenomena involve a continual shift between equilibrium and disequilibrium, tension and stability, and integration and disintegration. Neither structural-functionalism nor conflict theory can claim comprehensive and exclusive validity. There are sociological phenomena for the explanation of which functionalism is inherently more appropriate and there are social problems for the understanding of which conflict theory provides a better frame of reference. The choice between the two alternate theories is to be dictated by the nature of the problem to be investigated and explained. However, some sociologists have the tendency to put the cart before the horse when they set out to interpret sociological phenomena with a predetermined perspective anchored in their favourite theory. It seems appropriate to refer back to Dahrendorf, one of the most distinguished contemporary conflict theorists:

Just as the physicists can solve certain problems only by assuming the wave character of light and others, on the contrary, only by assuming a corpuscular or quantum theory, so there are problems of sociology which can be adequately attacked only with an integration theory and others which require a conflict theory for a meaningful analysis. Both theories can work extensively with the same categories, but they emphasize different aspects. While the integration theory likens a society to an ellipse, a rounded entity which encloses all of its elements, conflict theory sees society rather as a hyperbola, which, it is true, has the same foci, but is open in many directions and appears as a tension field of the determining forces.[54]

How do we, then, account for the dominance of structural-functionalism in contemporary American sociology? First, a spate of studies in small group research have almost idealized the 'principle of common interest' and treated conflict as a form of deviant behaviour. Second, the system theorists in general, and the Parsonian school in particular, have abstracted the order and regularity characteristic of modern complex organizations as manifested in the functional division of labour, chain of command, bureaucratic structure, and line matrices, and have extrapolated the same for society as a whole. The engineered consensus of formal organizations is applied to the equilibrated structure of mass society. Some sociologists, notably Lipset, stress the levelling influence of American affluence—as more and more Americans are able to reap the benefits of national prosperity wherein the quest for consensus is thought to be reinforced. Others argue that consensus in today's society is manufactured by rational bureaucratic structures by means of persuasion and manipulation. 'But perhaps the most powerful reason for the shift to consensus theory is the "enlightened" recognition that mass terror is not as powerful an instrument for extracting economic and political loyalties as mass persuasion.'[55]

NOTES

1. Don Martindale, *The Nature and Types of Sociological Theory* (Boston, Houghton-Mifflin Company, 1960), pp. 147–8. Reprinted by permission.

2. Gaetano Mosca, 'The Ruling Class', Quoted from William J. Chambliss (ed.), *Sociological Readings in the Conflict Perspective* (Reading, Mass., Addison-Wesley Publishing Co., 1973), p. 232.

3. Georg Simmel, *Conflict and the Web of Group Affiliations* (Glencoe, Free Press, 1955), p. 13.

4. Ibid., p. 14.

5. Lewis Coser, *The Functions of Social Conflict* (New York, Free Press, 1956), p. 49.

6. Ralf Dahrendorf, *Class and Class Conflict in Industrial Society* (Stanford, Stanford University Press, 1959), p. 159.

7. Irving Louis Horowitz, 'Consensus, Conflict, and Cooperation', in N. J. Demerath III and Richard A. Peterson (eds.), *System, Change, and Conflict* (New York, Free Press, 1967), p. 269.

8. Ibid., p. 275.

9. Ralf Dahrendorf, 'Toward a Theory of Social Conflict', in Amitai Etzioni and Eva Etzioni-Halevy (eds.), *Social Change* (New York, Basic Books, 1973), p. 102.

10. Ralf Dahrendorf, 'Out of Utopia: Toward a Reorientation of Sociological Analysis', in Lewis Coser and Bernard Rosenberg (eds.), *Sociological Theory* (New York, The Macmillan Company, 1969), pp. 222–40, 236, 237.

11. Pierre L. van den Berghe, 'Dialectic and Functionalism: Toward a Theoretical Synthesis', in Chambliss, op. cit., p. 47.

12. Dahrendorf, *Toward a Theory of Social Conflict*, op. cit., p. 105.

13. Karl Marx and Friedrich Engels, 'The Class Struggle', in Etzioni, op. cit., p. 32.

14. Karl Marx, *Selected Writings in Sociology and Social Philosophy* (translated by T. B. Bottomore, London, McGraw-Hill, 1964), pp. 51, 78.

15. Lewis Coser, *Masters of Sociological Thought* (New York, Harcourt Brace Jovanovich, Inc., 1971), p. 44.

16. See Raymond Aron, *Main Currents in Sociological Thought I* (Garden City, Doubleday Company, 1968), p. 152.

17. Marx, *Selected Writings*, p. 223.

18. For a detailed discussion and critique of Marx's theory of class conflict, see Chapters 1 and 4 of Ralf Dahrendorf, *Class and Class Conflict in Industrial Society*.

19. Aron, op. cit., p. 165.

20. Maurice Cornforth, *Historical Materialism* (New York, International Publishers, 1954), pp. 58–9.

21. Karl Marx, *Early Writings* (translated and edited by T. B. Bottomore, New York, McGraw-Hill, 1964), p. 122.

22. Marx and Engels, in Etzioni, op. cit., pp. 36–7.

23. Ibid., pp. 37–8.

24. Irving Howe (ed.), *Essential Works of Socialism* (New York, Holt, Rinehart and Winston, 1971), p. 7.

25. T. B. Bottomore, 'Marxist Sociology', in *The International Encyclopedia of the Social Sciences*, vol. 10, ed. David L. Sills (New York, Macmillan Company, 1968), p. 46.

26. T. B. Bottomore, 'Karl Marx: Sociologist or Marxist?' in Serge Denisoff

et al., *Theories and Paradigms in Contemporary Sociology* (Itasca, F. E. Peacock Publishers, Inc., 1974, pp. 304–5.

27. Herbert Marcuse, 'Re-examination of the Concept of Revolution', in Denisoff et al., op. cit., p. 319.
28. His works represent neo-colonialism and imperialism. See *Latin America: Underdevelopment or Revolution, Capitalism and Underdevelopment in Latin America, and Dependence and Underdevelopment*, co-authored with J. D. Cockeroft and D. L. Johnson.
29. Marcuse, op. cit., pp. 320, 322.
30. C. Wright Mills, 'The Higher Circles', in Chambliss, op. cit., p. 275.
31. Ibid., p. 288.
32. Robert V. Presthus, *Men at the Top: A Study in Community Power* (New York, Oxford University Press, 1964), p. 38.
33. C. Wright Mills, 'The Conditions of Modern Work', in Steven Deutsch and John Howard (eds), *Where It's At: Radical Perspectives in Sociology* (New York: Harper and Row Publishers, 1970), p. 291.
34. Ibid., p. 291.
35. Ibid., p. 292.
36. See Dahrendorf, *Class and Class Conflict*, op. cit., pp. 236, 166, and Etzioni, op. cit., p. 109.
37. van den Berghe, op. cit., p. 53.
38. Dahrendorf, *Class and Class Conflict*, p. 302.
39. Trent Schroyer, 'A Reconceptualization of Critical Theory', in Alan Wells (ed.), *Contemporary Sociological Theories* (Santa Monica, Goodyear Publishing Company, 1978), p. 253.
40. Ibid., pp. 254, 251.
41. Irving Louis Horowitz, 'Radicalism and Contemporary American Society', in Deutsch and Howard, op. cit., p. 569.
42. Ibid., pp. 5–6.
43. Ibid., p. 7.
44. Randall Collins, 'The Empirical Validity of the Conflict Tradition', in Alan Wells, op. cit., p. 169.
45. Ibid., p. 170.
46. Randall Collins, *Conflict Sociology* (New York, Academic Press, 1975), pp. 60, 89.
47. Lewis Coser, 'Social Conflict and the Theory of Social Change', in Etzioni, op. cit., p. 114.
48. Ibid., p. 115.
49. Coser, *The Functions of Social Conflict*, op. cit., pp. 151–6.
50. James T. Duke, *Conflict and Power in Social Life* (Provo, Brigham Young University Press, 1976), p. 176.
51. Quoted in Denisoff et. al., op. cit., p. 297.
52. Horowitz, 'Consensus, Conflict, and Cooperation', op. cit., p. 268.
53. Duke, op. cit., pp. 199, 205.
54. Dahrendorf, 'Toward a Theory of Social Conflict', op. cit., p. 106.
55. Horowitz, 'Consensus, Conflict, and Cooperation', op. cit., p. 277.

CHAPTER 6

Exchange Theory

The theory of social exchange is not one coherent theoretical system. It contains strains of British individualistic orientation and French collectivistic orientation in theory construction. It is a mixture of utilitarian economics, functional anthropology, and behavioural psychology. The classical traditions of the exchange theory are attributed to James Frazer, Malinowski, Marcel Mauss and Levi-Strauss; its contemporary variations were developed by George Homans and Peter Blau, two of the most outstanding exponents of current exchange theories.

Intellectual Background

The intellectual roots of exchange theory may be traced to the utilitarian thought which views men as rationally seeking to maximize their material benefits from transactions with others in a free and competitive market place. On the strength of their knowledge of the market situation, men would rationally choose between available alternatives based on a calculation of cost and benefits. However, classical as well as modern sociologists have always tried to devise alternatives to the utilitarian thought. Contemporary exchange theorists have recognized that men are not always rational, that they do not always try to maximize profit in every exchange and that their interactions are regulated by external constraints. Yet the fundamental assumption underlying all exchange theories is that men always seek to make some profit in their exchange transactions with others, which are to a significant extent governed by considerations of costs and benefits— material or non-material.

The first explicit formulation of exchange theory was the work of Sir James Frazer. In studying various kinship and marriage practices among primitive societies, Frazer was particularly struck by the strong preference of the Australian aboriginals for cross-cousin marriage and their prohibition of parallel cousin marriages. He sought to explain the custom in terms of the familiar utilitarian economic thought: the Australian aboriginal who had no equivalent in property to give for a wife, was obliged to get her in exchange for a female relative, usually a sister or daughter; in other words, men enter into institutionalized patterns of exchange to satisfy their basic economic needs. 'Thus the exchange of sisters, whether sisters in the full or in the group sense of the word, appears to have been the very pivot on which turned the great reformation initiated by the dual organization of society.'[1] Frazer also recognized the consequences of such exchange relations for status and power. He wrote: 'Since among the Australian aborigines women had a high economic and commercial value, a man who had many sisters or daughters was rich and a man who had none was poor and might be unable to procure a wife at all.'[2] Thus older men could procure a number of wives for themselves from among the younger women, forcing younger men who had no women to give in exchange to remain single or be content with the discarded wives of their elders. Such a system of exchange also enabled older men who possessed commodities of big economic value to gain power and social privileges in society.

Malinowski was the first to draw a clear distinction between economic exchange and social exchange. In his ethnography of the *Trobriand Islander*, he discussed an exchange system called the *Kula Ring* which involved the exchange of armlets and necklaces which travelled in opposite directions but always within a closed circle of individuals. In sharp contrast with the utilitarian perspective of Frazer, Malinowski recognized the symbolic meaning of the ceremonial exchange of armlets and necklaces which was intended to strengthen a network of interpersonal relationships. Moreover, *Kula* transactions could be done only between partners, and the exchange actors could not seek out the highest bidder in order to maximize material benefits. The exchange system was designed to meet various social psychological and functional needs of the individual and society.

Malinowski recognized the importance of basic psychological needs in explaining social behaviour but rejected the assumption of pervasive economic motives in social explanation. Malinowski goes to the very heart of the relationship between individual and society. Ekeh brings out the basic assumption underlying Malinowski's interpretation of the *Kula*: 'An institution that both meets the needs of individuals and helps to maintain the society as an ongoing concern will be more stable than an institution that insures the one but not the other of these two functions.[23]

Reacting to Malinowski's psychological interpretation, Marcel Mauss set out to reinterpret the *Kula Ring*. He sought to identify the force which compels the recipient to repay a gift. Mauss recognized that it was society which mandates and carries on exchange, not individuals, and that exchange transactions are normatively regulated by the collectivity. This recognition led to the first collectivistic or structural orientation in modern exchange theories.

Mauss' chief contribution to social exchange theory lies in his recognition that social exchange processes yield for the larger society a moral code of behaviour which acquires an independent existence outside the social exchange situation and which informs all social, economic, and political interpersonal relationships in society.[4]

Mauss de-emphasized the role of individuals in social exchange transactions. According to him, it is not individuals who are isolated unit actors but persons who are representatives of certain social roles who take part in the exchange. Mauss also stresses the morality of social exchange and relegates considerations of self-interest to the background.

The triple obligation of social exchange—to give, to receive, and to repay—are to be understood not in the idiom of self-interest but in terms of interpersonal, hence inter-group, relations. Every social exchange transaction creates social bonds that not only tie one person to another and to society but one segment of society to another. Moreover, the morality that emerges from these social bonds exists as reality *sui generis* and informs social interactions and activities in society.[5]

Levi-Strauss, one of the most influential structuralists, rejected both Frazer's utilitarian interpretation and Malinowski's psychological conceptualization, and in a manner similar to Mauss' analysis, formulated the most explicit and elaborate structural exchange perspective. Reacting sharply to the utilitarian assumption that social behaviour is motivated by calculated economic considerations, Levi-Strauss declared that

It is the exchange which counts and not the things exchanged. Everywhere we find again and again this double assumption, implicit or explicit, that reciprocal gifts constitute a means of transmission of goods; and that these goods are not offered primarily or essentially, in order to gain a profit or advantage of an economic nature.[6]

Obviously for Levi-Strauss, the items of exchange are culturally defined, and their values are not intrinsic but extrinsic and symbolic. And the primary function of exchange is structural integration of the larger society. He also emphasized that the patterns of exchange varied with types of social organization and that they are regulated by the norms and values of a society. Furthermore,

all exchange relations involve costs for individuals, but, in contrast with economic or psychological explanations of exchange such costs are attributed to society—to its customs, rules, laws, and values. These features of society require behaviours that incur costs; thus, the individual does not assess the costs to himself, but to the 'social order' requiring that costly behaviour be emitted.[7]

Ekeh identifies two assumptions which are central to Levi-Strauss' brand of social exchange: 'first, social exchange behaviour is human and therefore sub-human animals are incapable of social exchange and, correlatively, cannot provide a model of human social exchange. Secondly, social exchange is a supra-individual process and individual self-interests may be involved in it but they cannot sustain social exchange processes.'[8] Levi-Strauss' rejection of the psychological interpretation of social exchange behaviour is based on these theoretical assumptions: first, social exchange is a distinctively symbolic process which can neither be derived from nor ascribed to animal behaviour. 'Man may share certain attributes with infra-human animals, but it is what is unique to him as human not what he shares with animals, that enables him to engage in social exchange processes.'[9] Second, social exchange is normative behaviour governed by societal rules and norms. Third, exchange behaviour is creative and dynamic but animal behaviour, devoid of imagination, is static. As Levi-Strauss points out, 'in the sphere of culture, the individual always receives more than he gives, and gives more than he receives.'[10] Moreover, men attribute meanings and values to the things exchanged independently of the intrinsic value of the items involved. Fourth, exchange behaviour is carried on within well defined institutional frameworks. Ekeh spells out three propositions that define the institutional bases of social exchange behaviour.

(a) The principle of social scarcity and societal intervention.

If a product of symbolic value is limited in quantity society intervenes in its distribution, and hence the formulation of the rules of exchange. If a product is in abundance society leaves its distribution to chance or natural laws. But Levi-Strauss is talking about social scarcity, not economic scarcity, the meaning of which is defined by society. Sometimes, artificial scarcity is created by society by regulating the circulation of certain desired items. For example, incest and exogamy are social inventions designed to make a spouse scarce by disqualifying certain groups of persons as possible choice of mates.

(b) The principle of the social cost of exchange.

'The cost of social exchange is borne by individual givers and attributed to society, *outside of the exchange situation*'. Thus the cost of a banquet is attributed to the social custom which requires it and that of a Christmas gift to the institution of Christmas rather than to those who benefit from it. 'This principle frees particular social exchange transactions from the disruptive consequences of attributing the cost of social exchange activities to those who benefit from them.'[11]

(c) The principle of reciprocity.

This principle defines the pattern of reciprocation whereby an individual feels obligated to repay a gift received. But in Levi-Strauss' scheme this principle involves not only an individual rewarding his benefactor directly but by rewarding any other actors in the exchange situation interlinked by the norm of reciprocity.

The behavioural perspective: George Homans

George Homans is undoubtedly the most outstanding spokesman of the current individualistic exchange theory. Unlike his predecessors who restricted the items of social exchange to one kind, namely women, or armlets and necklaces, Homans expanded the range of social exchange to embrace all activities. Labelled as an individual self-interest theory, Homans' formulation represents a unique combination of elementary economics and behavioural psychology. Eminently influenced by Skinner's behavioural psychology, Homans argues that human behaviour and social organizations can be effectively explained only by invoking the principles of psychology yielded by the study of animal behaviour. It must be remembered that these elementary principles of animal behaviour were formulated by behavioural psychologists based on their observation of the responses of pigeons (in the Skinner box) to rewards and punishments systematically provided by the investigator. The fundamental assumption underlying Homans' exchange theory is that the principles of describing animal behaviour will form the core of a deductive system of propositions explaining social behaviour. Turner has neatly summarized those thoeretical generalizations in behaviourism that found their way into sociological exchange theory:

1. In any given situation, organisms will emit those behaviours that will yield the most reward and least punishment.
2. Organisms will repeat those behaviours which have proved rewarding in the past.
3. Organisms will repeat behaviours in situations that are similar to those in the past in which behaviours were rewarded.
4. Present stimuli that on past occasions have been associated with rewards will evoke behaviours similar to those emitted in the past.
5. Repetition of behaviours will occur only as long as they continue to yield rewards.
6. An organism will display emotion if a behaviour that has previously been rewarded in the same, or similar, situation suddenly goes unrewarded.
7. The more an organism receives rewards from a particular behaviour, the less rewarding that behaviour becomes (due to satiation) and the more likely the organism to emit alternative behaviours in search of other rewards.[12]

Thus proclaiming himself as an 'ultimate psychological reductionist', Homans has fashioned his exchange theory after the principles of conditioned animal behaviour rather than symbolic human behaviour. It is well known that these principles were formulated on the basis of behavioural psychologists' highly controlled observations of laboratory animals, whose needs could be inferred from deprivations imposed by the investigators. However, human needs are much more difficult to ascertain. Moreover, humans interact in group situations that defy experimental controls.

One of the most important adjustments of Skinnerian principles to fit the facts of human social organization involves the recognition that needs are satisfied by other people and that people reward and punish each other. In contrast with Skinner's animals, which only indirectly interact with Skinner through the apparatus of the laboratory and which have little ability to reward Skinner (except perhaps to confirm his principles), humans constantly give and take, or exchange, rewards and punishments.[13]

Let us now examine Homans, social exchange theory in detail. We will begin by defining the basic concepts that are essential to the understanding of Homans' propositions.

Activity   The kind of behaviour aimed at deriving rewards.

Sentiment	The activities by means of which the members of a particular verbal or symbolic community communicate feelings and emotional attitudes.
Interaction	Social behaviour in which people direct their activities towards each other.
Quantity	The number of units of the activity that the organism in question emits within a given period of time.
Value	The degree of reinforcement or punishment a man gets from the unit of an activity he receives.
Reward	Anything or any activity that a person receives that is positively evaluated by him.

To these terms borrowed from behavioural psychology Homans adds a set of terms taken from elementary economics.

| Cost | The cost of a unit of given activity is a value of the reward obtainable through a unit of an alternative activity foregone in emitting the given one, that is, the alternative reward foregone. (The cost of a cup of coffee is not the price you pay for it but whatever else you could have bought with that amount). |
| Profit | Reward minus cost for engaging in a certain activity. |

In terms of these basic concepts we may now summarize Homans' propositions:[14]

1. *The success proposition.* For all actions taken by persons, the more often a particular action of a person is rewarded, the more likely the person is to perform that action. The proposition does not say why the person performed the action in the first place. However, having done something, if the person finds the action successful in the sense of generating positive value to him, he is likely to repeat the same action expecting additional rewards. The frequency of action depends on the frequency of reward but there are built-in limits imposed by satiation. The frequency of action also depends on the pattern in which it is rewarded. Homans believes that:

man, like an experimental animal such as pigeon, will repeat an action less often if it is rewarded regularly—for instance, if it is rewarded every time it is performed—than he will if it is rewarded at irregular intervals of time or at irregular ratios between the number of times he performs the action and the number of times it is rewarded. Furthermore an action once regularly rewarded will, when the reward ceases, become extinguished sooner than one rewarded irregularly.

According to Homans, why people are willing to work so hard at gambling, fishing, or hunting, even when they have little success, is that such actions are characteristically rewarded irregularly. Similarly, if an action once rewarded is never rewarded again, the activity eventually becomes 'extinguished' until it is reinstated with fresh rewards.

2. *The stimulus proposition.* If, in the past, the occurrence of a particular stimulus, or set of stimuli, has been the occasion on which a person's action has been rewarded, then the more similar the present stimuli are to the past ones, the more likely the person is to perform the action, or some similar action, now.

The crucial variable in the stimulus proposition is the degree of similarity between present stimuli and those under which an action was rewarded in the past. And the reappearance of the circumstances under which an action was rewarded in the past will cause the repetition of the action. Thus a fisherman who has cast his line into a dark pool and caught a fish is more likely to fish in a dark pool.

3. *The value proposition.* The more valuable to a person is the result of his action, the more likely he is to perform the action.

Rewards are those results of a person's actions that have positive values for him, and punishments are those that have negative ones. According to the value proposition, an increase in the positive value of the reward makes it more likely that a person will perform a particular act, and an increase in the negative value of the punishment makes it less likely that he will do so. The things that men find rewarding are many and varied. Homans hastens to add that the rewards he is concerned with are not necessarily materialistic values but values that may be altruistic as well.

4. *The deprivation-satiation proposition.* The more often in the recent past a person has received a particular reward, the less valuable any further unit of that reward becomes for him. If a man has received the reward often, he becomes satiated with it; its value for him decreases and he becomes less inclined to perform an action which generates the same reward.

5. *The aggression-approval proposition.* This proposition is divided into two parts:

(a) When a person's action does not receive the reward he expected, or receives punishment he did not expect, he will be angry; he is more likely to perform aggressive behaviour, and the results of such behaviour become more valuable to him.

(b) When a person's action receives reward he expected, especially a greater reward than he expected, or does not receive punishment he expected, he will be pleased; he becomes more likely to perform approving behaviour, and the results of such behaviour become more valuable to him.

Homans stresses the historicity implied by these propositions, that is, the great importance of man's past experiences in shaping his present behaviour.

A man's past history of success, of stimulation, of the acquisition of values all affect the way he behaves now. The choices he made in the past may still be limiting the opportunities available to him today, or he may perceive them as limiting; hence the great weight attaches to a man's early experience by all schools of modern psychology. The ill effects of some early experiences may of course be overcome, but it may be difficult to do so—there is something to be overcome.

6. *The rationality proposition.* In choosing between alternative actions, a person will choose that one for which, as perceived by him at the time, the value, V, of the result, multiplied by the probability, P, of getting the result, is the greater.

This proposition involves two related elements. First, the value a man sets on the results of his action; second, the probability of success which is based on past experiences. Homans' favorite example is that of William the Conqueror who set a high value on becoming the king of England, but the odds were against him and his contemporaries might have judged his chance of success to be small. Now, Homans explains William's decision to go ahead with his invasion of England by invoking the success proposition: the almost unbroken series of William's military victories over the preceding twenty years.

And Homans regards these behavioural propositions as adequate for the explanation of not only animal and individual behaviour but complex social behaviour as well. Parsons and Eisenstadt, among others, question this assumption. According to Parsons, exchange transactions between individuals take place within a complex system of social relationships regulated by normative and symbolic systems. According to Eisenstadt, Homans has ignored the crucial distinction between institutionalized and non-institutionalized or informal behaviour; while Homans' behavioural theory may be suitable for the explanation of the latter, it certainly cannot explain the former (institutionalized behaviour).

Homans has completely ignored the science of culture which

deals with the uniqueness of man and the symbolic nature of human behaviour. As White has said, 'The symbol is the universe of humanity.'[15] Man is not always rational; he is not always after maximizing material benefits. Things, for him, have a symbolic value, not simply intrinsic value, because of the meaning bestowed on them by culture. Whereas a pigeon does not look for or feel rewarded by ceremonial objects, man is willing to die for a cross or a flag.

Ekeh brings out these other points:[16]

1. In conditioned behaviour, past experiences are necessary conditions of present activities. That is exactly why Homans emphasized the importance of past experiences in determining present behaviour. In symbolic behaviour, past experiences are neither necessary nor sufficient conditions of present activities. 'Although symbolic behaviour may include past experiences in its repertoire of responses, its chief characteristic is the capacity to relate present activities to future possibilities. If exchange behaviour were in fact to be conditioned behaviour, then we must assume that social exchange processes do not include future anticipations.' This is obviously not true, for exchange behaviour involves postponement of an act until the alternatives are more or less thoroughly tested symbolically. Moreover, with emphasis on past experiences Homans' theory simply cannot explain what an individual will do if he encounters new situations, or if his evaluation of future possibilities alters significantly because behavioural psychology which derives its principles primarily from animal behaviour is incapable of handling future calculations as the motive force in human behaviour.

2. 'Secondly, symbolic behaviour is behaviourally creative; conditioned behaviour is static. Symbolic behaviour can and does result in new behaviour; conditioned behaviour is repetitive of old behaviours.' Yes, animals can be taught sign language but they cannot teach.

3. 'Thirdly symbolic behaviour is normative behaviour shared by persons within a value system; conditioned behaviour is non-normative behaviour and is an attribute of the individual. Since conditioned behaviour is an individual experience, learned through sheer experience, it is non-transmissible.' While an intelligent animal may be taught to do someting ingenious by rewarding it, its off-spring cannot be socialized into this pattern of behaviour by the animal mother the way humans do.

4. 'Fourthly, symbolic behaviour makes use of time and space conceptions; on the other hand, conditioned behaviour cannot make use of time and space conceptions.'

5. In the final formulation of the exchange theory, Homans changed from being an 'ultimate psychological reductionist' to a psychological-with-economic reductionist. He began to extrapolate independently from behavioural psychology and elementary economics to elementary social behaviour. Thus his exchange theory represents a curious mixture of behavioural psychology and elementary economics. Neither of the two could by itself explain human exchange, for, 'there is a qualitative difference between them—with one specializing in the study of time-laden symbolic behaviour while the other, behavioural psychology, specializes in the study of non-symbolic behaviour with no conception of time—and that a combinaton of the two to form explanatory propositions for human or symbolic behaviour is not possible.' And Ekeh is emphatic that behavioural psychology and elementary economics do not mesh together.

Homans' propositions are derived from exchange transactions between two persons. Thus the theory itself is stated in dyadic terms but much of the evidence he invokes in support of his theory is in connection with multi-person interactions. Ekeh thus argues that 'there is a disjunction between Homans' dyadic propositions of social exchange and the empirical data to fit his theory by reducing multiperson interactions to multiple dyadic interactions.' Also the propositions derived from dyadic settings are claimed to have generalized validity for transactions in small groups as well as large collectivities.

Finally, Homans' concepts are so vaguely defined that the propositions couched in those terms are tantamount to tautologies. Turner observes:

Aside from the risk of generating tautologous propositions, Homans' critical concepts—activity, value, reward, cost, profit—are so generally defined that they can be used for virtually any *ad hoc* purpose. Homans has typically chosen to use the concepts to provide ex post facto interpretations of empirical studies . . . . With each interpretation, the concepts of activity, value, reward, cost, profit (and sometimes investment) are defined to 'fit the facts' of the cases under investigation.[17]

The Structural Perspective: Peter Blau

Blau begins his analysis of social exchange using basically the same psychological perspective on behaviour at the elementary level as Homans; hence, the basic principles underlying Blau's conception of exchange are strikingly similar to those of Homans:

An individual who supplies rewarding services to another obligates him. To discharge this obligation, the second must furnish benefits to the first in turn . . . . If both individuals value what they receive from the other, both are prone to supply more of their own services to provide incentives for the other to increase his supply and to avoid becoming indebted to him. As both receive increasing amounts of the assistance they originally needed rather badly, however, their need for still further assistance typically declines.[18]

Eventually the declining marginal utility of additional benefits is no longer worth the cost of obtaining them.

However, Blau's analysis of social exchange differs from Homans' in several significant ways. First, although Blau's exchange model encompasses a wide range of behaviour it 'is limited to actions that are contingent on rewarding reactions from others and that cease when these expected reactions are not forthcoming.'[19] Second, Blau rejects Homans' behavioural perspective and psychological reductionism. Third, having analysed the characteristics of interaction, Blau shifts the micro level analysis to incorporate macro structures such as social systems which have their own 'dynamics with emergent properties'. Thus Blau's 'problem is to derive the social processes that govern the complex structures of communities and societies from the simpler processes that pervade the daily intercourse among individuals and their interpersonal relations.'[20] In this endeavour he seeks to avoid the two dangers of 'the *Scylla* of abstract conceptions too remote from observable empirical reality and the *Charybdis* of reductionism that ignores emergent social and structural properties.' Fourth, unlike Homans, Blau does not state a formal set of propositions and is not interested in developing the higher-order axioms of a deductive theoretic system; he only aims to offer a theoretical 'prolegomenon', or a conceptual sketch. Finally, Blau dwells at length on the consequences of the patterns of exchange for power, social integration and so on in terms of all three major theoretical frameworks in modern sociology—symbolic interactionism, functionalism, and conflict theory.

'Social exchange . . . refers to voluntary actions of individuals that are motivated by the returns they are expected to bring and typically do in fact bring from others.'[21] Social exchange transactions are triggered by two psychological processes: the underlying feeling of attraction between individuals and their desires for various kinds of rewards. 'An individual is attracted to another if he expects associating with him to be in some way rewarding for himself, and his interest in the expected social rewards draws him to the other.'[22] Indeed, Blau regards social life as a 'market place' in which actors negotiate with each other in order to make a gain—a material benefit or a psychological reward. And the individual who has received some benefits is obligated to reciprocate in order to continue receiving them in the future. Thus the norm of reciprocity serves as a 'starting mechanism' of social interaction and group structure. What we have said so far about Blau's exchange theory may be formally stated as follows: (a) A person who enters into a particular social activity expects a reward. (b) The more he receives a valuable reward in return for an activity, the more he will emit that particular activity. (c) The more a particular activity brings expected rewards, the less valuable additional rewards become and the less likely the emission of the particular activity. (d) A person who receives a benefit in a social interaction is expected to reciprocate. (e) Reciprocal obligations cement bonds of social relationship and lead to social integration. (f) Violation of reciprocal obligations invites negative sanctions from the deprived parties.

Blau distinguishes between social exchange and economic exchange. The former entails unspecified obligations and generates feelings of personal obligation, gratitude, and trust but the latter rests on a formal contract that stipulates the exact quantities to be exchanged. Social exchange thus involves favours that create diffuse—and moral—future obligations whereas economic exchange is made possible by contractual obligations. 'In contrast to economic commodities, the benefits involved in social exchange do not have an exact price in terms of a single quantitative medium of exchange, which is another reason why social obligations are unspecific.'[23] Moreover, social exchange is more personalized than economic exchange.

Among the conditions that affect processes of social exchange, Blau includes the stage in the development and the character of the relationship between exchange partners, the nature of the benefits that enter into the transactions and the costs incurred in providing them, and the social context in which the exchanges take place. In more specific terms, the conditions of exchange may be enumerated as follows:

1. Making investments that constitute commitments to the other party;
2. Reciprocation by the other proving his trustworthiness;
3. Special mechanisms that perpetuate obligations and thus strengthen bonds of indebtedness and trust;
4. Provision of just rewards that compensate for cost.

Blau delineates the social context in which exchange transactions take place as follows:

First, even if we abstract the exchange transactions in a single pair, they are influenced by the 'role-set' of each partner, that is, by the role relations either has by virtue of occupying the social status relevant to the exchange, since these role relations govern the alternative opportunities of the two. The larger circle of acquaintances of the members of a clique who exchange invitations, for example, or the dating opportunities of two lovers, define the alternatives foregone by each and hence affect the cost each incurs in order to obtain rewards from his present association. . . . Second, the entire exchange transactions in a group determine a prevailing rate of exchange, and this group standard puts pressure on any partnership whose transctions deviate from it to come into line. These are not normative pressures in the sense of moral standards supported by group sanctions that enforce conformity but pressures resulting from existing opportunities. . . . Third, potential coalitions among the weaker members of a collectivity tend to restrain its stronger members from fully exploiting their advantageous position in exchange transactions . . . . Fourth, the differences in power to which exchange processes typically give rise in a group subsequently modify these processes, since established power enables an individual to compel others to provide services without offering a fair return, although the danger of the formation of coalitions to destroy his power may discourage its exploitative use . . . . Finally, the social situation exerts a subtle but important influence by making the transactions in a given exchange relation part of other exchanges that occur in the background and that may, nevertheless, be the more salient ones. A person may give a waiter a large tip to elicit the approval of his companions at the table for his generosity, not primarily to earn the waiter's gratitude.[24]

Having specified the conditions of exchange Blau turns to the differentiation of exchange relations leading to power. According to Blau, 'A person who commands services others need, and who is independent of any at their command, attains power over others by making the satisfaction of their need contingent on their compliance.'[25] The unilateral supply of important services on which others are dependent serves as a source of power. Thus the person on whom others are dependent for vital services has the power to extract compliance in an exchange relationship. His demands may be considered fair and just by those who receive the benefits. Such collective approval of power legitimates that power. According to Blau, individuals who need a service another has to offer have the following alternatives: they can supply him with a service that he needs badly so as to induce him to offer his service in return; they may seek to obtain the service from alternative sources; they may learn to resign themselves to do without this service or be content with some substitute for it; or, finally, finding no alternatives, they may comply with his wishes since he can make continued supply of the needed service contingent on their compliance.

Further differentiation of exchange processes leads to legitimation and organization culminating in emergent social structures. Reciprocal obligations and notions of legitimacy generate balancing forces that create a strain toward equilibrium. But there are also diverse balancing forces and elements of opposition which produce strain, imbalance, and change.

At the elementary level of direct exchange between individual men, interpersonal attraction determines the interaction pattern. But social systems at the macro level always involve indirect exchange relations between individuals and collectivities as well as between types of collectivities. Such complex exchange systems are typically mediated by 'shared values'. Turner observes:

As people and various forms of collective organization become dependent upon particular networks of indirect exchange for expected rewards, pressures for formalizing exchange networks through explicit norms increase. This formalization and regularization of complex exchange systems can be effective under three minimal conditions: (a) The formalized exchange networks must have profitable payoffs for most parties to the exchange. (b) Most individuals organized into collective units must have internalized through prior socialization the mediating values used to build exchange networks. And (c) those units with power in the exchange system must receive a level of rewards that moves them to seek actively the formalization of rules governing exchange relations.[26]

As Blau shifts his emphasis from elementary exchange to macro-level structures, the principle of 'interpersonal attraction' is replaced by the principle of 'shared values', and the processes of competition, differentiation, integration, and opposition assume greater significance. Exchange relations among complex structures are typically institutionalized, and largely patterned by common standards and values. Such values are viewed by Blau as 'media of social transactions'. They are internalized in the individual members in a society through the process of socialization. Institutionalized as common standards and judged as appropriate by the collectivity, they mediate complex exchange systems and define principles of reciprocity and fair exchange. In discussing 'mediating values' that regulate the processes of attraction, competition, and differentiation, Blau turns to Parsons' pattern variable, viz., universalism-particularism. Particularistic values serve as the media of 'integration' and 'solidarity' and 'unite members of a collectivity in common solidarity and extend the scope of integrative bonds far beyond the limits of personal feelings of attraction.'[27] Particularistic values thus represents a system of symbols which sets a particular group from other collectivities and serves as 'functional substitutes for sentiments of personal attraction that integrate the members of a face-to-face group into a cohesive unit'.[28] Universalistic values, on the other hand, help standardize the value of various types of activity across extended networks of exchange relations and render its comparison possible. They serve as the media of exchange and differentiation, provide for unequal but 'fair' distribution of rewards across extended exchange networks and thus allow ranking and stratification through an institutionalized system for the differential distribution of desirables.

In discussing the other two social processes—integration and opposition—Blau discovers two additional types of mediating values: 'legitimating values' and 'opposition values'. The former removes power from the realm of personal influence and assigns it to 'positions' and 'offices', and establishes as well as legitimizes authority structure. Opposition values serve as a rallying point for those who have suffered deprivations and injustice and channelize as well as legitimize their fight against 'entrenched powers and existing institutions in the society' that have not adhered to the norms of fair exchange.

As exchange relations become increasingly differentiated, common values and norms emerge to facilitate societal integration. Here Blau turns to functional analysis to explain the institutionalization of substructures within the macrostructure of society through value consensus and shared norms. In the first place, the norms of reciprocity obligate the recipient of a reward to make a return. Institutionalized systems of values and norms provide standards for judging rewards and what constitutes a fair exchange. They create bonds of trust and friendship between peers as well as produce and fortify status differences between superiors and subordinates. They also serve to legitimize power and authority through an institutionalized system of fair exchange. In the words of Blau, 'The legitimation of patterns of social conduct and social relations requires that common values and norms put the stamp of approval on them and reinforce and perpetuate them. Legitimate organizations and social relations are those of which the community approves whereas illegitimate ones violate the prevailing values in the community.'[29]

Blau, however, goes beyond the functional analysis of social integration through shared values. He also incorporates elements of the dialectical conflict theory into his formulation of social exchange model. There are always values in a society that are not institutionalized into the exchange system. These 'opposing values' provide a counter-institutional component in the macro-structure generating forces of dissensus and imbalance. 'There is a dialectic in social life, for it is governed by many contradictory forces,' claims Blau. Reciprocity on one level entails imbalances on others. The multiple consequences of a social force have contradictory repercussions in the social structure. The very forces that restore equilibrium in one respect, or in one segment of the social structure, are typically disequilibrating forces in other respects, or in other segments. The exploitative or oppressive exercise of power by those who command valued resources provokes social disapproval and, even hostility and rebellion. Similarly resistance to change by vested interests and powers also serve as a source of strain and imbalance. Moreover, institutions are accepted only as long as they are instrumental in extracting payoffs to individuals engaged in complex systems of exchange. But all institutionalized systems entail a 'counter-institutional component', 'consisting of those basic values and beliefs that have not been realized and have not found expression in explicit institutional forms, and which are the ultimate source of social change.'[30] So long as these values remain unrealized in institutional exchange relations, individuals who have internalized them will derive little payoff from existing structural arrangements and will thus feel deprived, forcing them to resort to strategies of change, ideological movements and open revolution. Blau writes:

Structural change, therefore, assumes a dialectical pattern. While social structures are governed by equilibrating forces, given the complex interdependence and incompatible requirements of intersecting substructures in a society, virtually every equilibrating force generates disequilibrium on other levels. In the process of creating readjustments in one respect, other dislocations are typically produced that necessitate further readjustments. Social imbalances may persist for prolonged periods, and social equilibrium is not constantly maintained, because a latency period intervenes before opposition forces have mobilized sufficient strength to effect adjustments. The current disequilibrating and re-equilibrating forces on many levels of social structure are reflected in the dialectical nature of structural change.[31]

Blau's analysis is a mixture of conceptual taxonomies and implicit theoretical generalizations that purports to stand at the cross-roads of the individualistic and collectivistic orientations in sociological theory. Rather than formulate explicit theoretical propositions as Homans does, Blau is content to furnish, like Parsons, 'bundles of concepts', which 'allow him considerable analytical leeway' and which can be bent and refined in an *ad hoc* fashion to fit whatever the facts may dictate.'[32]

Turner comments on the fact that Blau's conceptualization has been subjected to relatively few criticisms: 'Part of the reason for this dearth of critical review stems from the fact that, in synthesizing into an exchange perspective previously diverse theoretical traditions, Blau offers "something for everyone".' For the functionalist, Blau offers the concept of mediating values, types of institutions, and the counterpart of mechanisms of socialization and control that operate to maintain macro-social wholes; for the conflict theorist, Blau presents a dialectical-conflict perspective emphasizing the inevitable forces of opposition in relations of power and authority; for the interactionist, Blau's analysis of elementary exchange processes places considerable emphasis on role taking, role playing, and manipulation of self as actors compete for rewards; and, for the critic of Homans' reductionism, Blau provides an insightful portrayal of exchanges among emergent social structures which leave the 'integrity' of sociological theorizing intact.'[33]

Ekeh contends that:
in spite of this attempt to achieve a compromise between the indivi-

dualistic and the collectivistic orientations in sociology, Blau's social exchange theory is eminently individualistic—indeed it is nearer Spencerian and Frazerian individualism in its emphasis on economic self-interest as the motive force for social action than Homans' conditioned behavioural individualism.[34]

In both Blau's and Homans' schema, an individual enters into a social exchange relation with the primary purpose of profiting from it. However, 'Blau's model of social exchange is the behaviour of the economic man; Homans' is the behaviour of the economic pigeon.'[35] While Homans explains social structures in terms of basic psychological needs, Blau explains them in terms of basic economic needs.

Blau's attempt to integrate symbolic interactionism, functionalism and conflict theory into one logical framework is certainly commendable even if their logical integration is not fully realized. His analysis of the factors that contribute to cohesion and solidarity and the internalization of shared values is insightful. And unlike the functionalists, Blau has explicitly discussed the relationship between the individual and society. Unlike many conflict theorists, Blau is not content to assert that conflict is endemic to authority relations and that inherent predilections to change exist in every social system; rather he points up ways and means in which authority structures are created and maintained. His analysis of the sources of conflict and the forces of change are explicit and thoroughgoing. Moreover, Blau's conceptualization of macro-structures is also a definite improvement over Parsons' portrayal of institutionalisation which largely ignored the structural basis of conflict and change.

Reciprocity and Justice in Social Exchange

The norm of reciprocity

Although the principle of reciprocity has been employed by social scientists for decades, it is Alvin Gouldner who developed the most elaborate formulation of the principle so central to the conceptualization of social exchange theory. Gouldner begins by rejecting Parsons' equation of complementarity with reciprocity. According to Gouldner, complementarity connotes that one's rights are another's obligations and vice versa, the underlying assumption being that once a stable relation of mutual gratification has been established the system is self-perpetuating and not in need of any special mechanism to maintain it. Such a formulation neglects the importance of shared values as a source of stability in the social system.

Benefits exchanged by two parties may be identical or equal; one party may give nothing in return for the benefits received. Both of these are extreme cases. Usually, the parties return something more or less in value than the benefit received. This kind of generalized obligation which compels one person to make a return for the benefit received from other persons is institutionalized as the norm of reciprocity. Two aspects of the norm of reciprocity may be identified: expedient and moral. When a relationship is maintained purely for economic self-interest expedient considerations dominate the exchange transaction. However, benefits bestowed on a purely voluntary basis are more highly valued than those rendered because of situational constraint or moral obligation. Similarly, a return based on moral considerations is more valued than the one prompted by situational expediency.

The norm of reciprocity, which Gouldner regards as universal, makes two interrelated, minimal demands: (1) people should help those who have helped them, and (2) people should not injure those who have helped them. Generically, the norm of reciprocity may be conceived of as a dimension to be found in all value systems and, in particular, as one among a *number* of "Principal Components" universally present in moral codes.'[30]

Previous formulations of the principle of reciprocity—particularly those of Malinowski and Homans—emphasized gratification and equivalence; they imply that individuals who give something expect to receive something of equivalent value in return. But Gouldner is not so much concerned with why people conform to others' expectations as with why they reciprocate the benefit in the first place. According to him, 'the motivation for reciprocity stems not only from the sheer gratification which Alter receives from Ego but also from Alter's internalization of a specific norm of reciprocity which morally obliges him to give benefits to those from whom he has received them.' If gratification were the only motivation, then expedient considerations (of continuing to receive benefits) would suffice to bring about conformity. However, the norm of reciprocity is a concrete and special mechanism which serves the following stabilizing functions for the social system:

1. The norm of reciprocity checks the disruptive potentialities of

power differences. It safeguards powerful people against the temptations of their own power and prevents exploitation of the weak by the strong (such as sexual exploitation, or exploitation of students by the teacher).

2. It is not only the fulfilment of obligations that contributes to the stability of social systems but also the period when there is a pending obligation is also crucial in cementing social relationships. The norm of reciprocity structures social relations so as to create a shadow of indebtedness between the time of giving and the time of receiving payments which obligates the parties to continue the exchange. This is why neither the debtor nor the creditor is eager to break off mutual relations.

3. Unlike specific status duties associated with an office, the norm of reciprocity is indeterminate and does not require specific and uniform performances from people whose behaviour it regulates.

This indeterminancy enables the norm of reciprocity to perform some of its most important system-stabilizing functions. Being indeterminate, the norm can be applied to countless *ad hoc* transactions, thus providing a flexible moral sanction for transactions which might not otherwise be regulated by specific status obligations. The norm, in this respect, is a kind of plastic filler, capable of being poured into the shifting crevices of social structures, and serving as a kind of all-purpose moral cement.

4. Even when duties and obligations of a status-occupant are clearly defined by the status-system, the norm of reciprocity serves as a second-order defence of stability by providing an additional moral sanction for conforming with the obligations. In the words of Gouldner, 'the norm of reciprocity requires that if others have been fulfilling their status duties to you, you in turn have an additional or second-order obligation (repayment) to fulfil your status duties to them. In this manner, the sentiment of gratitude joins forces with the sentiment of rectitude and adds a safety-margin in the motivation to conformity.' Thus the chauffeur takes extra care with his boss's car not only because it is part of his duty but also because he has a particularly benevolent employer. This function of the norm of reciprocity also enables people to justify their claims against those who fail to reciprocate.

5. The norm of reciprocity also serves as a 'starting mechanism' which 'helps to initiate social interaction and is functional in the early phases of certain groups before they have developed a differentiated and customary set of status duties.'

The Theory of Distributive Justice

The theory of distributive justice seeks to explain the process of allocation of rewards among actors in a social system. Individuals in a social exchange context have what they regard as legitimate expectations about how rewards should be allocated. If such expectations are violated, there will be strain and pressures for change. Feelings of frustration and pressures for change depend not on the absolute level of reward received but on the relationship between rewards expected and rewards received. The exchange is conceived to be fair by an individual when his rewards are proportional to his costs and consistent with his expectations. When social actors in an exchange situation are rewarded by a third party, the theory of distributive justice dictates the following principles:

1. Similar actors must be rewarded similarly; and
2. Dissimilar actors must be rewarded dissimilarly.

These principles suggest that workers with the same training, experience and skills must be paid the same wages and that those with less qualifications must receive less.

Homans and Blau are the two outstanding exponents of the theory of distributive justice. We will consider Homans first. Homans summarizes the rules of justice implicit in social exchange as follows:

A man in an exchange relation with another will expect that the rewards of each man be proportional to his costs—the greater the rewards, the greater the costs—and that the net rewards, or profits, of each man be proportional to his investments—the greater the investments, the greater the profits . . . . Finally, when each man is being rewarded by some third party, he will expect the third party, in the distribution of rewards, to maintain this relation between the two of them.[37]

Homans proposes the following rules of justice:[38]

1. The proportionality of rewards: 'the value of what a member receives by way of reward from the members of the group in one field of activity should be proportional to the value to them of the activities he contributes in another field.'

2. The proportionality of rewards and investments: 'the value of what a member of a group receives from other members should be proportional to his investments.'

3. The proportionality of rewards, costs and investments: When two men in exchange are paid by the same third party, he should

maintain the proportionality of profit to investment. If the investments of the two are equal, their profits should be equal; if their investments are unequal, the one with greater investments should get greater profit.

Status congruence and social certitude of actors in a collectivity depend on the fairness of the system of exchange. The relative status of two men is congruent if both are justly rewarded, that is, if they are rewarded in accordance with the magnitude of their respective investments. If the investments (experience, skill, etc.) of the two are identical but their rewards different, the one who is paid less feels slighted, leading to status incongruence between the two. Homans regards status congruence as a condition of social certitude. And people will find incongruence costly because of the effects it may have on the future behaviour of others toward them.

Blau's concept of 'fair exchange' is fundamentally similar to Homans' rule of distributive justice. The main difference, as he sees it, is his own explicit emphasis on social norms which function to promote socially significant investments.

An important implication of this principle of justice is that people compare themselves in terms of their investments as well as in terms of their rewards and expect differences in the rewards to correspond to differences in the investments, and their satisfaction with their own rewards depends just as much on the fact that these expectations are not disappointed as on the actual quantity of the rewards.[39]

Blau seeks to bring out some flaws in Homans' conceptualization of justice in exchange. First, in the area of expertise profits are not always proportional to investments. Having previously invested resources, an expert can furnish advice at no cost to himself. Second, Blau takes exception to Homans' 'loose' use of the term investment which includes even age, sex and seniority. If men are paid more than women for the same job, the practice has nothing to do with investment or justice; it is socially so patterned, but not necessarily just. Third, Blau rejects Homans' contention that higher investments should receive higher reward not in one respect but in all cases. Blau feels that it is unjust that persons already rewarded for their investments in one case are equally rewarded in other cases. The alternative explanation is that persons rewarded with superior status in one area can use their wealth, status and power as investments in other areas and thus be rewarded further. Fourth, the rule of justice is a social norm which stipulates that people ought to receive a fair return for their investments in exchange transactions. Homans implies that it is a natural sentiment rather than a belief shared by members of a collectivity.

Following the economic principle governing the interaction between the forces of demand and supply, Blau formulates an equilibrium concept of fairness in social exchange. The prevailing norms in a community define in a rough fashion what constitutes a fair return for various services depending on the investments needed to supply these services and their significance in terms of the community's value system. But it is highly improbable that all social actors will receive a fair return for all their services and investments, for there are factors other than social norms such as conditions of demand and supply which influence exchange transactions. Blau observes:

In the course of social exchange, a going rate of exchange between two social benefits becomes established. This going rate is governed by supply and demand, though only in rough fashion, since considerations other than the two benefits in question influence exchange transactions, notably other benefits that simultaneously enter into exchange relations, such as social support and companionship. Thus, if the demand for advice in a work group is high and there are only few experts who can supply it, others will be under pressure to comply with the wishes of an expert to a considerable extent in order to induce him to devote his scarce time to consultations with them rather than someone else. The resulting high price of advice is likely to motivate experts to devote more time to giving it, thereby increasing supply. Should the supply of advice come to exceed the demand for it, experts will be under pressure to offer it for less compliance, because others can choose among many available consultants.[40]

In other words, the greater the demand for advice coupled with shortage of experts, the greater the price, namely respect for advice and compliance. Thus exchange tends to move towards the rate at which demand and supply are equal. But there is no exact equilibrium price in social exchange but only an approximate exchange ratio between two social benefits, because personal considerations and social norms influence the process of social exchange. Hence the difference between the actual rate of exchange in a specific transaction and the prevailing rate in a group.

A number of factors help bring about justice in social exchange. 'People whose standards of justice are violated feel angry as well as dissatisfied and give vent to their anger through disapproval of and sometimes hostility and hatred against those who caused it.'[41] Since distributive justice is a social norm its violation will bring about social disapproval which is a cost to those who indulge in injustice. Success in a competitive society largely depends on compliance with the principle of distributive justice. People who satisfy the public with valuable services prosper while others decline. Mobility and the availability of alternatives enable the deprived to seek justice elsewhere. Above all, internalized moral standards may make man feel guilty for treating others unjustly.

Yet justice does not always prevail—and not all men receive fair returns. Why? First, the actual conditions of demand and supply determine the rate of exchange. For example, scarce supply of a particular service and the great demand for it may extract a disproportionately higher return. Second, the exploitative use of power may tilt the balance of exchange, that is, the strong and the powerful may exploit the conditions of exchange to make unjust demands on those who are dependent on them. Blau concludes: unrewarding social disapproval (which is a cost) resulting from unfair treatment, and the rewarding social approval (which may be a reward in itself) elicited by unselfish fairness tend to restore equity by reducing the excessive profits in the former case and by increasing the possibly insufficient ones in the latter.

Looking Ahead

With its focus on social action and social relationships, exchange theory seeks to delineate the dynamics of social processes in terms of a variety of principles drawn from utilitarianism, economics, behavioural psychology, functionalism and dialectical sociology. The leading exponents of exchange theory like George Homans, Peter Blau, Thibaut and Kelley, Richard Emerson and Alfred Kuhn represent the fields of sociology, psychology, and economics. While their theories are definitely anchored to the substance of their respective fields, all of them are clearly cross disciplinary in character, although there is no explicit attempt to integrate the different perspectives from the diverse fields. However, Homans and Kuhn have tried to tie their work to other fields while Blau has attempted to integrate the different theoretical perspectives in his own field. The various theories also converge on their emphasis on the process of interaction, although the unit of analysis varies from individual act (Homans) to social relationship (Emerson). Another striking similarity between these diverse formulations is their treatment of social power and its consequences.

Exchange formulations have broadened our understanding not only of the process of social exchange but also all other social relationships namely cooperation, competition, conflict and coercion. By viewing individuals as goal-oriented social actors who make decisions to cooperate, accommodate, compete or manipulate, the exchange theory draws liberally from diverse and apparently conflicting theoretical perspectives, and thus 'offers something for everyone'. Moreover, exchange formulations seem to have a particular appeal to those social scientists who are interested in formal theory. They lend themselves to rigorous deductive systems and mathematical models and have led to the development of rigorous propositions and formal theorems. The exchange theory has also prompted the elaboration of various theoretical systems within social psychology. Within sociology, it has enhanced our understanding of the building blocks of social organization. Both Homans and Blau have contributed to our understanding of interaction patterns, normative regulations and reciprocal expectations that govern such patterns, conditions that make for cooperation or conflict in social life, and above all, the processes of institutionalization. Thus exchange theory has already become a substantive orientation and even a model in micro-sociology. It has enriched the methodology of various theories of the middle range. In the future, the exchange theory will continue to contribute substantially to such theories in sociology and social psychology as balance, relative deprivation, coalition, game, small group, social power and communication. Moreover, the exchange theory has developed an effective conceptual model to delineate social structures and processes from dyads and small collectivities to large-scale social systems. This could be a significant boom to, and an elaboration of, functionalism and dialectical conflict theory which have focussed primarily on macro-structures and generalized at the level of systems rather than the inner workings of smaller collectivities that determine the nature of macro-structures.

Looking ahead, Richard Emerson's[42] formalization of the exchange theory appears to offer a viable model that minimizes several of the tautological and substantive problems that confront the exchange perspectives developed by Homans and Blau. For instance, he sought to bypass the issue of tautology by viewing social relationships among actors, rather than individual actors, as the unit of analysis. Thus in dealing with the exchange relationship between an expert (A) who gives advice and the recipient (B) who rewards the former with respect, Emerson is not concerned with (as Homans and Blau are) why A or B entered the relationship; rather, he is interested in the events which would influence the ratio between advice and respect exchanged in the network of A-B relationship. In this formulation, the emphasis shifts from an individual actor's motivation (e.g. rational orientation to maximize profits) and values to the ratio of rewards exchanged among actors and the factors in the social environment that influence this ratio and make for the balancing of the exchange relationship. In this line of argument, neither the values nor the behaviour of the individual is the dependent variable. Instead the propositions seek to explain the variables outside the social actor, particularly the conditions that determine the nature of the network of relationships.

In attempting 'to address social structure and structural change within the framework of exchange theory', Emerson has developed a highly formalized mathematical model of exchange network analysis. Like Homans, Emerson also begins with a discussion of psychological behaviourism, selectively borrowing concepts and principles from the logic of operant psychology, but, unlike Homans, Emerson sought to elaborate these concepts and principles into a number of propositions, corollaries and theorems to analyse human social organization and its characteristic patterns. Consistent with the canons of mathematical models, Emerson's formalization is extremely rigorous. Propositions and theorems are stated in terms of covariance among concepts which are precisely defined and represented by symbolic notation. Jonathan Turner has provided a substantive summary of Emerson's mathematical model and our discussion is based on this summary.

In Emerson's scheme, it is a given that an exchange relation exists between at least two actors. This relationship has been formed from (a) perceived opportunities by at least one actor, (b) the initiation of behaviours, and (c) the consummation of a transaction between actors mutually reinforcing each other. If initiations go unreinforced, then an exchange relation does not exist. And unless the exchange transaction between actors endures for at least some period of time, it is theoretically uninteresting.[43]

Thus Emerson begins with an established exchange relation, rather than individual actors, and concentrates on such processes as the use of power and balancing that influence the network of exchange relationship. Emerson's basic position is that exchange transactions over time tend toward balance and that 'in complex exchange relations involving many actors, A, B, C, D . . . , the basic processes of dependence, power, and balance will ebb and flow as new actors and new reinforcers or resources enter the exchange relations.'[44]

Turner has summarized the initial theorems of Emerson as follows:

1. The greater the value of rewards to A in a situation, the more initiations by A reveal a curvilinear pattern, with initiations increasing over early transactions and then decreasing over time.
2. The greater the dependency of A on a set of exchange relations, the more likely A to initiate behaviours in this set of relations.
3. The more the uncertainty of A increases in an exchange relation, the more the dependency of A on that situation increases and vice versa.
4. The more the dependency of B on A for rewards in an A; B exchange relationship, the greater the power of A over B and the more imbalanced the relationship between A and B.
5. The greater the imbalance of an A; B exchange relation at one point in time, the more likely it is to be balanced at a subsequent point in time.[45]

Now Emerson goes on to identify several basic social forms such as unilateral monopoly, division of labour, social circles and social stratification; and new corollaries and theories are added as 'balancing operations' in these areas are analysed. To provide an illustration, let us consider unilateral monopoly. In the network outlined below, actor A provides valuable resources for actors B_1, B_2 and B_3 who, in return, reward A with their services. But while Bs have only A as a source for their rewards, A has multiple sources for rewards. Bs are thus dependent on A who is at a power advantage. Such a structure of unilateral monopoly often typifies interpersonal as well as intercorporate units. For example, A could be a particularly desirable marriage partner sought after by three different women, B_1, B_2, and B_3. Or A could be a corporation which is the sole supplier of certain raw materials for three manufacturing firms. Or A could be a governmental body and Bs dependent agencies. Thus, 'by focussing on the structure of exchange relationship, many of the micro versus macro problems of exchange analysis, as well as of sociological theory in general, are reduced.'

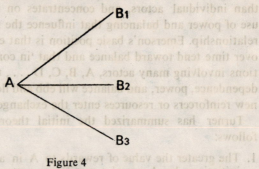

Figure 4

In terms of Emerson's line of argument, it must be remembered, the situation of unilateral monopoly which is an imbalanced state is subject to change. Emerson proceeds to examine various ways in which this unilateral monopoly can become balanced, and accordingly develops additional corollaries and theorems to account for them. Emerson predicts that a decrease in the value of the reward for those at a power disadvantage will operate to balance a unilateral monopoly when no alternative sources of reward exist and where Bs cannot effectively communicate. If other conditions exist, other balancing operations are possible. If Bs are in a position to communicate, they might form a coalition and force A to balance exchanges. Or Bs might find other sources for their reward, thus decreasing A's power advantage over them.

Emerson's network approach has a number of advantages. It has avoided the issue of reductionism that plagued Homans' exchange theory. It has bypassed the problem of tautology that characterized much of the earlier exchange formulations. It evidences considerably more deductive and methodological rigour than any previous exchange model. According to Turner, 'To a great extent the future of exchange theory hinges on how well these apparent advantages obviate the long-standing logical problem of tautology and substantive problems of vagueness and micro-macro discontinuity.'[46] However, it must be pointed out that, despite its many advantages, Emerson's network approach is too 'formalistic'. Any attempt to formulate the dynamics of interpersonal interaction and patterns of institutionalization in terms of well defined mathematical models ignores the subtleties and qualitative dimensions of social processes. In any case, Emerson's network approach is no substitute for the

more substantive exchange formulations; at best, it provides an
effective strategy that supplements the methodology and the definitional framework of other exchange models.

NOTES

1. Peter P. Ekeh, *Social Exchange Theory* (Cambridge, Harvard University Press, 1974), quoted from p. 23.
2. Ibid.
3. Ibid., p. 29.
4. Ibid., p. 58.
5. Ibid., p. 32.
6. Claude Levi-Strauss, 'The Principle of Reciprocity', in Lewis Coser and Bernard Rosenberg (eds.), *The Sociological Theory* (New York, Macmillan Company, 1971), p. 78.
7. Jonathan Turner, *The Structure of Sociological Theory* (Homewood, Dorsey Press, 1974), p. 220.
8. Ekeh, op. cit., p. 43.
9. Ibid., p. 45.
10. Ibid., p. 46.
11. Ibid., p. 47.
12. Turner, op. cit., p. 222.
13. Ibid., p. 234.
14. George C. Homans, *Social Behaviour: Its Elementary Forms* (New York: Harcourt Brace Jovanovich, 1974). For a summary of Homans' essential propositions, see his article, 'The General Propositions of Exchange Theory' in Alan Wells (ed.), *Contemporary Sociological Theories* (Santa Monica, Goodyear Publishing Company, 1978), pp. 131–45. Quotes taken from this article.
15. See Ekeh, op. cit., p. 103.
16. See Ekeh, op. cit., pp. 107–17, 125. Paraphrased and quoted.
17. Turner, op. cit., p. 246.
18. Peter M. Blau, *Exchange and Power in Social Life* (New York, John Wiley & Sons, 1964), pp. 89–90.
19. Ibid., p. 6.
20. Ibid., p. 2.
21. Ibid., p. 91.
22. Ibid., p. 20.
23. Ibid., pp. 94–5.
24. Ibid., pp. 104–5.
25. Ibid., p. 22.
26. Turner, op. cit., p. 282.
27. Blau, op. cit., p. 267.
28. Ibid.
29. Ibid., p. 220.

30. Ibid., p. 279.
31. Ibid., p. 338.
32. Turner, op. cit., p. 290.
33. Ibid., pp. 289–90.
34. Ekeh, op. cit., p. 167.
35. Ibid., p. 170.
36. Alvin Gouldner, 'The Norm of Reciprocity: A Preliminary Statement', *American Sociological Review*, **25** (April, 1960), 161–78. Quotes from pp. 171–6.
37. Homans, *Social Behaviour*, op. cit., p. 232.
38. Ibid., pp. 234–37.
39. Blau, op. cit., p. 156.
40. Ibid., pp. 151–2.
41. Ibid. p. 157.
42. See Richard M. Emerson, 'Exchange Theory, Part I: A Psychological Basis for Social Exchange', and 'Exchange Theory, Part II: Exchange Relations and Network Structures', in Joseph Berger et al. (eds.), *Sociological Theories in Progress* (New York, Houghton Mifflin Company, 1972).
43. Jonathan Turner, *The Structure of Sociological Theory* (Homewood, Dorsey Press, 1978), revised edition, p. 294.
44. Ibid., p. 295.
45. Ibid., p. 297.
46. Ibid., p. 305.

CHAPTER 7

Theories of Anomie and Alienation

In recent years, a great volume of literature* has come to be accumulated on the crisis of modern society which, in the words of Riesman, is a 'lonely crowd', or, according to Homans, 'a dust heap of individuals without links to one another'. The past decades have seen a systematic erosion of primary ties in the wake of urbanization and industrialization which brought forth the complex mass society based on 'cold, anonymous and formal relationships'. Individuals living in today's mass society acquire what Simmel calls the 'blasé attitude' which involves antipathy, repulsion, unmerciful matter-of-factness and utmost particularization. This attitude precludes them from interacting with other men as full, emotional and concerned human beings. Wirth's theory of urbanism depicted interpersonal contacts in the city as 'impersonal, superficial, transitory, and segmental' and emphasized the 'substitution of secondary for primary contracts, the weakening of bonds of kinship, and the declining social significance of the family, the disappearance of the neighbourhood, and the undermining of the traditional basis of social solidarity.'[1] Wirth writes:

Large numbers account for individual variability, the relative absence of intimate personal acquaintanceship, the segmentalization of human relations which are largely anonymous, superficial, and transitory, and associated characteristics. Density involves diversification and specialization, the coincidence of close physical contact and distant social relations, glaring contrasts, a complex pattern of segregation, the predominance of formal social control, and accentuated friction, among other phenomena. Heterogeneity tends to break down rigid social structures and to produce increased mobility, instability, and insecurity, and the affiliation of the individuals with a variety of intersecting and tangential social groups with a high rate of membership turnover. The pecuniary nexus tends to displace personal relations,

---

*Only works of general theoretical importance are treated in this volume; studies in deviant behaviour and other specialized applications are beyond the scope of the present chapter.

and institutions tend to cater to mass rather than individual require-ments. The individual thus becomes effective only as he acts through organized groups.[2]

Prevailing technoculture has upset man's balance with nature, failed to respond to real human needs and to draw out the best in the individual but has kept individuals from interacting with one another as full, emotional human beings. The result is that many individuals seek to form communal living groups, set up counter-cultures, experi-ment with new utopian communities or return to some fundamental religious expressions. There seems to be a general consensus that the root of psychic conflict and personal disorganization, of the malady of the maladjusted and the marginal, reside in the prevalent cultural and role conflicts operative in society, rather than in the personality's inner psychic dynamics. Retreatism of drug addicts, political activism of the young radicals, escapism of the hippie communes and the de-viant lifestyles of counter-cultures are only manifest expressions of the malady of 'all the lonely people'. Hence, as Kenneth Keniston points out, 'Most usages of "alienation" share the assumption that some relationship or connection that once existed, that is "natural", desi-rable, or good, has been lost.'[3] And contemporary social theory has, though belatedly, evinced great interest in the phenomena. The con-cepts of anomie and alienation are old but they gained wide currency only recently.

Theories of Anomie

The development of the concept of anomie may be traced to Emile Durkheim's first book, *The Division of Labor in Society*, published in 1893. But it was in his classic monograph, *Suicide*, that Durkheim formulated and used the theory of anomie in interpreting selected uniformities in rates of suicide.

Durkheim attributed anomie to unlimited aspirations and the breakdown of regulatory norms: 'No living being can be happy or even exist unless his needs are sufficiently proportioned to his means.'[4] In the animal, a condition of equilibrium between needs and means is established with automatic spontaneity because the needs of the animal are dependent on its body and on purely material conditions and it has no power of reflection to imagine other ends. The case of man is entirely different. Man's aspirations have constantly increased since the beginnings of history. Man's 'capacity for feeling is in itself an unsatiable and bottomless abyss'. There is nothing in man's organic structure or his psychological constitution which can regulate his unlimited desires.

But if nothing external can restrain this capacity, it can only be a source of torment to himself. Unlimited desires are insatiable by definition and insatiability is rightly considered a sign of morbidity. Being unlimited, they constantly and infinitely surpass the means at their command; they cannot be quenched. Inextinguishable thirst is constantly renewed torture.

Since the individual has no way of restraining his unlimited propensities, this must be done by some force exterior to him. Social desires can be regulated only by a moral force. Durkheim views the collective order as the only legitimate moral force that can effectively restrain the social or moral needs. 'Either directly and as a whole, or through the agency of one of its organs, society alone can play this moderating role; for it is the only moral power superior to the individual, the authority of which he accepts.'

However, occasionally this mechanism breaks down and normlessness ensues. Durkheim writes:

But when society is disturbed by some painful crisis or by beneficent but abrupt transitions, it is momentarily incapable of exercising this influence; thence come the sudden rises in the curve of suicides . . . . In the case of economic disasters, indeed, something like a declassification occurs which suddenly casts certain individuals into a lower state than their previous one. Then they must reduce their requirements, restrain their needs, learn greater self-control. All the advantages of social influence are lost so far as they are concerned; their moral education has to be recommenced. But society cannot adjust them instantaneously to this new life and teach them to practise the increased self-repression to which they are unaccustomed. So they are not adjusted to the condition forced on them, and its very prospect is intolerable; hence the suffering which detaches them from a reduced existence even before they have made trial of it.

Thus any abrupt transitions such as economic disaster, industrial crisis or sudden prosperity can cause a deregulation of the normative structure. That is why, Durkheim reasons, anomie is a chronic state of affairs in the modern socio-economic system. Sudden changes upset the societal scale instantly but a new scale cannot be immediately improvised. Collective conscience requires time to reclassify men and things. During such periods of transition there is no restraint on aspirations which continue to rise unbridled. 'The state of deregulation or anomy is thus further heightened by passions being less disciplined, precisely when they need nore disciplining.' Overweening ambition and the race for unattainable goals continue to heighten anomie. According to Durkheim, poverty protects against suicide because it is a restraint in itself: 'the less one has the less he is tempted to extend the range of his needs indefinitely.'

In analysing the consequences of anomie, Durkheim showed that there was a high rate of anomic suicide among those who are wealthy as well as among divorced persons. Sudden upward changes in the standard of living or the breakup of a marriage throw life out of gear and put norms in a flux. Like economic anomie, domestic anomie resulting from the death of a husband or wife is also the result of a catastrophe that upsets the scale of life. Durkheim also points out a number of factors that contribute to anomie in modern society. Economic progress has largely freed industrial relations from all regulation, and there is no moral strong enough to exercise control in the sphere of trade and industry. Furthermore,

Religion has lost most of its power. And government, instead of regulating economic life, has become its tool and servant. The most opposite schools, orthodox economists and extreme socialists, unite to reduce government to the role of a more or less passive intermediary among the various social functions. . . . On both sides nations are declared to have the single or chief purpose of achieving industrial prosperity; such is the implication of the dogma of economic materialism, the basis of both apparently opposed systems. . . .the appetites thus excited become freed of any limiting authority. . . . Ultimately, this liberation of desires has been made worse by the very development of industry and the almost infinite extension of the market. . . . Such is the source of the excitement predominating in this part of society, and which has thence extended to the other parts. There the state of crisis and anomy is constant and, so to speak, normal. From top to bottom of the ladder, greed is aroused without knowing where to find ultimate foothold. Nothing can calm it, since its goal is far beyond all it can attain . . . . A thirst arises for novelties, unfamiliar pleasures, nameless sensations, all of which lose their savour once known. Henceforth, one has no strength to endure the least reverse . . . . Weariness alone, moreover, is enough to bring disillusionment, for he cannot in the end escape the futility of an endless pursuit.

In short, Durkheim conceived of anomie as a social condition of normlessness or the deregulation of the normative structure, that is, the failure of the collective moral order to restrain the overweening ambition, greed and unlimited aspirations.

In his famous essay, *Social Structure and Anomie*, Merton broadened Durkheim's concept of anomie in an attempt to explain not only
suicide but various types of deviant behaviour as well as revolutionary upheavals. Unlike Durkheim who emphasized man's overweening ambition to achieve unattainable goals, Merton sought 'to
discover how some social structures exert a definite pressure upon
certain persons in the society to engage in non-conforming rather
than conforming conduct.'[5] In sharp contrast to the Freudian contention that social structure restrains the free expression of man's
innate impulses and that man periodically breaks into open rebellion
against these restraints to achieve freedom, Merton contends that
social structure is active, producing fresh motivations and patterning types of conduct. Thus Merton concentrated not on the individual but on the social order and stressed the importance of normative
structures in determining individual responses.

From among the several elements of social and cultural structures,
Merton analytically separates two: cultural goals and institutionalized means. The goals are more or less integrated and constitute a
frame of aspirational reference. They are the acknowledged desirables in any society such as success, money, power, prestige etc.
Institutionalized means are the acceptable modes of reaching out for
these goals. These are not necessarily the most efficient means but
those normatively regulated and approved by the social system.

Cultural goals and institutionalized means may vary independently
of each other. In this connection, Merton suggests two polar types
of cultures. 'There may develop a very heavy, at times a virtually
exclusive, stress upon the value of particular goals, involving comparatively little concern with the institutionally prescribed means of
striving toward these goals.' In this type of 'malintegrated culture',
the goals are held so important that any means—including the most
strictly forbidden ones—may be resorted to. 'A second polar type is
found in groups where activities originally conceived as instrumental
are transmuted into self-contained practices, lacking further objec-
tives. The original purposes are forgotten and close adherence to
institutionally prescribed conduct becomes a matter of ritual. Sheer
conformity becomes a central value.' Merton suggests that 'Between
these extreme types are societies which maintain a rough balance
between emphases upon cultural goals and institutionalized practices,
and these constitute the integrated and relatively stable though
changing, societies.'

Now Merton proceeds to define anomie as the disjunction between cultural goals and institutionalized means. In a tone reminiscent of Durkheim, Merton writes: 'The process whereby exaltation of the end generates a literal *demoralization*, i.e., a de-institutionalization, of the means occurs in many groups where the two components of the social structure are not highly integrated.' As an example he cites the contemporary American culture in which 'money has been consecrated as a value in itself.' He goes on to point out that there is no stopping point in the American dream and that the emphasis on success goals has become an internalized value. But the question is whether there is equally heavy emphasis on legitimate means and whether such means are open to all members of the society. Merton's answer is contained in his typology of modes of individual adaptation.

TABLE 1

A Typology of Modes of Individual Adaptation

Modes of adaptation	Culture goals	Institutionalized means
I. Conformity	+	+
II. Innovation	+	−
III. Ritualism	−	+
IV. Retreatism	−	−
V. Rebellion	±	±

(+) signifies 'acceptance', (−) signifies 'rejection' and (±) signifies 'rejection of prevailing values and substitution of new values'.

I. Conformity.   As the most common and widely diffused mode of adaptation, conformity to both cultural goals and institutionalized means renders stability and continuity to any social system. Since we are primarily concerned with anomie here, we will proceed to discuss the other four modes of adaptation that constitute Merton's anomie paradigm.

II. Innovation.   This type of adaptation occurs when the individual has assimilated the cultural emphasis on the goal without equally internalizing the institutional norms governing the means for its attainment. The individual accepts the success-goals but rejects the approved means; he resorts to institutionally proscribed but often effective means of attaining at least the simulacrum of success. Robbery, theft, embezzlement, forgery, cheating at the examination and all similar cases where success goals are sought to be attained by illegitimate means are examples of innovation. Merton notes that this type of deviant behaviour is particularly common among lower classes whose advance towards the success-goal is blocked by numerous structural barriers. Thus on the one hand, the great cultural emphasis on success is highly evaluated by all but, on the other hand, the social structure unduly limits practical recourse to institutional means for segments of the population which are thus forced to resort to any illegitimate means. But Merton hastens to add that a high frequency of deviant behaviour is not generated merely by lack of opportunity. Indeed, even greater structural barriers to mobility may be found in a caste system or a rigidly stratified class society. 'It is only when a system of cultural values extolls, virtually above all else, certain *common* success-goals *for the population at large* while the social structure rigorously restricts or completely closes access to approved modes of reaching these goals *for a considerable part of the same population*, that deviant behaviour ensues on a large scale.' In other words, it is not poverty or a widespread lack of opportunity alone that is responsible for deviant behaviour but their unique combination with a great emphasis on success and social mobility for all internalized as a positive value by sufficiently large numbers that induces innovation. This explains why poverty is less highly correlated with crime in other—even less developed—societies than in the United States.

III. Ritualism. 'It involves the abandoning or scaling down of the lofty cultural goals of great pecuniary success and rapid social mobility to the point where one's aspirations can be satisfied. But though one rejects the cultural obligation to attempt "to get ahead in the world", though one draws in one's horizons, one continues to abide almost compulsively by institutional norms.' This type of adaptation is fostered by a society which stresses achieved status. Men who are acutely aware of status anxiety and frustration that may be produced by ceaseless competitive struggle attempt to avoid or minimize such dangers by lowering their level of ambition or 'playing safe'. The overly cautious bureaucrat who wants to conform to every rule in the book and the receptionist at the emergency wing of the hospital who wants to have every proforma filled in before the patient is admitted are ritualists. 'It is, in short, the mode of adaptation of individually seeking a *private* escape from the dangers and frustrations which seem to them inherent in the competition for major cultural goals by abandoning these goals and clinging all the more closely to the safe routines and the institutional norms.' Merton expects members of the lower middle class to be more heavily represented among 'ritualists'.

IV. Retreatism. This is a privatized rather than a collective mode of adaptation of the socially disinherited. 'People who adapt (or maladapt) in this fashion are, strictly speaking, *in* the society but not *of* it. Sociologically, these constitute the true aliens.' Merton includes in this category the adaptive activities of psychotics, autists, outcasts, vagrants, vagabonds, skid-row bums, tramps, chronic drunkards and drug addicts. This mode of adaptation occurs when the individual has thoroughly assimilated both the culture goals and the institutional means but the available institutional means are not productive of success. At the same time, the interiorized moral obligations for adopting socially approved means conflict with the pressures to resort to illicit means; the individual has no access to means which are at once legitimate and effective. Defeatism, quietism and resignation-alienation set in and the individual drops out.

V. Rebellion. 'This adaptation leads men outside the environing social structure to envisage and seek to bring into being a new, that is to say, a greatly modified social structure. It presupposes alienation from reigning goals and standards.' When the prevailing structures and institutional arrangements are perceived to be unjust or stumbling blocks to the realization of legitimized goals, the stage is set for rebellion. Organized political action, populist movements, and revolutionary upheavals all represent degrees of rebellion.

Having identified the modes of individual adaptation, Merton defines anomie as:

a breakdown in the cultural structure, occurring particularly when there is an acute disjunction between the cultural norms and goals and the socially structured capacities of members of the group to act in accord with them. In this conception, cultural values may help to produce behaviour which is at odds with the mandates of the values themselves.

In other words, the condition of anomie or normlessness sets in when the social structure strains the cultural values, that is, when the cultural system calls for behaviours and attitudes which the social system precludes. Merton offers a distinction between 'simple' and 'acute' anomie. 'Simple anomie refers to the state of confusion in a group or society which is subject to conflict between value-systems, resulting in some degree of uneasiness and a sense of separation from the group; acute anomie, to the deterioration and, at the extreme, the disintegration of value systems, which results in marked anxieties.' In short, Merton sees the conflict between cultural goals and institutionalized means as the primary source of anomie.

Merton insists that anomie is essentially a sociological concept. 'Anomie refers to a property of a social system, not to the state of mind of this or that individual within the system.' He adds: 'Anomie, then, is a condition of the social surround, not a condition of particular people. People are *confronted* by substantial anomie when, as a matter of objective fact, they cannot rely upon a high probability that the behaviour of others will be in rough accord with standards *jointly* regarded as legitimate.'[7] For example, a degree of anomie has set in when men and women cannot frequent the parks or walk the streets without the fear of being mugged. The condition of anomie exists when there is a general loss of faith in the efficacy of the government, when contractual cooperation is characterized more by mistrust than trust, or when there is an uneasiness gripping the community because of alarming increase in crime rates, an insurgent movement or some other impending danger.

A number of sociologists, particularly Parsons, Cloward, Mizruchi and Srole have elaborated and extended Merton's theory of anomie. While dealing with the institutionalization of role-expectations and corresponding sanctions, Parsons portrays a continuum ranging from 'perfect integration' at one pole to anomie, 'the absence of structured complementarity of the interaction process or, what is the same thing, the complete breakdown of normative order in both senses.'[8] He identifies two components of the motivational structure relative to a system of complementary expectations: (1) the negative component called an alienative need-disposition, and (2) the positive component or a conformative need-disposition. 'Where alienative motivation is present, but the conformative component is dominant over the alienative, we may speak of *compulsive conformity,* where on the other hand the alienative component is dominant over the conformative, we may speak of compulsive alienation.'[9] Parsons subdivides the conformative and the alienative types according to whether the interaction itself is primarily active or passive.

TABLE 2

	Activity	Passivity
Conformative dominance	Compulsive performance orientation	Compulsive acquiescence in status-expectations
Alienative dominance	Rebelliousness	Withdrawal

This classification is, as Parsons himself acknowledges, a restatement in motivational terms of Merton's formulation. Merton's 'conformity' is what Parsons calls the equilibrated condition of the interactive systems without conflict on either side or alienative motivation. Merton's 'innovation' and 'ritualism' are Parsons' two compulsively conformative types, while 'rebellion' and 'retreatism' are the two alienative types. Parsons suggests that Merton's paradigm is best suited for the analysis of social systems where achievement values are prominent. Where ascriptive values are institutionalized, especially in combination with particularism, Merton's paradigm may not be readily applicable. For this reason and because of his inclusion of the motivational element, Parsons contends that his own version is more general and culture-free.

Richard Cloward who evaluated Merton's paradigm in terms of its applicability to studies of deviant behaviour has added a new dimension to the conceptualization of anomie—the concept of the differential distribution of illegitimate means. In Merton's theoretical statement, 'innovation' is defined as a mode of adaptation whereby individuals are forced to resort to illicit means. But Cloward points out that there are also differentials in access to illegitimate means and that the structure of opportunity plays a significant part in the distribution of deviant adaptations.

According to Merton differing rates of ritualistic and innovating behaviour in the middle and lower classes may be attributed to imperfect socialization.

The 'rule-oriented' accent in middle-class socialization presumably disposes persons to handle stress by engaging in ritualistic rather than innovating behaviour. The lower-class person, contrastingly, having internalized less stringent norms, can violate conventions with less guilt and anxiety. Values, in other words, exercise a canalizing influence, limiting the choice of deviant adaptations for persons variously distributed throughout the social system.[10]

The underlying assumption is that illegitimate means are freely available to all members of the social system. The reality is, however, different. Cloward writes:

The availability of illegitimate means, then is controlled by various criteria in the same manner that has long been ascribed to conventional means. Both systems of opportunity are (1) limited, rather than infinitely available, and (2) differentially available depending on the location of persons in the social structure.

When we employ the term 'means', whether legitimate or illegitimate, at least two things are implied: first, that there are appropriate learning environments for the acquisition of the values and skills associated with the performance of a particular role; and second, that the individual has opportunities to discharge the role once he has been prepared. The term subsumes, therefore, both *learning structures* and *opportunity structures*.

Cloward illustrates his point with reference to careers in the rackets. The youngsters who grow up in neighbourhoods where the rackets flourish as stable, indigenous institutions have necessary learning environments and opportunity which would facilitate their recruitment. Similarly several white collar crimes such as embezzlement and forgery are adaptive behaviours confined to certain segments of society.

Merton acknowledges Cloward's theory to be a clarification and substantial extension of his own theory of structural strain toward anomie.

Mizruchi tested the Durkheim-Merton hypothesis of the correlation between anomie and class structure and found that 'anomie had greater effects as we descended the class structure, independently of the degree to which success values were shared by the class groups'.[11] Thus, while there was generally strong evidence to support the hypothesis, Mizruchi argues that blocked efforts to reach culturally defined goals cannot provide the full explanation for the progressively greater demoralization observed in the lower classes. His

'data on the relationships between social class', social participation, and personal demoralization supported (his) hypothesis that the lower classes are, in addition to being blocked in their success aspirations, cut off from those sources of the community structure that provide both a sense of integration with the community and access to values that motivate striving for life goals.

Mizruchi also found that the middle classes striving toward occupational goals experienced greater anomie than anticipated by Merton. When success goals are perceived as blocked, the middle classes tend to become more demoralized than do the lower classes. Mizruchi suggests

that the effects of disparity between aspiration and achievement may possibly be smaller in the lower classes than in the higher classes, because there is a greater familiarity with failure among the former and greater opportunity to rationalize. Furthermore, work does not have the same significance for those who are on the lower rungs of the occupational hierarchy.

In terms of these findings, Mizruchi proposes some revision of Merton's theory of anomie. More specifically he suggests that there are at least two sets of causal factors that operate to produce personal demoralization. According to him there is more than one type of anomie. Mizruchi has carefully identified two types of anomie which he has labelled as 'bondlessness' and 'boundlessness'.

'Bondlessness represents a type of structured strain in which socially structured goals are incompatible with the various socially structured means by which they may be sought.' This type corresponds to Merton's 'innovation' and results from a disparity between internalized success goals and structured opportunities for their realization. 'Boundlessness', on the other hand, corresponds to Durkheim's conception of anomie based on deregulation or normlessness. This type results from what Durkheim calls 'overweening ambition' or what Mizruchi calls 'the myth of infinite elevation' which is more characteristic of the middle, rather than lower, classes. The success goals of the middle classes are often more difficult to attain than the concrete goals of the lower classes. Their achievement goals are nebulous and without limit. Moreover, since achievement is very difficult to assess, the middle classes place greater emphasis on status symbols which only money can buy. Thus middle classes suffer to a greater extent than lower classes from the type of anomie induced by the pursuit of unattainable goals.

In 1956 Leo Srole developed the first systematic scale to measure anomie. Using the opinion-poll format representing the individual's perception of his social world, Srole devised a measure of interpersonal alienation or 'anomia'. Known as the 'eunomia-anomia continuum', the scale depicted 'the individual's generalized, pervasive sense of "self-to-others belongingness" at one extreme compared with "self-to-others distance" and "self-to-others alienation" at the other pole of the continuum.'[12] Srole viewed individual eunomia-anomia as 'a variable contemporary condition having its origin in the complex interaction of social and personality factors, present and past. In short, the condition is regarded as a variable dependent on both sociological and psychological processes.'

The measure of anomie involved simple agree-disagree type responses to the following five statements of opinion:

1. There is little use writing to public officials because often they aren't really interested in the problems of the average man.
2. Nowadays a person has to live pretty much for today and let tomorrow take care of itself.
3. In spite of what some people say, the lot of the average man is getting worse, not better.
4. It's hardly fair to bring children into the world with the way things look for the future.
5. These days a person doesn't really know whom he can count on.

Srole regarded social dysfunction as the independent variable, the individual's state of self-to-group alienation as the intervening variable, and change in personality (Fromm's theory) or adaptive modes (Merton's theory) as the dependent variable. And his findings supported 'the general hypothesis of an interactive process linking the individual state of anomia and interpersonal dysfunction in the social realm'.

Using Srole's scale, Wendell Bell[13] found that anomie is inversely related to economic status when the latter is measured by individual or neighbourhood factors. This is consistent with Srole's findings and Merton's theoretical position that differential access to success goals, together with a generally uniform expectation of success, will result in anomie among those persons with the least opportunity to attain such success. He also found positive correlation between anomie and social isolation. In a later sudy,[14] Meier and Bell showed that:

anomia results when individuals lack access to means for the achievement of life goals. Such lack of opportunity follows largely as a result of the individual's position in the social structure as determined by such factors as type of occupation, amount of education, income, age, sex, ethnicity, marital status, the type and amount of association in both formal organizations and in informal groups of friends, work associates, neighbours, and relatives, and the degree of commitment of particular belief, attitudes, and values.

Consistent with these conclusions, Robert Angell[15] found that 'people of high occupation tend to have low anomia scores and to be somewhat permissive, non-interfering, and unprejudiced. Those of low occupation and high anomia score, the reverse.' And David Gottlieb seems to concur: 'the more restrictive the social system is, in the perception of the individual, the less likely he is to depend on traditional means of goal attainment.'[16]

Just as Parsons argued that Merton's conceptualization of anomie is culture-bound, Simon and Gagnon[17] argue that it is time-bound as well. Developed during the period following the great depression, Merton's theory was influenced by the economic and social conditions that created a society of scarcity; hence Merton's formulation applies to the anomie of scarcity. In the society of scarcity upward mobility was a trial and a risk. The contemporary world projects a different social reality—the one that involves both the anomie of scarcity and the anomie of affluence. The idea of economic success as a fixed, modal goal toward which everyone struggled is no longer tenable. The Mertonian reformulation of Durkheim is essentially a frustration theory of deviant adaptations which takes commitment to success goals for granted and treats the institutionalized means as problematic. However, the very co-existence of affluence and scarcity has transformed the social world portrayed by Merton. Accordingly, Simon and Gagnon suggest a reversal of the emphasis between goals and means. 'Since effective means for social achievement are now generally available to sectors within *certain* classes and cohorts in the population, it is the commitment to and the gratification to be derived from the achievement that become problematic.' In contrast to the old social order which inculcated the culturally defined success goals in most individuals but blocked their realization by structural barriers, modern society makes promises and proceeds to keep them for many segments of the population. But then success and status symbols tend to be evaluated differently; they have lost much of their old glory. And precisely because 'the objects or experiences that have symbolized achievement (in the past) become part of the easily accessible and therefore unspectacular, everyday quality of life', they no longer 'confirm competence, moral worth, and/or good fortune.' Thus, with the growth of affluence, the significance of the ownership of objects has declined, and the demystification of success has grown more general. Hence the need for a new theory of the anomie of affluence.

It must be noted that Simon and Gagnon's notion of the anomie of affluence takes institutional means for granted. Commitment to goals and the ability of goal achievement to generate adequate levels of gratification are assumed problematic. The following paradigm is offered:

TABLE 3
TYPOLOGY OF ADAPTIVE RESPONSES

Type	Commitment to goals	Gratification by goal achievement
1. Optimal conformist	Plus	Plus
2. Detached conformist	Minus	Plus
3. Compulsive achiever	Plus	Minus
4. Conforming deviant	Plus	Innovative
5. Detached person	Minus	Minus
6. Escapist	Minus	Innovative
7. Conventional reformer	Innovative	Plus
8. Missionary	Innovative	Minus
9. Total rebel	Innovative	Innovative

1. The Optimal conformists are 'those individuals most thoroughly attached to the society: those for whom the society both appears to be working and is experienced as working. They are committed to its major goals and experience their realization of them as gratifying.' There is little pressure for them to engage in deviant behaviour.

2. Detached conformists 'find the sources of gratifications associated with achievement adequate but are not particularly committed to the goals. They engage in achievement-oriented behaviour without passion or enthusiasm but rather with a kind of bland acceptance.' Those who prefer 'social ethic' to the 'work ethic' fit this category.

3. The compulsive achiever is 'totally committed to achievement but lacking a capacity for experiencing congruent gratifications, this type must achieve compulsively. Certifications or rewards, it should be observed, serve not only to encourage achieving behaviour but also to constrain excessive achievement.' A mirror image of Merton's 'ritualist', this type has little capacity for experiencing the gratifications of achievement outside the process of achievement itself.

4. The conforming deviant

Having acquired the means of gratification, such persons must explore the dimensions of pleasure in search of modes of gratification; given the overdetermined character of their pursuit of the unreachable, their quest for new experiences, of which Durkheim spoke, begins to consume them. Reinforcing this quest for the extraordinary, which by definition should bring them quickly to the margins of deviance, is the fact, neglected by Durkheim, that one of the frequent rewards of achievement is an immunity to many of the sanctions that constrain and punish the less successful.

5. The detached persons come closest to Merton's 'retreatists' but they are not permanent drop-outs. With cool responses to both the values of achievement and the gratifications attending it, they 'drift' through a transitional phase of adaptation. A large number of middle and upper middle class youths who are mistakenly identified in a more markedly deviant category fall in this group.

6. The escapist who rejects the values of achievement and, unlike the detached vagrant, accepts innovative and possibly deviant styles of gratification, also resembles Merton's description of the 'retreatist'. There is one crucial difference, however. Merton's 'retreatists' are social outcasts who suffer hopeless deprivation but the affluent escapist is a member of the higher social classes and can seek escape in ways that are less self-destructive than those we associate with lower class retreatism. The continuing drug subcultures of middle and upper middle class youths illustrate this type of adaptation.

7. The conventional reformer

combines a desire to replace the major goals of the society with an acceptance of the qualities of life that constitute the content and style of the successful life. This type tends to give rise to the 'loyal opposition', whose capacity to pursue radically the changes they desire in societal goals is basically limited by their shared commitment, which tends to have a more immediate existential aspect. In effect, they accept conventional images of the 'good life', but would alter the routes to its achievement in order to make it more universally available.

8. The missionary resembles the conventional reformer very closely but may demonstrate a wider set of political styles and even resemble the compulsive achiever. The overzealous missionary may view himself as 'an instrument of history' and may 'seek to trans-

form "the great march" born of strategic necessity into a permanent social and political system.'

9. The total rebel seeks to replace both the goals of the social order and the quality of life associated with success within that order; yet the range and quality of their political action are largely determined by the definition of the quality of gratification in the future order. 'Rather than focus on new political goals, such rebels may seek to transform politics into an attractive lifestyle, developing in turn a commitment to confrontational politics or the politics of immediate and dramatic personal experiences.'

McClosky and Schaar contend that the standard explanatory model for the analysis of anomie* is both oversimplified and over-elaborate; the literature on anomie has almost exclusively focussed on sociological variables and has failed to take account of personal and psychological factors. The fundamental logic underlying both Mertonian and Durkheimian conceptualization of anomie is the same: social condition → psychological state → deviant behaviour. Both focus on the two outside links of the causal chain but say nothing about the middle. McClosky and Schaar question the prevailing assumption that the factors associated with contemporary mass society such as division of labour, bureaucratization, abrupt social changes, high mobility and the weakening of traditional institutions produce anomie, and argue that many forces that appear on *a priori* grounds to induce anomie may in fact be counteracted by the prodigious advances in communication, education, and economic well-being. 'Moreover, the leap from the subjective feelings expressed by individuals to statements about objective social conditions is a perilous one.'[18] What people believe about a society may not necessarily reflect its true character. Just because some people feel anomic, the society cannot be described as anomic.

McClosky and Schaar conceptualize anomie as:

a state of mind, a cluster of attitudes, beliefs, and feelings in the minds of individuals. Specifically, it is the feeling that the world and oneself are adrift, wandering, lacking in clear rules and stable moorings. The anomic feels literally *de*-moralized; for him, the norms governing behaviour are weak, ambiguous, and remote. He lives in a normative 'low pressure' area, a turbulent region of weak and fitful currents of moral meaning. The core of the concept is the feeling of moral emptiness.

---

*They spell 'anomie' with a 'y' (anomy) but we will be consistent.

Just as the norms of a society are learned, so too are the anomic feelings of normlessness. While persons who are in an effective social position to learn the norms do not exhibit a high incidence of anomie, those who are cut off from the mainstream of social life experience intense anomic feelings. McClosky and Schaar contend that 'whatever interferes with one's ability to learn a community's norms, or weakens one's socialization into its central patterns of belief, must be considered among the determinants of anomy.' While some of these determinants are obviously sociological, others are, indeed, psychological and personal. Since sociological factors have been largely accounted for McClosky and Schaar attempted to identify the key personality factors that contributed to anomie. They divided these factors into 'three categories': (1) *Cognitive factors* that influence one's ability to learn and understand; (2) *Emotional factors* that tend to lower one's ability to perceive reality correctly; (3) *Substantive beliefs and attitudes* that interfere with successful communication and interaction.

The researchers found that, of the three scales in the study, the 'Material aspirations' scale which measures the desire for wealth and status symbols, and the 'aspiration-ambition' scale which assesses the strength of a person's actual commitment to the values of success and prestige are not significantly correlated with the anomie scale. But there was a highly significant positive correlation between 'status frustration' and anomie. McClosky and Schaar concluded that anomie

is governed not only by one's position and role in the society but also, in no small measure, by one's intellectual and personality characteristics. Anomie feelings, we have said, result when socialization and the learning of the norms are impeded . . . . Thus, persons whose cognitive capacity is for some reason deficient are more likely to view the society as disorderly and bewildering, and to deplore the incoherence of its value system. Similarly, persons strongly governed by anxiety, hostility, and other aversive motivational and affective states suffer not only from impaired cognitive functioning but also from a tendency to distort their perceptions of social 'reality', to accommodate poorly to social change, complexity, and ambiguity, and—through the projection of their anxieties, fears, and uncertainties—to perceive the world as hostile and anxiety-ridden.

McClosky and Schaar suggest that the standard explanatory concept usually employed in the conceptualization of anomie, namely social dysfunction, disjunction between cultural goals and institutional means, overweening ambition, etc., may not point up necessary or sufficient conditions for anomie. They think that 'an alternative and possibly more useful approach might be to regard anomie as a by-product of the socialization process—as a sign of the failure of socialization and of the means by which socialization is achieved, namely, communication, interaction, and learning.'

THEORIES OF ALIENATION

The development of the notion of alienation may be traced to German idealistic philosophy, especially exemplified in Hegelian thought. But it was Karl Marx who first made use of the concept as a powerful diagnostic tool for sociological inquiry. For Marx, the history of mankind is not only a history of class struggle but also of the increasing alienation of man. The notion of alienation is central to Marxian thought. While alienation is commonplace in capitalist society and dominates every institutional sphere such as religion, economy, and polity, its predominance in the work place assumes an overriding importance for Marx. Estranged or alienated labour involves four aspects: the worker's alienation from the object he produces, from the process of production, from himself and from the community of his fellow men. According to Marx, 'alienation appears not merely in the result but also in the *process of production*, within *productive activity* itself.... If the product of labour is alienation, production itself must be active alienation .... The alienation of the object of labour merely summarizes the alienation in the work activity itself.'[19]

The worker is a victim of exploitation at the hands of the bourgeois. The more wealth the worker produces, the poorer he becomes. Just as labour produces the world of things, it also creates the devaluation of the world of men. This devaluation increases in direct proportion to the increase in the production of commodities. The worker sinks to the level of a commodity and becomes indeed the most wretched of commodities.

This fact expresses merely that the object which labour produces—labour's product—confronts it as *something alien*, as a *power independent* of the producer. The product of labour is labour which has been congealed in an object, which has become material: it is the *objectification* of labour. Labour's realization is its objectification. In the conditions dealt with by political economy this realization of labour appears as *loss of reality* for the workers; objectification as *loss of the object* and *object-bondage*: appropriation as estrangement, as *alienation*.[20]

The more the worker spends himself, the less he has of himself. The worker puts his life into the object he creates but the very object becomes an instrument of alien purpose and strengthens the hands of his exploiters. The worker becomes a slave of his object. 'The *alienation* of the worker in his product means not only that his labour becomes an object, and *external* existence, but that it exists *outside him*, independently, as something alien to him, and that it becomes a power on its own confronting him; it means that the life which he has conferred on the object confronts him as something hostile and alien.' In short, the worker spends his life and produces everything not for himself but for the powers that manipulate him. While labour may produce beauty, luxury and intelligence, for the worker it produces only the opposite—deformity, misery and idiocy. Marx summarizes the alienation of labour in the following inimitable words:

First, the fact that labour is *external* to the worker, i.e., it does not belong to his essential being; that in his work, therefore, he does not affirm himself but denies himself, does not feel content but unhappy, does not develop freely his physical and mental energy but mortifies his body and ruins his mind. The worker therefore only feels himself outside his work, and in his work feels outside himself. He is at home when he is not working, and when he is working he is not at home. His labour is therefore not voluntary, but coerced; it is *forced labour*. It is therefore not the satisfaction of a need; it is merely a *means* to satisfy needs external to it. Its alien character emerges clearly in the fact that as soon as no physical or other compulsion exists, labour is shunned like the plague. External labour, labour in which man alienates himself, is a labour of self-sacrifice, of mortification. Lastly, the external character of labour for the worker appears in the fact that it is not his own, but someone else's, that it does not belong to him, that in it he belongs, not to himself, but to another. Just as in religion the spontaneous activity of the human imagination, of the human brain and the human heart, operates independently of the individual—that is, operates on him as an alien, divine or diabolical activity—in the same way the worker's activity is not his spontaneous activity. It belongs to another; it is the loss of his self.

Thus Marx has identified two 'hostile powers' which render labour and its product alien. One is the 'other man', the capitalist, who commands production. The other is the economic system, the market situation, which governs the behaviour of capital and the process of production. The former is a human power and the latter an 'inhuman power'. As a worker, I am at the mercy of the 'other man' who decides what I should make and how I should make it. My product bears no relation to my personality and interests; it ceases to be an expression of my creative powers. Indeed, it never is my product at all; it is an alien object produced at my expense, at the cost of my self-realization and physical well-being, and against my will but at the bidding of 'another alien, hostile, powerful and independent man'. Once the object is finished, it belongs to the other man who is free to use it in whatever manner he chooses. As it becomes an instrument of his will, he becomes all the more powerful. And my product becomes an 'alien, hostile, powerful and independent object', an instrument of my own oppression at the hands of the other man who is 'lord of this object'. To Marx, 'alienation is apparent not only in the fact that *my* means of life belong to *someone else* . . . , but also that . . . an *inhuman power* rules over everything.'[21] The impersonal forces of the market economy are alien to the worker; they make him 'dependent upon all the fluctuations in market price and in the movement of capital'. They have no regard for his welfare, are independent of his will, and, ultimately produce his 'beggary or starvation'.

Schacht, in his detailed evaluation of Marxian thought, suggests that Marx's concept of alienation implies two meanings: alienation from other men, and self-alienation. The first meaning is reflected in Marx's treatment of estranged labour, alienation of the worker from the process of production and its product, and alienation in relation to the two 'hostile powers' discussed above. Schacht writes:

A man is self-alienated for Marx if his true 'human' nature is something alien to him—if his life fails to manifest the characteristics of a truly human life. There are three such characteristics for Marx: individuality, sociality, and cultivated sensibility. Self-alienation thus takes the form of dehumanization in the spheres of life which correspond to them: production, social life, and sensuous life. It may best be understood in terms of dehumanization in each of these areas.[22]

Since the worker's own activity does not belong to him because it is a coerced activity, the entire process of production, of estranged labour, is performed in the service and under the yoke of a powerful and hostile force. The man who regards himself as a species being and a free being feels doubly deprived. Moreover, the condition of subservience to another man engenders his relation to other men.

'Through *estranged, alienated* labour, then, the worker produces the relationship to this labour of a man alien to labour and standing outside it. The relationship of the worker to labour engenders the relation to it of the capitalist, or whatever one chooses to call the master of labour. *Private property* is thus the product, the result, the necessary consequence, of alienated labour, of the external relation of the worker to nature and to himself."[23] And, the alien being to whom labour and the product of labour belong continue to dominate the life of the worker. He manipulates the political structure, lends legitimacy to the system of production and distribution, and seeks to solidify his privileged position. And the cycle of exploitation continues.

Thus, in summary, several elements are involved in the Marxian concept of alienation: estrangement or man's alienation from himself and from nature, powerlessness or political alienation, religious alienation and the worker's alienation in relation to the process of production and the object they produce. And estranged labour constitutes the most recurrent theme in the Marxian conception of alienation.

In his analysis of the white-collar world, following Marx's lead, C. Wright Mills demonstrates how the modern professionals and managers of bureaucracy are internally fragmented and dependent on larger forces and are afflicted with conditions of alienation from product as well as processes of work. Mills writes:

In almost any job, this employee sells a degree of his independence; his working life is within the domain of others; the level of his skills that are used and the areas in which he may exercise independent decisions are subject to management by others . . . . The objective alienation of man from the product and the process of work is entailed by the legal framework of modern capitalism and the modern division of labour. The worker does not own the product or the tools of his production. In the labour contract he sells his time, energy, and skill into the power of others . . . a person instrumentalizes and externalizes intimate features of his person and disposition. In certain white-collar areas, the rise of personality markets has carried self and social alienation to explicit extremes.[24]

The world of work in today's capitalist society is a bureaucratized enterprise. Centralized administrative decisions regulate the process of work. Mechanization has transformed the office and the sales-room; automation has routinized the individual in the name of rational division of labour. Yet:

the more and the harder men work, the more they build up that which dominates their work as an alien force, the commodity; so also, the more and the harder the white-collar man works, the more he builds up the enterprise outside himself, which is, as we have seen, duly made a fetish and thus indirectly justified. The enterprise is not the institutional shadow of great men, as perhaps it seemed under the old captain of industry; nor is it the instrument through which men realize themselves in work, as in small-scale production. The enterprise is an impersonal and alien Name, and the more that is placed in it, the less is placed in man.

This passage exemplifies the striking similarity between the conceptualizations of alienation by Marx and Mills.

Treating alienation from the personal standpoint of the actor Melvin Seeman found five basic ways in which the concept of alienation has been used:

1. *Powerlessness.* The most frequent usage in current literature, the concept of alienation as powerlessness is defined 'as the expectancy or probability held by the individual that his own behaviour cannot determine the occurrence of the outcomes, or reinforcements, he seeks.'[25] It is a distinctly social psychological view which deals with the individual's perception of lack of control over sociopolitical events; it is not necessarily an accurate reflection of the objective condition in society. This notion of alienation originated in the Marxian view of the workers' condition in capitalist society but 'clearly departs from the Marxian tradition by removing the critical, polemic element in the idea of alienation.'

2. *Meaninglessness.* This type of alienation 'refers to the individual's sense of understanding the events in which he is engaged. We may speak of high alienation, in the meaninglessness usage, when the individual is unclear as to what he ought to believe—when the individual's minimal standards for clarity in decision-making are not met.' The individual's psychic system wanders in search of meaning, of new experiences, of belief systems. His perception of existing meaning structures is confused. He cannot predict with confidence the consequences of acting on a given belief and he is unsure about the future outcomes of behaviour. The popularity of communitarian communes and the new religious experiments attests to the pervasiveness of meaninglessness.

3. *Normlessness.* Based on Durkheim's conception of the breakdown of normative regulations, this variant of alienation 'may be defined as one in which there is a high expectancy that socially un-

approved behaviours are required to achieve given goals.' Merton's anomie paradigm illustrates the notion of alienation as normlessness.

4. *Isolation.* 'The alienated in the isolation sense are those who, like the intellectual, assign low reward value to goals or beliefs that are typically highly valued in the given society.' This type of alienation refers to the estrangement from society such as the detachment of the intellectual from popular cultural standards or the orientation of the 'rebel' who fails to identify with existing goals and standards.

5. *Self-estrangement.* This type of alienation, defined as the individual's engagement in activities that are not intrinsically rewarding, may be measured as 'the degree of dependence of the given behaviour upon anticipated future rewards, that is, upon rewards that lie outside the acitivity itself.' This notion of the loss of intrinsically meaningful satisfactions, regarded as an essential feature of modern society, is embodied in the writings of Marx, Mills and Mannheim.

In a later version, Seeman carved out an additional category called 'cultural estrangement' from 'isolation' and defined it as the individual's rejection of commonly held values in the society, and introduced the concept of 'social isolation' to mean the sense of exclusion or rejection. However, we feel that the original classification amply conveys the essential meanings of 'alienation'.

Melvin Kohn set out to test two related hypotheses suggested by Marx's analysis of the occupational sources of alienation — one emphasizing control over the product of one's labour, the other emphasizing control over the work process. Treating alienation as a concept standing at the intersection of socio-cultural conditions and psychological orientation, he sought to examine the relationship between occupational structure and the subjective experience of alienation under the conditions that exist in a large-scale, technological economy. Kohn wanted to test two hypotheses in particular: first, emphasizing the loss of control over the *products* of one's labour posits that ownership and hierarchical position are of crucial importance with respect to alienation. 'The other hypothesis, emphasizing loss of control over the *process* of labour, suggests that ... such determinants of occupational self-direction as closeness of supervision, routinization, and substantive complexity overshadow ownership, hierarchical position, and division of labour in their effects on alienation.'[26] As for the concept of alienation, Kohn used the four distinguishable facets of alienation suggested by Seeman, namely, powerlessness, self-estrangement, normlessness and isolation.

Kohn identified three aspects of occupational structure: (1) ownership and position in the supervisory hierarchy (based on actual ownership and on the respondent's estimate of how many people are 'under' him; (2) division of labour (based on the number of levels of supervision); and (3) occupational self-direction (based on closeness of supervision, routinization, and substantive complexity).

Kohn found no significant correlation between ownership and the type of alienation most germane to Marx's analysis, powerlessness. Bureaucratization is negatively correlated with powerlessness. Contrary to the commonplace assumption that division of labour is itself conducive to powerlessness, this finding suggests that employees of highly bureaucratized firms and organizations are less likely to feel powerless than those of non-bureaucratized firms and organizations. All three of the conditions determinative of the degree of occupational self-direction are positively related to powerlessness. The same pattern of relationships is repeated for self-estrangement and normlessness.

Ownership per se is of minor importance at most, a position in the supervisory hierarchy is of greater importance, division of labour (as inferred from bureaucratization) is negatively related to alienation, and the three conditions that impede the exercise of occupational self-direction are consistently related to feelings of alienation. In each instance, the conditions determinative of occupational self-direction are more strongly related to alienation than are ownership and hierarchical position.

These findings support the double assumption inherent in Marx's analysis: both control over the product of one's labour and control over the process of one's labour are related to feelings of powerlessness, self-estrangement and normlessness. Kohn concluded: 'the conditions of work determinative of occupational self-direction—closeness of supervision, routinization, and substantive complexity—bear meaningfully on three major types of alienation—powerlessness, self-estrangement, and normlessness. The findings provide evidence not only for an interconnection between these conditions of occupational life and men's orientations to non-occupational social reality, but even for a causal effect.' Contrary to the widely held assumption that there is little carryover from occupational experience to non-occupational alienation, the data indicate:

that there *is* carryover from occupational experience to alienation in non-occupational realms, and that this carryover is of the logically simplest type ... the lessons of the job are directly generalized to non-occupational realities. Occupational experiences that limit workers' opportunities to exercise self-direction in their work are conducive to feelings of powerlessness, to self-estrangement, and even to normlessness.

As Walter Gerson points out:

The term alienation has been used by psychologists and sociologists to refer to an extraordinary variety of psychologial disorders, including loss of self, anxiety states, anomie, despair, depersonalization, rootlessness, apathy, social disorganization, loneliness, atomization, powerlessness, isolation, pessimism, and the loss of beliefs or values. Among social groups that have been described as alienated—in addition to those already mentioned—are women, migrant workers, immigrants, suicides, addicts, consumers, sex deviates, the prejudiced, bureaucrats, exiles, and recluses. This is still by no means a complete listing; yet even allowing for duplication, it includes a sizable *majority* of persons living in our advanced industrial society.[27]

Gerson suggests that a fundamental distinction between structural conditions and states of individual estrangement is central to the understanding of the concept of alienation. 'It seems appropriate to limit the term alienation to mean an individual feeling or state of dissociation from self, from others, or from the world at large.' The social conditions that produce alienation are not to be confused with the psychological condition of the individual. Gerson defines alienation 'as the loss of identity. The alienated person is not only out of touch with other persons but also out of touch with himself.'

Gerson identifies four social conditions which may be conducive to the development of alienation:

1. The Techno-industrial revolution. Mechanization has largely routinized work relations and made man a servant of the machines. With the tremendous growth of mechanical power and the demoralization of the worker, the industrial society has speeded up the alienation of human labour.

2. The Bureaucratic reorganization. Just as machines routinize labour, elaborate bureaucratic structures 'rationalize' the conduct of human affairs and render it impersonal and devoid of emotions. This

is what Max Weber referred to as the dehumanizing effect of bureaucracy.

3. Consumption and leisure life. Work has declined as a central activity which enables man to express himself; rather, work has primarily become the means which make enjoyment of leisure and expansion of consumption possible. Acquisition of status symbols and conspicuous consumption have assumed a new significance. Yet, although the 'idols of leisure' have replaced the 'idols of work', leisure has become relatively meaningless and less creative.

4. Disenchantment and the Freudian ethic. Loss of certain ideational values, general weakening of faith and the decline of the influence of religion have undermined the basis of social solidarity creating general disenchantment in the individual. And since the Freudian man is fundamentally socially irresponsible and in a position of antagonism to his society, the Freudian ethic cannot fill the vacuum created by disenchantment. Thus 'man remains incomplete, without identification, alienated.'

However, people desire a certain completeness and meaning to their existence. Therefore, they develop, consciously or unconsciously, a number of responses to the prevailing condition of alienation. Gerson cautions that the several conditions prevailing in society such as apathy, resignation, deviant behaviour, etc., are not responses but symptoms of alienation. Gerson counts the following as the most common responses: exaltation of science as the faith of our age, 'the increased emphasis on the nuclear family not as an economic or even educational unit but as a recreational, play, companionship group', participation in 'publics', proliferation of voluntary associations, the increased importance of the 'play group' in adult society, the do-it-yourself trend and the popularity of numerous hobbies, suburban 'ruralization' in search of 'neighbourliness', and the tremendous expansion of the social welfare functions of the government.

Schacht classifies sociological literature on alienation under four headings:

I. *Alienation and Others*

In this perspective, alienation may mean any of the following:

(a) Loneliness—lack of supportive primary relationships, social isolation, absence of interpersonal attraction.

(b) Lack of solidarity—'non-belonging', 'non-sharing', exclusion from social and cultural participation, lack of identification with other's views, interests and tastes.

(c) Dissatisfaction in social relations—dissatisfaction with one's associates such as supervisors, fellow workers and others.

II. *Alienation and Work*

(a) Lack of job satisfaction—'feeling of disappointment' concerning one's position and employment.

(b) Lack of the intrinsic reward of work—working merely for livelihood, work is not engaging or rewarding in itself.

(c) Lack of control, meaning and self-expression in work—absence of personal control over the product of labour, process of production and managerial activities; meaninglessness of work because of extreme standardization, and lack of opportunity for self-expression.

III. *Alienation, Events and Structures*

(a) The feeling of powerlessness—individual's sense of inability to influence the course of socio-political events, feeling of helplessness in solving today's problems.

(b) The wrongness of powerlessness—the idea that one is alienated not simply because he feels powerless but because this powerlessness is regarded in some sense illegitimate; the feeling that one has been wrongly denied his right to 'control'.

(c) Distrust and apathy—inaction, distrust of political leaders, political apathy.

(d) The incomprehensibility of events—meaninglessness of life or overall purposelessness, inability to understand the very events upon which one's life and happiness are known to depend.

(e) Meaningless choices—not meaninglessness itself or feeling of powerlessness, but individual's awareness that he has to choose from among a set of alternatives between which there are no real differences or the feeling that he lacks adequate information to reach an intelligent decision.

IV. *Alienation, Culture, and Society*

(a) Disassociation from popular culture—individual's rejection of, indifference to or disenchantment from popular cultural standards, measured in terms of estrangement from conventional religion, indifference to mass media, popular education, etc.

(b) Dissociation from societal values—lack of identification with the fundamental values of one's society, rejection of the most basic assumptions and assignations of values which are taken for granted by most members of a society, rather than dissociation from a few aspects of popular culture.

(c) Rejection of societal behavioural norms—normlessness, rejection of established standards of behaviour, Merton's disjunction between cultural goals and institutional means.

(d) Anomie—alienation being subsumed under the discussion of the societal condition of anomie by Durkheim, Parsons, Merton, Cloward and others.

Sociologists formulate their conception of alienation in terms of widely differing feelings and attitudes. An individual is not considered alienated unless he has the appropriate feelings. As social scientists anxious to develop objective criteria, sociologists seek to operationalize their conceptions of alienation by developing ways of 'tapping' the feelings in question. This is usually accomplished with the help of a series of opinion statements to which the subjects are asked to respond. Schacht questions whether it is possible to construct tests which have the degree of sensitivity required to elicit the feelings—the wide variety of attitudes with which the numerous writers are concerned. It may be even more difficult to develop a culture-free test.

Anomie and Alienation: A Synthetic View

While Durkheim, Merton and others have treated anomie as a structural phenomenon, a number of sociologists particularly Robert MacIver and David Reisman have developed a psychological conception of anomie. To MacIver:

Anomy signifies the *state of mind* of one who has been pulled up by his moral roots, who has no longer any standards but only disconnected urges, who has no longer any sense of continuity, of folk, of obligation. The anomic man has become spiritually sterile, responsive only to himself, responsible to no one. He derides the values of other men. His only faith is the philosophy of denial. He lives on the thin line of sensation between no future and no past.[28]

Grodzines suggests that alienation will particularly afflict certain types of personalities and persons at certain levels of society. He defined alienation as 'the state in which individuals feel no sense of "belonging" to their community or nation. Personal contacts are neither stable nor satisfactory.'[29] To Eric Fromm, man's separation from nature is the essence of alienation. He talks about 'the process of individuation' and man's 'emergence from a state of oneness with the natural world to an awareness of himself as an entity separate from surrounding nature and men'. Alienation results from man's inability to relate himself fully to nature. 'To transcend nature, to be alienated from nature . . . finds man naked, ashamed'.[30] It must be reiterated that the alienated, according to Fromm, are not estranged from society. To the contrary, they are in complete unity with society. It is precisely the person who is in complete harmony with the social order whom Fromm labels alienated. This is in sharp contrast to the sociological view, particularly that of Parsons who regards anomie as the polar antithesis of complete institutionalization. Lasswell's concept of anomie refers to the 'lack of identification on the part of the primary ego of the individual with a "self" that includes others. In a word, modern man appeared to be suffering from psychic isolation. He felt alone, cut off, unwanted, unloved, unvalued.'[31] Thus the psychological conception of anomie has its focus on the individual and his psychic condition. 'But', according to Merton, 'the psychological concept is nevertheless a counterpart of the sociological concept of anomie, and not a substitute for it.'[32]

The notion of alienation implies the individual's feeling that he has lost control of his own life. The feeling of alienation manifests itself in the following areas:

(a) In the work place, the person feels that he has lost control over the process of production. With extreme specialization and bureaucratization, work is no longer a creative activity to which individual gives his best. Mechanization has made man a cog in the machine; routinization has made it impossible for him to fulfill himself in his work.

(b) Man feels that he has lost control over the product of his labour. The product no longer represents his achievement or craftsmanship; it is no longer a part of himself. It is a mass-produced commodity intended for a remote market whose forces, with the strength of his produce, come back to haunt and manipulate him.

(c) Man feels that he is alienated from society. He is unable to identify himself with the anonymous, impersonal mass society. Formal and routinized social relationships, devoid of emotions, make him feel lonely and rootless; he thinks he does not belong.

(d) Man feels estranged from himself. He suffers from a sense of the loss of identity and personal meaning. Traditional institutions such as family and religion which are supposed to give meaning to life have declined in influence. Man experiences a crisis of identity and questions the purpose of his being, the very existence.

(e) Finally, man feels that he is not in a position to change things for the better. He perceives a tremendous loss of personal efficacy and experiences inability to change the prevailing social system, political institutions, work situation, normative order, or meaning structure.

As the preceding discussion demonstrates anomie and alienation are two of the least clearly defined concepts in sociology. Some have equated anomie and alienation and used them interchangeably. Some have defined both as exclusively social phenomena while others have conceptualized them primarily as psychological phenomena. Those who have differentiated between anomie and alienation, see the former as a sociological and the latter as a psychological phenomenon. A few sociologists have proposed a straight-line causation from social condition to anomie; others have introduced an intervening variable in the form of psychic state. Although there is a general tendency to equate anomie and alienation with types of deviant behaviour, this is not always the case. Nettler observes:

Not merely the definitions, but also the evaluations of the alienated may vary with what he appears to be estranged from, and how: if he is a foreigner to himself, this is usually 'bad', although this may be called 'good' if he loses himself in an approved manner as through religious ecstacy or art. If, however, he is discomfited by his own society, this is called 'good' or 'bad', depending upon the society, or the critic, or whether the estrangement leads to 'creative insights' or to immersion in the mass media, and, allegedly, it does both.[33]

Having reviewed the various conceptual formulations of anomie and alienation, it seems appropriate to conclude that anomie is primarily a sociological phenomenon and alienation a psychological phenomenon. The two are related and involve reciprocal relationships in the causal chain. The appropriate explanatory model for the analysis of anomie and alienation may be graphically presented as follows:

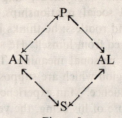

Figure 5.
P = Psychic State; S = Social State; AN = Anomie; AL = Alienation

The interrelationship among the variables is reciprocal. This formulation enables us to maintain the distinction between causes and consequences (which is especially important considering the oft-repeated tendency among sociologists to confuse anomic behaviour *in* society with the prevailing conditions *of* society).

Psychic state. This refers to the personal traits and psychological characteristics of the individual, predispositions such as anxiety, jealousy, and frustration; attitudes such as racial prejudice and ethnocentrism; poor cognitive capacities and resulting inability to evaluate events with confidence; emotional factors such as extreme hostility toward others and mistrust.

Social state. This involves conditions and characteristics associated with the modern complex society, especially the factors attributed to mass society: anonymity, impersonality, matter-of-factness and atomistic nature; extreme division of labour, bureaucratization and mechanization; routinization of work and social relationships; weakening of traditional integrative forces such as family and religion, rapid changes, high mobility and frequent migration.

Anomie. This is the breakdown of the normative structure of society in the broadest sense of the term: state of 'anarchy' and social disorder; cultural confusion; higher rates of crime and suicide; lawlessness; the phenomenon of drop-outs, drug-subcultures, communes, deviant lifestyles and various countercultures, recluses and new religious experiments; revolutionary upheavals, disruptive anti-social behaviours, lack of social integration.

Alienation. This refers to the personal demoralization and psychic disorganization of the individual: the feeling of powerlessness, meaninglessness, rootlessness and isolation; psychological disorders such as extreme anxiety states, despair, and pessimism; perception of a loss of self, of beliefs and values, and of the sense of purpose and attachment; behavioural adaptations that demonstrate apathy, distrust, aggression, and withdrawal symptoms.

NOTES

1. Louis Wirth, 'Urbanism as a Way of Life', *American Journal of Sociology*, **44** (July, 1938), 1–24.
2. Ibid., p. 9.
3. Kenneth Keniston, *The Uncommitted: Alienated Youth in American Society* (New York, Harcourt, Brace and World, 1965), p. 452.
4. Emile Durkheim, *Suicide*, translated by Spaulding and Simpson (New York, Free Press, 1951), quotes from pp. 246–56.
5. Robert K. Merton, *Social Theory and Social Structure* (Glencoe, Free Press, 1957), pp. 132–4, 136, 146, 149–51, 151, 155, 162.
6. Robert K. Merton, 'Anomie, Anomia, and Social Interaction: Contexts of Deviant Behavior', in Marshall B. Clinard (ed.), *Anomie and Deviant Behavior* (New York, Free Press, 1964), p. 226.
7. Ibid., p. 227.
8. Talcott Parsons, *The Social System* (New York, Free Press, 1951), p. 39.
9. Ibid., p. 254.
10. Richard A. Cloward, 'Illegitimate Means, Anomie, and Deviant Behaviour', *American Sociological Review*, **24** (April, 1959), pp. 164–76, quotes from 167, 168.
11. Ephraim H. Mizruchi, 'Success and Opportunity', in Lewis Coser and Bernard Rosenberg, *Sociological Theory* (New York, Macmillan Company, 1969), 545, 546.
12. Leo Srole, 'Social Integration and Certain Corollaries: An Exploratory Study', *American Sociological Review*, **21** (December, 1956), p. 711, 716.
13. Wendell Bell, 'Anomie, Social Isolation, and the Class Structure', *Sociometry*, **20** (June, 1957), 105–106.
14. Dorothy L. Meier und Wendell Bell, 'Anomie and Differential Access to the Achievement of Life Goals', *American Sociological Review*, **24** (April, 1959), 189–208, p. 190.
15. Robert C. Angell, 'Preferences for Moral Norms in Three Areas', *American Journal of Sociology*, **67** (1962), p. 660.
16. David Gotlieb, 'Some Comments on Comments', *American Journal of Sociology*, **70**, 478.
17. William Simon and John H. Gagnon, 'The Anomie of Affluence: A Post-Mertonian Conception', *American Journal of Sociology*, **82** (September, 1976), quotes from pages 361, and 370–4.
18. Herbert McClosky and John Schaar, 'Psychological Dimensions of Anomy', *American Sociological Review*, **30** (February, 1965), pp. 18–21, 39.
19. Karl Marx, *Early Writings* (Trans. and ed. by T. B. Bottomore, New York, McGraw-Hill, 1964), p. 124.

20. Karl Marx and Friedrich Engels, 'On Alienation', in C. Wright Mills (ed.), *Images of Man*, New York: George Braziller Inc., 1960, p. 498, 500.
21. As quoted by Richard Schacht, *Alienation* (Garden City, Doubleday and Company, 1970), p. 95.
22. Ibid., p. 110.
23. Marx and Engels, op. cit., p. 505.
24. C. Wright Mills, *White Collar* (New York, Oxford University Press, 953), pp. 224–5, 226.
25. Melvin Seeman, 'On the Meaning of Alienation', *American Sociological Review*, 24 (December, 1959). Reprinted in Coser and Rosenberg (ed.), op. cit., quotes from pages 512, 514, 517, 518 and 520.
26. Melvin L. Kohn, 'Occupational Structure and Alienation', *American Journal of Sociology*, 82 (July 1976), 111–30, quotes from pp. 113, 120, 127.
27. Walter M. Gerson, 'Alienation in Mass Society: Some Causes and Responses', in Clifton D. Bryant (ed.), *Social Problems Today* (Philadelphia, J. B. Lippincott and Company, 1971), pp. 24–5.
28. Robert M. MacIver, *The Ramparts We Guard* (New York, The Macmillan Company, 1950), pp. 84–5.
29. Morton Grodzines, *The Loyal and the Disloyal* (Chicago, University of Chicago Press, 1956), p. 134.
30. Erich Fromm, *Escape from Freedom* (New York, Avon Books, 1941), p. 50.
31. Harold Lasswell, 'The Threat to Privacy', in Robert MacIver (ed.), *Conflict and Loyalties* (New York, Harper and Brothers, 1952).
32. Robert Merton, *Social Theory*, op. cit., p. 162.
33. Gwynn Nettler, 'A Measure of Alienation', *American Sociological Review*, 22 (December, 1957), 670–7, p. 671.

CHAPTER 8
Symbolic Interactionism*

Towards the end of the nineteenth century, there developed a shift in the interests of social theorists away from the study of large-scale social structures and processes as initially explored by Marx, Spencer, and the social Darwinians who employed such concepts as social evolution, class conflict, and the body social. The turn-of-the-century social thinkers began to focus their attention upon the complexities of the individual's relationship to the large-scale structures of society. The interactional nature of man-in-society began to be thought of and looked at, not from the point of view of social institutions so much as from that of the individual person within society's institutions. One of America's first social psychologists has written, 'Social psychology falls into two very unequal divisions, viz., social ascendancy and individual ascendancy, the determination of the one by the many and the determination of the many by the one; the moulding of the ordinary person by his social environment, and the moulding of the social environment by the extraordinary person.'[1]

Symbolic interactionism is essentially a social-psychological perspective that is particularly relevant to sociological enterprise. Instead of dealing with abstract social structures, concrete forms of individual behaviour or inferred psychic characteristics, symbolic interactionism focuses on the nature of interaction, the dynamic patterns of social action and social relationship. Interaction itself is taken as the unit of analysis: attitudes are relegated to the background. Both the human being and the social structure are conceptualized as more complex, unpredictable and active than in the conventional sociological perspectives. Societies are composed of interacting individuals who not only react but perceive, interpret, act and create. The individual is not a bundle of attitudes but a dynamic and changing actor, always in the process of becoming and

---

* This chapter was written in collaboration with John Henry Morgan.

never fully formed. Social milieu is not something static 'out there', always influencing and shaping us but essentially an interaction process. The individual has not only a mind but also a self which is not a psychological entity but an aspect of social process that arises in the course of social experience and activity. Above all, the entire process of interaction is symbolic, with meanings constructed by human ingenuity. The meanings we share with others, our definition of the social world and our perception of, and response to, reality emerge in the process of interaction. Herbert Blumer, one of the chief architects of symbolic interactionism, writes:

The term 'symbolic interaction' refers, of course, to the peculiar and distinctive character of interaction as it takes place between human beings. The peculiarity consists in the fact that human beings interpret or 'define' each other's actions instead of merely reacting to each other's actions. Thus, human interaction is mediated by the use of symbols, by interpretation, or by ascertaining the meaning of one another's actions. This mediation is equivalent to inserting a process of interpretation between stimulus and response in the case of human behaviour.[2]

In European circles, it was sociologist Georg Simmel who began first to explore a heretofore untapped region of man's social life, viz., the 'sociability' or social interaction which must necessarily exist among individuals in order that macro-structures in society can exist at all. To Max Weber, the central concern of sociology was social action which is intentional, meaningful and symbolic. Like Simmel and Weber, the first generation of American sociologists began to understand that the phenomena of large-scale social structures and processes studied so diligently by functional and conflict theorists, viz., class, the state, family, religion, social evolution, were essentially demonstrations of specific interactions among individuals. However, the historical complexity of the development of ideas disallows any simple claim that this thought or that idea is genuinely unique and unrelated to any other idea. In the development of the perspective known as 'symbolic interaction', numerous thinkers can be cited as contributing to its emergence, such as the philosophers James W. Baldwin, William James, and John Dewey, and the sociologists Georg Simmel and W. I. Thomas, and they each in turn owe their intellectual development to Kant, Hegel, and German romantic idealism as well as to Spencer, Comte, and Marx. Of those who number among the pioneers in interactionist theory, Charles Horton Cooley and George Herbert Mead are unquestionably the most prominent.

CHARLES HORTON COOLEY

Being a truly liberally educated man, Cooley's thought was influenced by Spencer's social evolutionism, though Cooley was critical of Spencer's social determinism and naieveté, as well as inspired by Darwin's biology, Goethe's philosophy, and Emerson's romanticism. Particularly, Cooley admired John Dewey. Dewey's argument for an organic quality in social life and his analysis of the nature and function of language reinforced Cooley's own work in these areas. Cooley's passion to grasp the nature of social life led him more and more to the realization that only in understanding man, i.e., human nature, could he ever hope to understand society, i.e., the social order. In 1902, Cooley published his first book, entitled, unsurprisingly, *Human Nature and the Social Order*.

Organic Evolution

Cooley's sociological theory was necessarily influenced by his social thought. His philosophical assumptions and predispositions set the intellectual stage for his scientific work. The social thought of Cooley consisted of two profound and enduring assumptions about the nature of social life, i.e., that it is fundamentally an organic evolution, and that society is ideally democratic, moral, and progressive. Intimated in Spencer's 'social physic', in Simmel's 'sociability', and in Dewey's notion of the organic quality of social life, the organic view of society did not take on its full potential as a theoretical axiom until Cooley focused his attention upon the complex relationship which exists between the individual and society. In any serious consideration of this relationship, contended Cooley, it must be kept in mind that man does not stand alone as an individual and that society does not exist without individuals. That is, the 'isolated person' and the non-individual society are both equally mystical illusions. The organic view of society affirms the indispensable reciprocity between the individual and society. They are not empirically separable but are a differentiated coincidence of the same phenomenon—no society without individuals and no individual apart from society. Cooley wrote: 'If we say that society is an organism, we mean . . . that it is a complex of forms of processes of which in living and growing by interaction with the others, the whole being so unified that what takes place in one part affects all the rest. It is a vast tissue of reciprocal activity.'[3]

Cooley's organic evolution differed in an important way from that of Spencer and the nineteenth century social scientists. Whereas the early thinkers were concerned with large-scale collective aspects of development, of class struggle, of the body social, etc., Cooley was in quest of a deeper understanding of the individual—not an entity apart from society, but a particular psycho-social and historical instancing of society's constituent ingredients. 'Our life is all one human whole', wrote Cooley, 'and if we are to have any real knowledge of it we must see it as such. If we cut it up it dies in the process.'[4]

By redirecting attention from the grand historical sweeps of cultural events to a more systematic and sympathetic concern for the individual, Cooley perceived each individual as a 'fresh organization of life' constituting a two-fold emergent reality of genetic heredity and social past. This stream of human emergence or 'social transmission' included language, interaction, and education for each person in his own time and culture. Organic evolution, then, is the creative interplay of both the individual and society as two expressions of the same phenomenon, which are mutually reinforcing and coincidental though differentiable. Cooley's affirmation of the individual's integrity within the on-going society while simultaneously contending for the creative interplay between society and the individual led him to reject both the American and English tradition of utilitarian individualism and Spencerian sociology. 'Society', he explained, 'is an interweaving and interworking of mental selves. I imagine your mind, and especially what your mind thinks about my mind, and what your mind thinks about what my mind thinks about your mind . . . .'[5]

Thus, for Cooley, the fundamental task of sociology was to understand the organic nature of society as it evolves through the individual's perceptions of others and of themselves. If sociology is to understand society, it must concentrate its attention upon the mental activities of the individuals who make up society. 'The imaginations people have of one another', explained Cooley, 'are the solid facts of society . . . . Society is a relation among personal ideas.'[6]

The Looking-Glass Self

We have noted the historic shift for which Cooley is credited in re-directing attention, if not away from large-scale social institutions, at least to more substantive considerations of the nature of the individual, especially conceived of as 'mind', within society's institutions. The major social institutions for Cooley were language, the family, industry, education, religion, and law. To the extent that these institutions constitute the 'facts of society' available for sociological study, they are defined and established products of the public mind. They are, says Cooley, the outcome of organization and crystallization of thought around the forms of customs, symbols, beliefs, and lasting sentiments.' As we can see plainly here, Cooley did not attribute to an abstraction, i.e., society, real needs, but rather located them correctly within individuals who create society. Therefore, institutions are mental creations of individuals and are sustained by human habits of mind almost always held unconsciously due to familiarity. As Cooley has pointed out, when society's institutions are understood primarily as mental creations, the individual is thus not merely an 'effect' of the social structure, but is a creator and sustainer of it as well.

Primarily, Cooley concentrated his analytical skills upon the development of his fundamental dictum—'The imaginations people have of one another are the solid facts of society.' In his first book, *Human Nature and the Social Order*, he focused upon a theory of the social self, i.e., the meaning of the 'I' as observed in daily thought and speech. This primal idea of 'I' refers not so much to one's body as to 'my feelings'. This mental picture of oneself is what Cooley came to call the 'looking-glass self'. Having been greatly influenced by William James' definitions of psychology as the study of states of consciousness, Cooley adopts this definition and expands it by establishing the sociality of selfhood as it relates to the thoughts of others.

The *social self* is an *empirical self*—verified by observation. It is not an *a priori* Cartesian assumption nor a metaphysical abstraction. It is a product of social interaction, emerging from one's perception of one's self as reflected in the perceptions of others. It is, as social institutions, a quality of mental habit. In a word, it is generated in and verified by the mind—one's own mind and the minds of others. The concept of mind as employed by Cooley is rather specific:

Mind is an organic whole made up of cooperating individualities, in somewhat the same way that the music of an orchestra is made up of divergent but related sounds. No one would think it necessary or unreasonable to divide the music into two kinds, that made by the whole and that of particular instruments, and no more are these two kinds of mind, the social mind and the individual mind.[7]

A favourite expression of Cooley, and one which best portrayed his enduring sensitivity to the reciprocal relationship of self and society was 'self and society are twin-born'. For Cooley, to be aware of oneself was to be aware of society—thus, social consciousness and self-consciousness are inseparable. Self-image can only emerge with a reference group. And these consciousnesses of society and self, says Cooley, are located in the mind, i.e., human imagination. Unlike the natural sciences, all data of the social sciences are located in the human mind, in man's imaginative propensities. As Cooley observed: 'The imaginations which people have of one another are the solid facts of society, and that to observe and interpret these must be a chief aim of sociology.'[8]

For Cooley, the best way of talking about man's imaginative propensities, i.e., mind, was by paying attention to the emergence of the 'self'. As an individual develops a sense of 'I' he also develops simultaneously an awareness of and sensitivity to others as 'you', 'he/she', and 'they'. Through interaction with other selves, the self emerges. The self is not either individual or social primarily or firstly, but rather is a creation of dialectics between the individual and his social environment. An individual's awareness of himself is reflection of his perception of other's ideas of who he is, a process of one mind responding to other minds. This phenomenon Cooley came to call the 'looking-glass self.'

As we see our face, figures, and dress in the glass, and are interested in them because they are ours, and pleased or otherwise with them according as they do or do not answer to what we should like them to be, so in imagination we perceive in another's mind some thought of our appearance, manners, aims, deeds, character, friends, and so on, and are variously affected by it.[9]

In a real sense, for Cooley, social interaction with its concomitants of self and society, is a genuine 'meeting of the minds'. The concept of the 'looking-glass self', which probably constitutes the single most important and enduring contribution of Cooley to sociology and social psychology, is composed of three principal dimensions: (1) How we imagine our appearance to others; (2) How we imagine others' judgement of that appearance; (3) Our personal feeling about that judgement. When a child reaches the age of reflective self-awareness, an evolutionary progression in the early months and years, he becomes increasingly aware of others' recognition and evaluation of him. From the first, his mother, then his father, and then siblings and more and larger groups of people, his social arena develops. As he perceives others' estimations of his appearance, his 'self' develops accordingly. Not only is he aware of or able to imagine how he appears to others, he becomes also conscious of others' judgements and evaluations of his appearance. The result of this dual mental image, that is, of how he appears to and is evaluated by others, is a responsive feeling on his part to this evaluation—of pride or mortification or self-doubt, etc. Cooley gives a simple illustration of this process by using the example of an encounter between Alice, who has a new hat, and Angela, who just bought a new dress. He suggests that we then have the following sequence of perceptions:

(1) The real Alice, known only to her maker. (2) Her idea of herself, e.g., 'I (Alice) look well in this hat'. (3) Her idea of Angela's idea of her, e.g., 'Angela thinks I look well in this hat.' (4) Her idea of what Angela thinks she thinks of herself, e.g., 'Angela thinks I am proud of my looks in this hat.' (5) Angela's idea of what Alice thinks of herself, e.g., 'Alice thinks she is stunning in that hat.' And of course six analogous phases of Angela and her dress.[10]

The Primary Group

The logical extension of this 'looking-glass self' concept as descriptive of fundamental human social relationships is Cooley's idea of the 'primary group', which constitutes the fundamental meaning of all social organizations. The primary group is the seedbed of society and is indispensable in the forming of social nature, i.e., man's ideals, the experience of love and need for freedom and justice. The primary group is characterized by intimacy, face-to-face interaction, emotional warmth, and cooperation. Through the coincidental development of self-consciousness and social consciousness there is similarly the emergence of a sense of 'I-me' and 'us-we'. This sense of we-feeling fosters a strong identification of the self with group-life, for example, children's play groups, family, etc. Of course, all social interaction does not occur within a close-knit primary group, and, therefore, Cooley characterized the 'secondary group' as essentially and necessarily impersonal, contractual, formal, and rational, e.g., professional associations, corporations, bureaucracies, governments, etc.

The primary groups—the most important ones being the family, the play group of children, and the neighbourhood—is the universal breeding ground for the emergence of cooperation and fellowship. 'In these (primary groups)', explains Cooley, 'human nature comes into existence. Man does not have it at birth; he cannot acquire it except through fellowship, and it decays in isolation.'[11] The group forces the individual to give up individualistic interests in favour of group concerns and nurtures in-group feelings of sympathy and affection. Fundamentally, these groups are harmonious and affectionate, but competition, self-assertion, and passionate contentions also emerge. 'These passions', Cooley suggests, 'are socialized by sympathy, and come, or tend to come, under the discipline of a common spirit. The individual will be ambitious, but the chief object of his ambition will be some desired place in the thought of the others.'[12]

Cooley's social thought centered upon a confidence in human progress of an ever-widening expansion of human sympathy—a movement beginning in the primary groups of family and neighbourhood and moving outwards to encompass the community, the state, and the world. Not only was he an optimist and romantic idealist, he was thoroughly humanitarian, arguing cogently that the sociologist must display a sympathetic concern in his portrayal of the human predicament. Here is an excerpted quotation taken from Cooley by Edward C. Jaudy, which sums up Cooley's sentiment:

A sociologist must have the patient love of truth and need to reduce it to principles which all men of science require. Besides this, however, he needs the fullest sympathy and participation in the currents of life. He can no more stand aloof than can the novelist or the poet. He cannot be a specialist in the same way that a chemist or a botanist can, because he cannot narrow his life without narrowing his grasp on his subject. To attempt to build up sociology as a technical tradition remote from the great currents of literature and philosophy, would, in my opinion, be a fatal error. It cannot possibly avoid being difficult, but it should be as little abstruse as possible. If it is not human, it is nothing.[13]

Methodology

As with Weber, but independently of him, Cooley argued that the study of social life must be concerned with the 'meanings' which individuals attribute to their actions and circumstances. Sociology, quite necessarily, then, must go beyond the mere study of behaviour. The sociology of the rabbit hutch must necessarily be strictly a behavioural description. But the sociology of human life can and must rise above simple behavioural data to a higher place of analysis since it can effectively probe beneath the surface behaviour into the subjective meanings of human actions. 'Although our knowledge of people is behaviouristic', observes Cooley, 'it has no penetration, no distinctively human insight, unless it is sympathetic also.'[14]

When sociology and social psychology rule out the efficacy of a close examination and sympathetic analysis of 'motivation' in human behaviour, they are deprived of a valuable, even an indispensable, tool for human understanding. Cooley simply points out that the difference between our knowledge of a dog and our knowledge of individuals is our ability to have a 'sympathetic understanding' of his (the individual's) motivations. 'Knowledge requires both observation and interpretation, neither being more scientific than the other. And each branch of science must be worked out in its own way, which is mainly to be found in the actual search for truth rather than *a priori* methodology.'[15]

Similar to Weber's 'verstehen' and Sorokin's 'logico-meaningful' methodology, Cooley used the concept of 'sympathetic introspection' as his methodological label. Sympathetic introspection is the process of putting oneself in touch with various other persons, attempting to imagine how the world appears to them, and then recollecting and describing as closely as subjective, but, Cooley argues, since human behaviour, unlike instinctual animal behaviour, is fundamentally subjective, the method fits the data under investigation. The looking-glass self and the primary group, then, are not only the object of analysis, they are also the tools used in the analysis. 'In general,' explains Cooley, 'the insights of sociology are imaginative reconstructions of life whose truth depends upon the competence of the mind that makes them to embrace the chief factors of the process studied and are produced or anticipate their operation.'[16]

GEORGE HERBERT MEAD

Mead never wrote a book, but a handful of scattered papers. However, his greatness as a creative thinker and social theorist is reflected in the accomplishments of his students, many today being the leaders in their discipline. Soon after Mead's death, his students undertook to collect, edit, and publish in book form his formal university lectures. This effort resulted in four books consisting of Mead's thought, published at two-year intervals beginning in 1932. They are: *The Philosophy of the Present* (1932); *Mind, Self, and Society* (1934); *Movements of Thought in the 19th Century* (1936); and *The Philosophy of the Act* (1938).

Social psychology and the social act

At the turn of the century, when Mead began his teaching career, sociologists by and large had just begun to turn their attention, due somewhat to the proddings of Simmel in Germany and Cooley in America, to the specific issues and complexities of the individual in society. Up to this time, as we noted earlier, social theorists and the early sociologists were more concerned with large-scale social organizations, with social structures and their functions. With the coming of Cooley and Mead, analytical concern also began to include the small units of individual interaction. Mead called his sociology, 'social psychology'. It was primarily concerned with the study of the relationship between society and the individual, as we saw earlier in Cooley. Mead was interested in the nature and significance of group membership to individual behaviour. 'For social psychology', explained Mead, 'the whole (society) is prior to the part (the individual), not the whole in terms of the part or parts.'[17]

For Mead, that which constitutes the data of society is the 'social act', and, therefore, the fundamental task in social psychology was the analysis of the action in human encounter. The social act, for Mead, meant simply a transaction between two or more individuals who possess an established division of labour. The focus of concern is upon the behaviour of human interaction. 'Social psychology', Mead wrote, 'is behaviouristic in the sense of starting off with an observable activity—the dynamic, on-going social process, and the social acts which are its component elements—to be studied and analysed scientifically.' However, because Mead was in essential sympathy with Cooley, Simmel and Weber with respect to the 'subjective' uniqueness of human behaviour resulting from man's rationality and freedom of thought, he argued eloquently for the centrality in behaviour of the 'inner experience of the individual'.

Whereas Cooley relied heavily upon his concept of human imagination, i.e., man's mental cognizance of his social world, Mead concentrated upon the resulting 'act' of this consciousness awareness. Both Cooley and Mead, however, understood that the sociological challenge in the study of human social life was the sympathetic analysis and understanding of the 'interactional processes' of individuals in society. For Mead, 'symbolic interaction' was an evolutionarily developed social skill necessary for any kind of meaningful encounter of individuals. Language, says Mead, is one, and a major social act evolving out of the need for individuals to cooperate in a rational way. Language had its beginning in the 'gesture'—a primordial social act. Gestures, Mead points out, are either 'preparatory—beginnings of acts—social acts, i.e., actions and reactions which arise under the stimulation of other individuals, such as clenching the fists, grinding the teeth, assuming an attitude of defense—or else . . . outflows of nervous energy which sluice off the nervous excitement or reinforce and prepare indirectly for action.'[18]

The physical gesture, for example, the wink of an eye, the motion of a hand, the curl of a lip or raised eye-brow, become social gestures, i.e., social significants in human encounter, when they initiate and facilitate meaningful interaction, or mutually understood symbolic communication. Social gestures are significant symbolically when members of a social group mutually agree as to their specific meanings. A raised eyebrow may mean any number of things or communicate any number of messages in a specific group or in several different groups, but so long as the message communicated at any single instance is mutually perceived by the group, significant interaction can occur. The main function of these gestures, says Mead, is to facilitate rational behaviour and to stabilize social organizations. Gestures not only constitute the seed bed of language, but are also the essential prerequisite of all intellectual activity.

Rationalism and romanticism

Before we move to a systematic inquiry into the conceptual foundation of Mead's social psychology, a word should be said about his thorough-going rationalism and his romantic idealism. Philosophically speaking, rationalism is a perception of the world and a method of inquiry in which the criterion of truth is intellectually intelligible and deductively logical. Mead's rationalism, suggest Collins and

Makowsky, 'consisted of his theoretical joining of self and society in the ongoing social process, such that the individual was neither isolated from his fellows nor wholly determined by any abstract system.'[19] By this balance between the individual and society, Mead was able to avoid the pitfalls both of social determinism in which man is a pawn of social forces and of solypsism, in which man is treated as an isolated speck in a sea of chaos. In addition to his rationalism Mead was also a romantic of the German idealism which he encountered in his young years travelling and studying in Europe. Romanticism, especially the Kantian philosophies of the Schegels, Schelling, Novalis, and others, is a philosophical school of thought which attempts to texture knowledge to the realm of noumena (i.e., that dimension of reality which is not empirically observable), believing that all reality is ultimately spiritual, derived from a living spirit and thus knowable by the human spirit. Romanticism, furthermore, holds that Spirit, or the Absolute, is essentially creative and that the ultimate ground of all things is primarily an urge to self-expression; all that has been brought into being is but a means to its fuller self-realization. Therefore, for Mead, the self, explains Collins, 'is not a static unity that exists in *vacuo*; it is a dynamic, historical process that involves a subject-object relationship and arises as a result of interaction with other selves. The more we become aware of ourselves in the continuing social process, the more we increase our 'species consciousness'.[20] Armed with the confidence supplied by rationalism and the optimism of romanticism, Mead could approach the analysis of social life with an air of expectancy and hopefulness in understanding the human predicament.

The Coherent Theory: Mind, Self, Society

On more than one occasion, John Dewey, the father of American instrumental pragmatism and of a progressive educational philosophy, observed that Mead was the most creative philosophical mind of his day. William James, C. H. Cooley, and James Mark Baldwin all influenced Mead in some manner, but none so much as Dewey himself. And yet, Mead's contributions to human understanding resulted from his own creative capacity to spin out of his thoughts, gleaned from broadly and deeply developed ideas, a coherent theory of social life. Primarily this was done by linking together the emergence of the human mind, the social self, and the structures of society as these three elements conspire in the initiation and fostering of social interaction. This synthesis, which we shall subsequently explore in detail, made two overriding assumptions, viz., (1) that the bio-physiological frailty of the human organism necessitated cooperation as a deterrent to special extinction, and (2) that those social mechanisms (verbal, gestural, etc.) which evolved through cooperation among individuals would endure through time.

Mind: The three-fold foundation upon which Mead built his theory was Mind, Self, and Society, and the second in the series of posthumously published lectures of Mead bore this trilogy in its title. Mind, says Mead, is an emergent phenomenon of personal awareness on the part of the infant individual, of meaningful gestures selected out of a whole range of indiscriminate, experiential physical motions. Mind develops with the child's capacity to distinguish his and others' non-sense motions and significant gestures, the latter Mead calls 'conventional gestures'. A wink, for example, takes to itself a 'common meaning' which the mind discovers and employs within society. The child experiments with this gesture until he can mimic not only its physical appearance but can convey to others its symbolic meaning. As the child's mind develops (Cooley, it will be recalled, would be speaking here of human imagination), there is a simultaneous increase in social communication skills. Just as his physical dexterity develops with practice, such as climbing a ladder or riding a bicycle, so also his capacity to interact meaningfully through symbolic interaction by means of conventional gesturing develops. The more developed the mind in terms of symbolic interaction skills, the more sophisticated the level of meaningful communication among individuals. This ability to use and interpret social gestures greatly facilitates the development of mind, self, and society.

Mind emerges out of this maturing capacity of the child to distinguish and discriminate the symbols of interaction, by perceiving, conceiving, and interpreting gestures and language. By so doing, the child develops the capacity to assume the posture or perspective of the one with whom he is interacting, that is, the child is able to conceptualize another person's point of view. Mead calls this the ability to 'take the role of the other'. As we have seen, for Mead, the mind evolves when the child is able to (1) understand and use 'conventional gestures', (2) 'to employ the gestures' to 'take the role of the other', and (3) to imaginatively rehearse alternative lines of action. This third point, what Mead liked to call 'imaginative rehearsal', illustrates his conception of mind as a 'process' of intellectual activity, not as a static structure. In order for an individual to 'think about' what he will do before he actually does it, and to consider alternative forms of action before making a choice of action, he must 'rehearse' his decision, i.e., he must imagine his action before he acts. For this, says Mead, mind must be present. In order that society might exist and persist, mankind must have developed the capacity to imaginatively rehearse alternative lines of behaviour. Otherwise, no self could have evolved and no society could have developed. Man is not primarily an animal with instinctual behaviour of stimulus-response, but is human with a mind for rational judgment and freedom of decision. In this context, Mead distinguished between 'stimulus' and 'object'—animals respond to stimuli whereas man responds to objects. A stimulus, explains Mead, does not have an intrinsic character that acts upon individuals whereas the meaning of an object is conferred upon it by the individual. Animals and human beings alike *react* to stimuli, but only man *acts toward* an object. 'The individual is not surrounded by a world of pre-existing objects that coerce him; rather, he builds up his environment of objects according to his ongoing activity.'

The Self: Whereas Cooley focused upon mind (human imagination), as the primary factor in human interaction, Mead argued for a conception of mind as an emergent concomitant of society—that is, mind and society as coincidental phenomena. And if forced into a causal statement of which came first, Cooley would say that mind produces communication, and Mead would argue that mind arises within communication. Communication as meaningful interaction, for Mead, begins in random gesturing—both verbal and non-verbal—which, through a process of selective experimenting, evolves a repertoire of 'significant gestures' and spoken sounds converging so as to create mind.

As the father of symbolic interaction, Mead made a distinction between gesture and symbol. Gesture is a social act that operates as a stimulus for the response of another organism (animals) engaged in the same act. Symbol is a 'significant gesture' which conveys a 'meaning' to which only human beings can respond. Therefore, whereas a gesture may produce a stimulus in an animal, only man can act toward a gesture's meaning, i.e., a symbol. Therefore, only man is truly symbol-using, symbol-making animal, i.e., animal symbolicum. When a gesture, e.g., a wink of an eye, evokes the same meaning from the receiver of the gesture, i.e., the wink, as from the sender (of the wink), this gesture is a 'significant gesture', or symbol. When vocal gestures (speech) reach this receiver-sender consensus of meaning, language is the result. At the point where gestures employed in communication take upon themselves this symbolic function of conveying not just stimulus but consensual meaning, human inter-action is not just social as set forth by Cooley, but is more—it is symbolic interaction, according to Mead.

Symbolic interaction as meaningful communication occurs prima-rily through the capacity of individuals to take the role of the other, or simply 'role-taking'. Significant gestures, i.e., symbols, are signi-ficant because of their 'self-conscious' quality in man whereas non-significant gestures are non-significant, i.e., nonsymbolic, due to their 'non-self-conscious' quality in animals. Significant gestures as meaning-conveying symbols rely upon 'an arousal in the individual himself of the response which he is calling out in the individual, a taking of the role of the other, a tendency to act as the other person acts.'[21]

'I' and 'Me' As we have pointed out, one of Mead's most not-able contributions to the study of human relationships was his com-prehension of self-consciousness, its genesis and its sociality. Often, in explaining the complex nature of a child's ability to take the role of the other and to visualize his own performance from their point of view, Mead would say, 'the symbol arouses in one's self what it arouses in the other individual.' The mature self, he continues, arises when a 'generalized other' is internalized so that 'the community exercises control over the conduct of its individual members.' The self's essence is its reflective self-awareness, and with this essential capacity, an individual can be both an object 'me' and a subject 'I' to himself. This dual capacity is the essence of being social.

Mead was not a social determinist by which is meant a belief that what the individual is or becomes is fundamentally determined by his social environment. Mead was more organic and dynamic in his theory of man in society. The self for Mead was not simply a bag of social attitudes picked up in the environment. He used such concepts as 'self-image', 'self-concept', 'taking the role of the other', and 'significant others' to explain the creative balance which exists between the individual and society. His suggestion that through development of a mature self-consciousness, the individual becomes both an object and a subject to himself is a profound insight. He points out: 'It is the response of the organism (individual) to the attitudes of others, the "me" is the organized set of attitudes of the others which one assumes. The attitudes of the others constitute the organized *"me"* and then one reacts toward that as an "I".'[22]

Thus, according to Mead, the 'self' is made up of the 'I' and the 'me'. The 'I' represents the impulsive tendencies and the spontaneous behaviour of the human infant—that behaviour which is unconditioned and undisciplined whereas 'me' is the social component of self—the internalized demands of society. Over time, the process of continuous interaction with parents and significant others gives rise to the concept of 'me' which enables the individual to restrain and regulate the behaviour of 'I' in accordance with the established norms of the group or society.

Though Mead differed from Cooley in terms of the proper sequence in the initial emergence of mind and communication, they did concur that self-consciousness and social-consciousness were coextensive. For Mead, not so much the nature but the evolutionary process of self-consciousness was of primary interest. The basic process, of course, was human interaction in a social context. Says Mead: 'The self is something which has a development, it is not initially there, at birth, but arises in the process of social experience and activity, develops in the given individual as a result of his relations to that process as a whole and to other individuals within that process.'[23]

And in this connection, Mead suggested that self-consciousness emerges in three evolutionary stages, viz., (1) the stage of imitative acts, (2) the play stage, and (3) the game stage. The imitative stage, says Mead, occurs about the second year of life during which time the young child mimics the mannerisms and behavioural patterns of his parents, siblings (brothers and sisters) and other 'significant others', i.e., people in his immediate social environments. The play stage begins about the third year which is characterized by the child's growing interest in assuming various roles of his 'significant others', for example, playing mother, father, big sister, etc. The third and final stage of self-consciousness development during which time a unified self emerges is called by Mead the game stage. At this time, the child had developed the capacity to 'take the role of the others', not just of one other and not just of one role, but he is able to assume the attitudes of several people comprising his social group all at one time. Whether it be perceiving the various and conflicting attitudes of his parents and siblings during a moment of family feuding or an ability to really play in a baseball game or chess, he is able to enter into the human interaction because he can 'imagine' the role of others.

This third stage is, of course, very complex and indicates real maturity in consciousness of the self and others. Rational, adaptive behaviour is an indicator of mature self-consciousness. This maturity occurs when an individual is able to mentally perceive, understand, and employ the symbolic meanings of his own gestures and those of others. During this process, says Mead, the self has the unique quality of being an object to itself. Mead believed with Cooley that an individual cannot experience himself except through the eyes of gestures of others. Mead put it this way:

The individual enters his own experience as a self . . . not directly or immediately, not by becoming a subject to himself, but only in so far as he first becomes an object to himself just as other individuals are objects to him or in his experience, and he becomes an object to himself only by taking the attitudes of other individuals toward himself within a social environment or context of experience and behaviour in which both he and they are involved.[24]

In short, as a 'me' the individual is aware of himself as 'object'; as an 'I' he is aware of himself as a subject. Because the impulsive behaviour of the 'I' cannot be predicted, Mead argued with William James that the self is not determined by social environment but is forever open to alternative behaviours. Due to this balancing of the 'me' as the generalized other internalized, and the 'I' as incalculable spontaneity, human behaviour is fundamentally free and only irregularly predictable.

The Generalized Other

The pragmatic freshness and practical rationalism of Mead, those qualities which earned him the admiration of John Dewey, are especially reflected in his notion of the social self. The social self, says Mead, is a dynamic and changing relationship between the individuals and others between the 'I' and the 'me' of every individual. It is not the static intellectual monad of Descartes' mental 'I' nor is it the defense mechanism of Freud's executive 'ego'. The effectiveness of Mead's rational conception of the balancing duality of self and society, or self-consciousness and social consciousness, is illustrated in his explanation of social institutions and social control. Social institutions are essentially products of social habits which have evolved as effective means of establishing and fostering social order. Social control, which is necessarily operative in any viable social order, exists fundamentally as a social expression of individual self-control. Self-control is a social consciousness inevitability when individuals feel inwardly or subjectively obliged to honour the rights of others within the social group.

But for the emergence of 'the generalized other', social institutions, social order, and social control could not be. Through the growth and development of the self, the generalized other represents that stage at which the individual is finally able to relate to himself—as object and subject, as 'I' and 'me'—the attitudes and values of his social environment. As noted above, the generalized other is identified with an organized community or social group which fosters a sense of, and commitment to, an individual's self-unity. The generalized other nurtures a sense of enduring selfhood, of continuous self-integrity and personal identity through a continuously expanding number of social circles. The larger community (from small cohesive groups to giant bureaucracies) can express an attitude or value, says Mead, only because it is present in each individual's mind as the attitude or value of the generalized other.

In summary, Mead insists that 'self' is neither a psychological organism nor a biological entity but essentially a social process which arises in social experience and activity. Social interaction, communication and group processes introduce the self into which the individual organizes all his experiences. Thus an individual forms the concept of self in the process of meaningful interaction with significant others. How does an individual, for instance, come to acquire his self-concept of being 'intelligent'? According to the symbolic interaction theory, he is not intelligent because he thinks he is intelligent, he is not intelligent because others think he is intelligent, but he is intelligent because he thinks others think he is intelligent. It is the response of others who seek his advice and expertise and his perception of this experience with them that gave him his self-concept of being intelligent. Thus individuals come to acquire a variety of self-concepts such as 'beautiful', 'timid', 'honest', 'outgoing', etc. from their experience with the significant social group.

Mead has spoken with insightful sensitivity of the relationship of the adaptable 'self-image' to the more stable 'self-conception', realizing that though individuals rightly and necessarily attempt to fit in a social group by 'defining the situation' and adapting to it, they nevertheless have an enduring sense of their continuous self-hood throughout a variety of different social situations. Jonathan H. Turner offers this synopsis:

(As an individual matures) the transitory 'self-images' derived from specific others in each interactive situation eventually become crystallized into a more or less stabilized 'self-conception' of oneself as a certain type of object. With the emergence of these self-conceptions, actions of individuals are seen by Mead to take on consistency, since they are now mediated through a coherent and stable set of attitudes, dispositions, or meanings about oneself as a certain type of person.[25]

Functions of the Self

1. Communication. The self serves as an object of communication. Mead declares that 'the essence of the self . . . is cognitive: it lies in the internalized conversation of gestures which constitutes thinking, or in terms of which thought or reflection proceeds.'[26] Since human communication is essentially symbolic, without the self man would not be able to communicate with himself or others, because, as Mead observes: 'What is essential to communication is that the symbol should arouse in one's self what it arouses in the other individual.'[27]

2. Analysis of the situation. The self enables the individual to analyse each situation and to decide what line of action to take. Since the individual experiences himself not directly but in terms of the self, the most basic person in the situation, he takes stock of all elements in the situation in relation to the self. In other words, 'self-hood allows us to examine situations and how they affect us and to determine the kind of action we might take by imaginatively testing proposed action first on its effects on the self, that object we seem to know the best.'[28]

3. Self-direction and self-control. The importance of the self lies in the recognition that the individual can be the object of his own actions. He can act toward himself in much the same way he acts toward others. Just as he might control and manipulate others, he can direct and control the self. Indeed, the individual must be able

to respond to a self-image before he seeks to control himself or others. Thus in the symbolic interactionist perspective, the individual does not passively react to external stimuli; he perceives, interprets, organizes his thoughts, considers his options and chooses a line of action.

4. Self-judgement. The individual evaluates his self-image in terms of his experience with others. In the words of Shibutani:

Like other meanings, sentiments toward one-self are formed and reinforced in the regularized responses of other people. Through role-taking a proud man is able to visualize himself as an object toward which others have feelings of respect, admiration, or even awe. If others consistently address him with deference, he comes to take it for granted that he deserves such treatment. On the other hand, if someone is consistently mistreated or ridiculed, he cannot help but conclude that others despise him. If a person is always ignored, especially in situations in which others like himself are given attention, he may become convinced that he is a comparatively worthless object. Once such estimates have crystallized, they become more independent of the responses of other people.[29]

5. Identity. To furnish our identities is one of the essential functions of the self. In the process of social interaction and experience, the self receives the labels, names and other aspects of identity which others have for us and transforms them as our own. The self organizes our knowledge of 'who we are' and what we think of ourselves in terms of our perception of others' responses. Thus the individual comes to think of himself as 'shy', 'handsome', or 'timid' because these are precisely the labels which he thinks the social world has attributed to him.

6. Mind and problem-solving. The self not only activates the mind; indeed, it makes that activity possible at all. Because of mind, human beings develop an active relationship to their environment; rather than just responding to stimuli, they evaluate environmental stimuli and consciously select appropriate responses. Mead notes: 'Consciousness is involved where there is a problem, where one is deliberately adjusting one's self to the world, trying to get out of difficulty or pain. One is aware of experience and is trying to readjust the situation so that conduct can go ahead. There is, therefore, no consciousness in a world that is just there . . . .'[30] When the self interprets an identity as unacceptable (a timid or boring person) or perceives the attainment of a prized reward (honour or money) as being blocked, mind treats it as a problem and proceeds to work out

a strategy to deal with the situation.

Society. The third dimension in Mead's perception of the social world is society, and self and mind serve as the interaction ingredients which eventuate in social order. Society, says Mead, is a human construction. Society is an organized activity which is essentially regulated by the generalized other and the arena within which individuals make adjustments and cooperate with one another. It emerges out of the complex interactional adjustments—conflict, compromise, innovation, cooperation—which occur in human communications. As mind and self negotiate the parameters and operational rules of social discourse, society's order and institutions are sometimes altered, reconstructed, or disassembled. Social change, consequently, says Mead, is both likely and unpredictable—likely due to the dynamics of human interaction and unpredictable due to the freedom of spontaneity in mind and self.

The institutions of society which represent the organized and patterned interaction among a variety of individuals, are dependent for both their emergence and persistence upon mind and self. Through the agency of mind, by means of which the individual takes roles and imaginatively rehearses optional and alternative actions, coordinated activity among several individuals is made possible. Through the agency of self, especially the self's ability to critically evaluate its own attitudes and behaviour from the point of view of the generalized other, the social control needed in any meaningful and sustained coordinated activity would be impossible. For Mead, the fundamental process to be studied and understood, in addition to the emergent processes of self-consciousness, is the dynamic relationship, sometimes creative, sometimes destructive, but always organic, which exists between mind and self out of which society is generated. Mead's view of this dynamic relationship led him to believe that society, due to its constituent elements of mind and self is constantly in a state of flux and rife with potential change.

Methodology and Criticism

Every social theorist, whether he is research oriented or not, necessarily has a methodology. Some have only indirectly and implicitly suggested a methodological approach to the study of social phenomena in their writings, as for example the social philosophers of the classical period, and others have dwelt with some considerable seriousness upon the methodological issues in their work, as for example Weber and Sorokin. Mead fits into the latter category. With his philosopher-friend, John Dewey, Mead argued that in order for the human community to make progress in the quality of social life, it must apply scientific method to social problems. A position somewhat at odds, it should be recalled, with that of Herbert Spencer. Mead, like Dewey, was a thoroughgoing pragmatist and nowhere is this philosophical predisposition better reflected than in his scientific method.

For Mead, there are two sources of sociological understanding of man's social world. First, there is behaviouristic psychology—not positivistic behaviourism—which enables the social scientist to apprehend intelligence in terms of human activity. Without this capacity of the scientific community to perceive and understand not just behaviour as activity but human behaviour as social activity, the social scientists would be relegated to a simplistic analysis of human behaviour in terms of animal stimulus-response. But man can understand human behaviour by *looking* at 'action' and by *apprehending* 'intelligence'. The second source for understanding man's social world, says Mead, is the process of scientific research, a rigorous and non-doctrinal method which is self-revising and consistently critical of its findings, of its hypotheses, and of its conclusions. Through this dual emphasis upon behaviouristic psychology (action and intellection) and scientific method (critical research), the social scientist is able to approach the data of the social world with both confidence in method and expectation in understanding. As explained by Collins, Mead's methodological pragmatism included three assumptions or stages. First, as with the whole school of pragmatic philosophy, a hypothesis is considered true if it works when tested. Second, there was a fundamental belief that within human conduct there lies a process of knowing. And third, there was a confidence that knowledge is a process of acquiring the necessary 'scientific apparatus' (including ideas, concepts, units of analysis, theoretical models, paradigms, equations, etc.) to carry out the desirable task of social reconstruction in a democratic state.

As with any creative venture in the frontier regions of theory-building, Mead's profound legacy in American sociology was not without its shortcomings. It is probably more fair to say that his theory necessitated further clarifications which he himself did not make, either because he was unable to see them or because of time. Though his insights were often profound in terms of the evolution of self-consciousness in society, he was not sufficiently clear in his explication of the nature of social organization in society. Also, and as a result of this particular imprecision, the points of contact between the individual and society were occasionally unclear. His major contribution, viz., that mind and self generated society and that society affected mind and self, needs much work in order that its full implications might be realized. Of course, Mead could not cover all fronts in his sociological work. The field is too broad. However, it is to be regretted that he did not turn his inquiring mind to the problems of power and social stratification, of class and social mobility. Nevertheless, though his methodology sometimes defies duplication and is often too rationalistic and optimistically progressive for our day, his theories of mind, self, and society and of the social consequences of personal change are still main-line theories without which modern sociology would be considerably less than it is.

Symbolic Interaction—An Overview
Defining the Method

If not legitimately called 'the father' of symbolic interaction, Mead can certainly and justly be called the major pioneer in this new methodology. Of course, such names as Charles Horton Cooley, John Dewey, William James, James B. Baldwin, and W. I. Thomas must also be mentioned as fellers of trees in this frontier of social thought. However, it is from the classrooms of Mead that the major figures have come, doing more work and expanding the depth and breadth of symbolic interaction as a specific theoretical system. Of those who came to present this theoretical system, three broadly-defined schools of interpretation arose, viz., what might be called Herbert Blumer and the Chicago School, Manford Kuhn and the Iowa School, and Erving Goffman and dramaturgy. This text would be less than complete if these variants and elaborations of symbolic interaction were not at least summarized, but before that happens, a summary of symbolic interaction as a general theoretical perspective is in order.

Symbolic interaction, as we have seen both in Cooley's 'looking-glass self' and Mead's 'generalized other', is fundamentally interpretative and definitional. Human communication is interpretative due to its capacity to ascertain the 'meaning' of other persons' actions, and it is definitional in that it attempts to convey an indication, i.e., significant gesture—verbal or non-verbal, as to how other individuals can be said to be conceptualizations of social interaction as a complex of strategic adjustments, negotiations, compromises, innovations, etc., between individuals in the human environment.

Interaction: The Key Concept

The capacity to purposefully take a role, a skill resulting from self-conscious maturation, involves a variety of complex processes. The ability to both emit and interpret significant gestures is the ability to interact meaningfully. This ability is a development of the individual's 'objectifying' propensities. That is a mature self involved in meaningful communication necessarily must perceive himself not only as 'subject', but also as 'object'. No self can emerge without the balancing and I-me. In addition to self-objectification, a mature individual can objectify virtually any phenomenon of his social world, whether it be mental, physical, or emotional. Therefore, so long as there is a mutual agreement within the group as to the specific meanings of particular objectified phenomena, e.g., norms, ideas, persons, etc., symbolic interaction can occur. Therefore, so long as an individual is aware of the world of objects which his social group has selected as symbolically important, he can employ them in meaningful communications.

This process of objectification of selected phenomena in the social world as symbolically important implies the necessity for a mutual agreement within the group as to the exact selection. Symbolic interactionists call this selection process a 'definition of the situation' or a 'working consensus'. Until a group of individuals mutually agree upon the cluster of objects symbolically meaningful in their communication, no significant interaction can occur. A society evolves out of a complex history of compromise, innovation, and experimentation within a group seeking to reach a mutual agreement about significant gestures and meaningful symbols. By reaching a working consensus about gestures and symbols, a society establishes the general framework of references within which interaction can occur and be judged. Drawing up this social framework of gestures is called, in symbolic interaction, 'mapping'.

The process of mapping the social framework for symbolic interaction is an unending task, for there is a continuous flow of innovation, compromise, renegotiation in gesture-usages which necessitate redefinition of the situation in order that a working consensus can be maintained. Without this remapping and continual maintenance of the working consensus, a society would necessarily dissolve, either violently or by entropy. As a theory and method of analysis, symbolic interaction employs interpretation, evaluation, definition, and remapping as concepts which call attention to the interrelationship of self, mind, and society. As a theory, it calls attention to the symbolic nature of human interaction which necessitates social change due to the shifting definitions of the situation in society and culture.

Social Organization

Unlike the somewhat static view of organization and institution in the structural-functional approach, symbolic interaction conceives of social organization more in terms of an organic process since human behaviour is illustrative of the individual's interpretation, evaluation, definitional, and mapping processes. Social organization, then, represents the mental task, what Cooley called 'imagination', of fitting together a complex system of significant gestures in interaction. Therefore, the social structure for symbolic interaction becomes important as a focus of analysis when defined as a pattern of social organization which is the concomitant social reality of a perpetual interlacing of individual behaviours. Social structures can exist through time because of the repetition of their clear-cut expectations and common definitions of the situation in the interactional processes of individuals. But because social structures owe their existence and perpetuity to repetitious human interaction which is essentially 'symbolic' in nature and not simply to stimulus-response, there necessarily exists in social structure the potential for change through the introduction of new objects as significant and meaningful. Social structures, therefore, like interaction, are essentially organic and dynamic, never staying in the same for long, due to the inevitable process of reinterpretation, re-evaluation, redefinition, and remapping in human behaviour. Social structures are defined as patterns of social organization which can serve as mental objects which establish a working consensus within a social group. And, such redefinitions in turn result in altered social structures.

Human Nature

Just as symbolic interaction makes certain assumptions about the

234 of social organization, so likewise it claims

nature and function of social organization, so likewise it claims certain characteristics to be true of man's nature. The social life of man, say the symbolic interactionists, is essentially a result of the interpretative, evaluative, definitional, and mapping activities of individuals. Therefore, the study of social life must necessarily concentrate upon the nature of the individual units in interaction, i.e., individual himself and his symbolizing behaviour. First, it is asserted that humans have an ability to conceive of themselves as both subject and object, and by extension, to claim and label any object—mental, emotional, physical—as significant in interaction. Consequently, individuals are seen as actively involved in the creation and maintenance of their own social world, and not simply relegated to pawns pushed and pulled around by psychologically and sociologically determining factors. Therefore and finally, symbolic interaction claims that only by concentrating attention upon the individual's capacity to create symbolically meaningful objects in his world can human interaction and the resulting patterns of social organization be understood. Contrary to structural-functionalism, symbolic interaction contends that social organization does not emerge from such things as system forces, societal need, and structural mechanism; but rather from individuals engaged in a mutual interpretation, evaluation, definition, and mapping of the social world. These symbolic processes operative between individuals constitute the medium through which social patterns are created, maintained, and altered. Because of man's capacity to alter, substitute, and innovate symbolic gestures, he is capable of freely and intentionally as well as inadvertently and unintentionally altering and shifting behaviour and thus social organization. Contrary, then, to the visual imagery of behaviour being 'released'—such as might be employed in behaviouristic psychology, symbolic interaction portrays behaviour as being an intentional 'construction' of individuals. Man is creator and innovator, not manipulated and deterministic.

A Formalization

John Kinch attempted to frame the interactionist notions of self-concept into a formalized theory.[31] The self-concept, i.e., the individual's conception of himself, is that organization of qualities which the individual attributes to himself. The essence of the symbolic interaction theory is this: the individual's conception of himself emerges from social interaction and, in turn, guides or influences the behaviour of that individual.

Kinch proposes three postulates inherent in symbolic interaction theory:

1. The individual's self-concept is based on his perception of the way others are responding to him;
2. The individual's self-concept directs his behaviour.
3. The individual's perception of the responses of others toward him reflects the actual behaviour of others toward him.

By simple logic other propositions may be derived from these basic postulates:

4. The way the individual perceives the responses of others towards him will influence his behaviour.
5. The actual responses of others towards the individual will determine the way he sees himself (his self-concept).
6. The actual responses of others towards the individual will affect the behaviour of the individual.

These propositions imply four variables:

(S) the individual's *self-concept*
(P) His *perception* of the responses of others toward him
(A) *Actual responses* of others toward him
(B) His *behaviour*

Now the theory may be formally stated thus: The actual responses of others to the individual will be important in determining how the individidual will perceive himself. This perception will influence his self-conception which, in turn, will guide his behaviour. Symbolically it means: $A \rightarrow P \rightarrow S \rightarrow B$ (where $\rightarrow$ means leads to). However, there is another aspect of the interaction process which is often ignored. When the individual changes his behaviour according to his perception and the actual responses of others, then this change may affect the others' actual behaviour toward him also. That is, others' behaviour may change causing a reciprocal interactional cycle which may be depicted as follows:

Blumer and the Chicago School

A great teacher, though sometimes judged to be so merely by virtue of his writings, is more truly deserving of such a characterization on the basis of the ongoing success of his students. Such was the case with George Herbert Mead, for though he wrote and published ever so little, he did produce a group of students who would make any teacher in any age proud. But, as is too often the case with disciples, when the master is gone, there emerges a dispute over the correct and orthodox interpretation of the master's teachings. Let us look briefly at the resulting variations and elaborations upon Mead's thought. After completing his studies in sociology under Mead at the University of Chicago, Herbert Blumer, in 1952, moved to the University of California at Berkeley. Agreeing with Mead that society is continuously modified through the interactions of individuals, Blumer continued to emphasize the 'processual' nature of society over the somewhat rigid structural analysis of the functionalists. Society is essentially not a structure with a function but a dynamically unfolding process. Social structures exist—roles, statuses, norms, authority, etc.,—not as determinants of action but as the results of interaction. For Blumer, meaning does not inhere in objects, rather objects have meaning attributed to them by individuals in a definition of the situation. Significant meaning exists only to the extent that individuals have mutually agreed upon a particular definition of a specific object—whether it be a rock, chair, or an idea. Research methods, therefore, says Blumer, must attempt to get at the definitions of those individuals interacting in the social environment under analysis, by means of such materials as personal documents, case studies, participant observation, and life histories.

Blumer considers the following to be the central features of symbolic interactionism: (1) Human society is made up of individuals who have selves. The self constitutes the central mechanism which enables the human being to make indications to himself of things in his surroundings, to interpret the actions of others and to guide his own action by what he notes. (2) Individual action is constructed or built up instead of being a mere release; it is built up step by step by the individual through a process of self-indication, through noting and interpreting features of the situation in which he acts. (3) Group or collective action consists of the aligning of individual actions, brought about by the individuals' interpreting or taking into account each other's actions. In taking a role, the individual ascertains the intention or direction of the acts of others and forms and aligns his own action on the basis of such interpretation of the acts of others.

Blumer distinguishes between what he calls 'definitive concepts' and 'sensitizing concepts'. The former 'refers precisely to what is common to a class of objects, by the aid of a clear definition in terms of attributes or fixed bench marks.'[32] However, since the empirical world is not fixed but in a continuous process of redefinition through intrepretation and judgment, the use of definitive concepts is of limited value in sociological analysis. Blumer suggests that sociologists rely more on 'sensitizing concepts' which, although lacking in specification of attributes or bench marks, provide general orientation and guidance in dealing with empirical reality. 'Whereas definitive concepts provide prescriptions of what to see, sensitizing concepts merely suggest directions along which to look.'[33] This is entirely consistent with Blumer's position that only qualitative methodologies are appropriate for interactional, or general sociological, analysis.

Kuhn and the Iowa School

Manford Kuhn and his followers at the State University of Iowa share much of the same substantive orientation of symbolic interactionism with Blumer and his associates of the Chicago School. But they are very much critical of the methodology of the Chicago School which they consider to be too vague and intuitive to allow for scientific precision. Kuhn and his associates insisted that sociological methods should seek to measure actors' symbolic processes with reliable instruments. They constructed methodologically rigorous operational definitions of key concepts in symbolic interactionism such as 'self', 'social act', and 'generalized other', and developed structured measuring instruments, such as questionnaires, to get reliable and valid measures of key variables. One example is Kuhn's own attempt to objectify the study of the self through the utilization of his Twenty Statements Test (TST) in which the subject is asked to answer the question, 'Who am I?' in twenty statements. The most popular type of the TST reads as follows:

In the spaces below, please give twenty different answers to the question, 'Who am I?'. Give these as if you were giving them to yourself, not to somebody else. Write fairly rapidly, for the time is limited.

Whereas Chicago scoffed at such quantitative and static attempts to objectify what is essentially a dynamic and organic process, Iowa argued against the soft-headed approach of Chicago.

There are also other important differences between the two schools. Blumer emphasized the processual nature and changing character of the self; Kuhn stressed the 'core self' and defined it as a relatively stable set of meanings and attitudes. Blumer attributed the potential for spontaneity and indeterminacy to human behaviour and treated men as active creators of the world; Kuhn saw personality as structured and comparatively stable and stressed the continuity and predictability of human behaviour. Whereas Blumer saw action as 'construction' through active self-direction, Kuhn saw it more or less as a 'release' under the influence of collectivity. Similarly, Blumer emphasized the processual aspects of social organization; Kuhn emphasized its structural properties. The seemingly indeterministic view of the former portrayed social structures as objects to be intrepreted, mapped out and transformed, but the latter argued that the social world is determinate and that the 'core self' is largely shaped by it.

Erving Goffman and Dramaturgy

The dramaturgical approach, best exemplified by its founder Erving Goffman, is an extension of fundamental symbolic interaction. Goffman' major works include *The Presentation of Self in Everyday Life* (1959); *Asylums* (1961); *Interaction Ritual* (1967); *Frame Analysis: An Essay on the Organization of Experience* (1974). The social World, Goffman observes, is not self-ordered and meaning is not inherent in behaviour. Rather, the social order and the meaning of a particular behaviour are significant because people attribute significance to them. In interaction, therefore, individuals not only present themselves to each other, they also attempt to 'manage' the image they present. In fact, Goffman's primary focus is the process of impression management, that is, the ways in which actors manipulate gestures to create an impression in a particular social scene. Social behaviour, therefore, is somewhat analogous to theatrical drama. Not surprisingly, Goffman employs such terms as script, audience, identity kits, performer, performance, part, onstage, downstage, mask, props and other theatrical references. Thus by utilizing the language of drama, Goffman has provided an insightful account of the presentation of self in everyday life, demonstrated how actors validate self-conceptions, how they justify their actions through gestures, how prescriptions governing proper dress, tone of voice and choice of vocabulary represent overt aspects of interaction which display the salient features of the silent dialogue, and how people manipulate different social situations and adjust to them. Goffman has concentrated primarily upon face-to-face interaction. Like the Chicago School, he utilizes personal observations and experiences as his primary source of data. His writings are often criticized not so much because they display a genuinely humanistic concern for the feelings of others as for the too subjectivistic method which seems to defy objectification and verification.

An Assessment

To Blumer the conceptualization of the process of constructing action through self-indication is a unique symbolic interactionist orientation which is different from any sociological or psychological perspectives. The self is different from ego, the psychic characteristics, environmental pressures, external stimuli and psychological or biological drives. The process of self-indication stands over against them since it is 'a moving communicative process in which the individual notes things, assesses them, gives them a meaning, and decides to act on the basis of the meaning'; it is through this process that the human being constructs his conscious action. This perspective is an effective counter to sterile structuralism and concrete behaviourism in that it deals with covert as well as overt actions; symbolic interactionism is concerned not only with what the individual does but also with his perceptions, thought processes and self-indication. Instead of treating individuals as organisms that make up such organizations as the 'social system', 'culture', 'institutions', the 'social situation' or the 'status-role bundle', symbolic interactionism treats humans as dynamic and rational problem-solvers who, rather than being simply shaped by their social milieu, interpret, cooperate, take roles, communicate and align their acts. Moreover, conventional wisdom in sociology treats social action as an expression of forces playing on them rather than as acts which are built up by people through the process of interpretation. Thus symbolic interactionism is a powerful antidote to structural determinism. Above all, this is probably the only general sociological perspective that can most effectively handle one of the most difficult problems in contemporary sociological theory-building, namely, the relationship between the individual and the society.

Symbolic interactionism has refined a number of sociological concepts and enhanced their scientific value in analysing the interactional process. In particular, it has systematically made use of such central concepts as cooperation, conflict, role-playing, role taking, rehearsal of action, social situation, definition of the situation, self-direction, social objects, symbols and identity.

Symbolic interaction has made substantial contributions to almost every branch of sociology. By describing the nature of reality and its social construction and through the exploration of the areas of concern to Phenomenology and ethnomethodology, symbolic interaction has enriched the sociology of knowledge. By the systematic treatment of the stages through which the child acquires culture, attitudes and self-image, symbolic interaction has proved to be the most effective theory in explaining the process of socialization. In the study of deviance, it has been primarily responsible for the elaboration of the labelling theory which shows how deviant behaviour results from the judgement of others, which eventually becomes the judgement we have of self.

Mead's conceptualization marked a welcome departure from the conventional psychological behaviourism which generalized from animal behaviour (for example, based on the observation of the conditioned behaviour of rats) for human beings. But symbolic interactionism formulated a social psychological framework of the theory based on assumptions about man's distinct characteristics—his possession of self and his ability to use symbols. Animal intelligence does not involve the conception of a self or the use of symbols. Mead's notion of self is an effective counter to Freudianism and individual psychologies that concentrate on psychic systems and biological drives. By viewing man as an active agent rather than a passive recipient of external stimuli, Mead has emphasized the notion of 'emergence' in socal relations. However, it is unfortunate that many sociologists, especially some of the leading functionalists, have transformed Mead's self—essentially a process—into some sort of a static structure; they borrow selectively from Mead to explain how norms are internalized. They have also redefined the 'generalized other' to fit the reference group theory. This is unfair to Mead who defined self as a process and viewed men as freer and more active agents than conventional sociology did.

NOTES

1. E. A. Rose, *Social Psychology* (New York, Macmillan, 1911), p. 5.
2. Herbert Blumer, 'Society as Symbolic Interaction', in Arnold Rose (ed.), *Human Behaviour and Social Processes* (Boston, Houghton Mifflin Company, 1962), p. 179.
3. C. H. Cooley, *Social Process* (Carbondale, Southern Illinois University Press, 1966), p. 28
4. C. H. Cooley, *Social Organization* (New York, Schocken Press, 1962), p. xxi.
5. C. H. Cooley, *Life and the Student* (New York, Alfred A. Knopf, 1927), p. 201.
6. C. H. Cooley, *Human Nature and Social Order* (New York, Schocken Press, 1968), pp. 119, 121.
7. Cooley, *Social Organization*, p. 3.
8. Cooley, *Human Nature and Social Order*, pp. 121–2.
9. Ibid., p. 184.
10. Cooley, *Life and the Student*, pp. 200–1.
11. Cooley, *Social Organization*, pp. 23–4.
12. Ibid., p. 24.
13. As quoted by E. C. Jaudy, *Charles Horton Cooley: His Life and His Social Theory* (New York, Dryden Press, 1942), p. 96.
14. C. H. Cooley, *Sociological Theory and Social Research* (New York, Holt, Rinehart and Winston, 1930), p. 290.
15. As quoted by Richard Dewey, 'C. H. Cooley: Pioneer in Psychosociology', in *An Introduction to the History of Sociology*, ed. by H. E. Barnes (Chicago, University of Chicago Press, 1948), p. 844.
16. Cooley, *Sociological Theory and Social Research*, p. 307.
17. G. H. Mead, *Mind, Self and Society* (Chicago, University of Chicago Press, 1934), p. 7.
18. As quoted by A. J. Reck (ed.), *G. H. Mead: Selected Writings* (Indianapolis, Bobbs-Merrill, 1964), p. 109.
19. Randall Collins and Michael Makowsky, *The Discovery of Society* (New York, Random House, 1972), p. 149.
20. Ibid.
21. George Herbert Mead as quoted in Lewis Coser, *Masters of Sociological Thought* (New York, Harcourt, Brace, Jovanovich, 1977), p. 334.
22. Mead, *Mind, Self and Society*, p. 175.
23. Ibid., p. 135.
24. Ibid., p. 138.
25. Jonathan Turner, *The Structure of Sociological Theory* (Homewood, Dorsey Press, 1974), p. 154.
26. For a detailed discussion, see Joel M. Charon, *Symbolic Interactionism* (Englewood Cliffs, Prentice-Hall, 1979), pp. 71–8.

27. Mead, *Mind, Self and Society*, p. 149.
28. Charon, op. cit., p. 72.
29. Tamotsu Shibutani, *Society and Personality: An Interactionist Approach to Social Psychology* (Englewood Cliffs, Prentice-Hall, 1961), pp. 434–5.
30. G. H. Mead, *The Philosophy of the Act*, ed. by Merritt H. Moore (Chicago, University of Chicago Press, 1938), p. 657.
31. Summarized from Research Notes by John W. Kinch on 'A Formalized Theory of Self-concept,' *American Journal of Sociology*, 481.
32. Herbert Blumer, 'What is Wrong with Social Theory?', *American Sociological Review*, 19 (1954), 150.
33. Ibid.

CHAPTER 9
Phenomenological Sociology
by John H. Morgan

General Introduction

From the earliest records of human reflection, we learn that man has laboured valiantly, fearlessly, and tirelessly to understand his world, his place in it, and his relationship to it. The incomparable Greek philosopher, Aristotle, expressed in his *Ethics* the unquestionable truth that all men seek to know. Man, like all other animals, is equipped with sensory receptors and motor effectors sufficient to respond to the demands of the physical world. But, unlike other animals, man seems not driven merely to live a life of stimulus-response, ever receiving signals and reacting accordingly. Man is unquestionably bent upon not only living life but grasping it, of owning it not simply as provider of room and board but as a matrix within which his living has meaning—value, purpose, duty.[1] Man's world is not strictly a physical environment; rather, it is a symbolically endowed world of meanings, a world that man not only encounters, but a world he seeks to understand. His world is not so much a given as it is a discovery or a created panorama of interpretable symbols of meaning.[2] Man not only encounters, he interprets; he not only responds, he discovers and creates as well. He seeks not merely to know the world, but is driven to understand it and his relationship to it, to his fellow men, and to himself. The more he encounters and is confronted by his environment—physical, social, ideational—the more determined he is to understand it and interpret its meaning. Truly it can be said that man is the interpreting animal—*homo hermeneuticus*.[3]

To understand and to interpret the multidimensional world is man's chosen vocation—a commitment made early when the cave man took up paints to capture the mystery and the wonder of the hunt on the walls of his dwellings and a commitment which still thrives in the medical laboratories and the halls of the academy today. Man seeks to know and understand his world and himself as he relates to it, and most recently, sociology as fledgling science has joined in the great adventure of learning more about humankind. A youthful science in many respects, as compared to three thousand years of systematic philosophy and a half-millenium of astronomy, sociology has come along quickly in its own special parameters of research gaining acceptance and even respect from more established fields of learning. And like all other fields of research, as sociology has gained acceptance and flexed its scientific skills, it has produced sub-disciplines which claim specialized expertise in designated areas of the phenomena of social life. From an early sociology which aspired simply to study human social behaviour in interactional constellations of organizational settings, sociology has, in a brief period, given rise to specialized languages, research methodologies, and theoretical schools of thought which require advanced training and rigorous application in order to grasp their full interpretive potentials.

Within this framework has emerged phenomenological sociology and ethnomethodological sociology. Unlike the more traditional approaches in sociological theory and methodology which emphasize the historical and functional character of social behaviour, phenomenological sociology and ethnomethodological sociology are interpretive approaches to social life which emphasize 'the need to understand social action from the point of view of the social actor.'[4] In keeping with man's primordial urge to know and understand himself and his relationship to others, these two approaches attempt to identify (1) the meanings people find in their world—things, persons, events; (2) the perspectives from which people see themselves and others, and (3) the motives that underlie their behaviour. We might even suggest that these approaches exemplify the best motives and the most correct purpose for any social and behavioural science. 'Some have argued', say Chinoy and Hewitt, 'that this is the essential core of sociology.'[5]

If it is true that even original ideas have intellectual roots in the past reflections of thoughtful people, then it is fair to say that the ideational matrix within which phenomenological sociology and ethnomethodological sociology found roots and sprang to life is Husserlian philosophy and Mannheimian sociology. Though more will be said about both of these schools of thought later, a handy distinction is justified here between the traditional sociology of knowledge and phenomenological sociology as is practised today. The distinction is not so much a kind as it is an emphasis in analytical approaches and perspectives, for whereas 'phenomenological sociologists are interested in the foundations in intersubjective consciousness (individual's own personalistic reflections) of everyday life, the traditional sociology of knowledge has dealt with the relationship between socio-historical circumstances and knowledge, particularly intellectual knowledge.'[6] The most readily acclaimed expositor of the sociology of knowledge, Karl Mannheim, did not intend nor was he ever aware that from within his intellectual dominion two sub-disciplines were destined to spring—especially from his major work, *Ideology and Utopia* (1949),[7] providing the seedbed for further and divergent ideas. Mannheim drew heavily from his German countryman, Dilthey, whose philosophical writings in hermeneutics, i.e., the art of interpretation, produced in Mannheim the notion that knowledge is a product of one's own social and cultural setting. 'For Mannheim', wrote Sjoberg and Nett, 'knowledge is a product of one's social position, especially one's social class, within a society.'[8] Whereas Mannheim was almost exclusively interested in the socio-historical matrix of intellectual knowledge, later phenomenological and ethnomethodological sociologists turned their interest and attention to extremely subjectivistic, privatistic, and individualistic phenomena in the social arena.

A highly regarded extrapolation of Mannheim's early work coupled with phenomenological sensitivity to interpretation is found in Berger and Luckmann's work. 'Their basic assumption', explain Wallace and Wolf, 'is that everyday reality is a socially constructed system in which people give phenomena a certain order of reality....'[9] Though Berger and Luckmann consider themselves revisionist sociologists of knowledge, their work is quite frequently cited as a good example of phenomenological sociology. They have explained rather carefully the duplicity of people's socially constructed reality—its objective as well as its subjective characteristics. With respect to the former, society, though admittedly a human product, is nevertheless and undeniably an objective reality which is another way of saying that society is external to the individual person who, in a real sense, is actually a product of society. However, as regards the subjective quality of reality socially constructed, Berger and Luckmann have written this: 'Everyday life presents itself as a reality interpreted by men and subjectively meaningful to them as a coherent world. Thus, society is actually constructed by activity that expresses meaning.'[10] Because both phenomenological and ethnomethodological sociologists are predicated on the 'point of view of the actor', it is easy to see how the sociology of knowledge, particularly as done by Berger and Luckmann, gets unsolicited credit for nurturing the rise of these two sub-disciplines. When in an earlier book, Berger says, 'Worlds are socially constructed and socially maintained'[11], he is articulating the perimeters of phenomenology and ethnomethodology; and when he goes on to say, 'their continuing reality, both objective (as common, taken-for-granted facticity) and subjective (as facticity imposing itself on individual consciousness), depends upon specific social processes, namely those processes that ongoingly reconstruct and maintain the particular worlds in question'[12], he corroborates their predisposition to study reality as interpreted by people in their everyday activities. Particularly, phenomenological sociology is sensitive to the inevitable threat to people these interpretations of social worlds cause, and the realization that a social base for continued interpretation is necessary for the sociologist himself is of special concern and interest to phenomenological sociologists. Within this context, we are later to discuss the practical as well as scientifically necessary employment of brackets around certain presumptions of phenomenologists and ethnomethodologists in order for them to be able to do their work.

Before we move on to a rather careful evaluation of each of the two sub-disciplines under discussion here, it might be helpful to compare and contrast briefly basic attitudes which characterize the phenomenologists' and the ethnomethodologists' perceptions of each other and their sociological colleagues outside their particular schools of thought and activity. Both for the traditional sociologist and the layman in the street, objects, events, and persons of the domain of everyday life are believed to exist independently of the mode of inquiry addressed to them—a simple philosophy of commonsense reality. For phenomenological and ethnomethodological sociologists, there is neither necessity nor justification for the constructing or the assuming of such a position about the 'real' world. Rather, for analytical purposes, what 'really' *is there* is irrelevant; but what *is thought to be there* by a social group is central. 'Both phenomenologists and ethnomethodologists', explains Heap and Roth, 'suspend or "bracket" the belief that such objects are independent of the mode of inquiry used to make the objects observable.'[13]

Therefore, instead of taking phenomena from the 'natural order' for analysis as do the sociohistorical and functional schools of sociologists, the ethnomethodologists and the phenomenological sociologists hold in abeyance any truth-valid-real judgment about that order and concentrate their attention upon the 'real' world as it is thought, believed, and perceived to be by a social group. As Heap and Roth have carefully pointed out, another discernible difference between phenomenological and ethnomethodological sociology is their variant forms of reductionism. In the former, for instance, things in the 'real' world are *reduced* to things of immediate consciousness and are understood as being constituted 'in and through' intentional acts of consciousness. However, for ethnomethodology, the objectivized things of the social environment are *reduced* to the interpretational operations which assemble and reassemble 'things' for the on-going constitution of the real world according to varying situations. Thus, conclude Heap and Roth, for phenomenological sociology, 'the foundational nexus of meaning' in man's world is that of 'immediate consciousness', whereas for ethnomethodology, 'the foundational nexus of meaning' is to be found in the 'immediately present, directly observed social situation' in the real world.[14] But, we should be quick to point out that anything which supposedly transcends this nexus (whether thought of as outside immediate consciousness or objects outside social situations) is bracketed, held in suspension, or 'put out of play' as relates to any analytical description or interpretation of the social world of human experience. The domain of phenomenological inquiry necessarily is limited to the analysis and interpretation of recognizable structures of immediate consciousness while the domain of ethnomethodological inquiry is focused specifically upon the limited perimeter of human activity which tends to construct, for the actors in the social matrix, a sense of objective realness about the world.

Phenomenology

The term 'phenomenology' as it is used by Edmund Husserl (1859–1938) in his most notable philosophical treatise, *Ideas: Introduction to Pure Phenomenology* (1913), designates first of all a principle of philosophical and scientific method. The usual method of natural science proceeds from a body of accepted truth and seeks to extend its conquest of the unknown by putting questions to nature and compelling it to answer. The phenomenological method adopts a softer approach. Setting aside all presuppositions and suppressing hypotheses (as far as humanly possible through rigorous self-examination), it seeks to devise techniques of observation, description, and classification which will permit it to disclose structures and connections in nature which do not yield to experimental techniques. *Ideas* was written with a view to clearing up the distinction between phenomenological psychology, which Husserl regarded as a legitimate, but secondary, science, and phenomenological philosophy, which, he was prepared to maintain, is the foundation of all science. When a sociologist or psychologist conducts a phenomenological investigation, he puts aside all the usual theories and assumptions which have governed research in that field; but he cannot rid himself of all presuppositions (such as, for example, the belief in the existence of the external world, the constancy of nature, etc.). As Plato saw, every science (except philosophy) must proceed upon some assumptions. To fulfill its promise, the phenomenological approach must bring us at last to an absolutely presuppositionless science. Pure phenomenology, or phenomenological philosophy, is, in Husserl's opinion, precisely that. (It has long been the aspiration of philosophers to make their science an absolute one, one that rids itself of all presuppositions and stands with open countenance before pure Being. Husserl stands in this tradition.)

Husserl pointed out that it seems innocent enough to explain consciousness in terms of natural causes until we recollect that matter and the laws which govern its behaviour are themselves part of our experience. This, according to Husserl, is the point at which the philosopher must step in. His primary task, in fact, will be to distinguish within experience the part that *experiences* from the part that is *experienced*. He talks, for example, of 'suspending' our natural beliefs, including the fundamental conviction of every healthy mind that there is a world 'out there', that there are other selves, and so on. We are asked to 'alter' this natural standpoint, to 'disconnect' our beliefs about causation and motion, to 'put them out of action'. This is, of course, only a methodological procedure, in order to help us overcome our animal bias and make it possible for us to take a coolly intellectual view of things. Greek philosophy used the term *epoche* to indicate the suspension of judgment. Husserl presses this term into his service.

As we shall immediately see, the phenomenological approach in sociology is based upon this particular philosophical foundation. Its beginnings can be detected in earlier periods of the discipline's development, but only in the third quarter of this century has it become a major theoretical and methodological school of thought gathering prominent and numerous followers and making grand efforts to contribute to the science. Husserl's phenomenology, as implied above, is as Timascheff suggested 'a critique of positivism or naturalistic empiricism which assumes that scientists through their five senses can investigate the world and build a body of knowledge that accurately reflects the objective reality of the world.'[15] This kind of naive empiricism is severely criticized by phenomenologists because it simplistically views the human mind as merely an empty container, or, as Edie has observed, the human mind is perceived to be nothing but 'the passive receptor of discrete, simple, atomic impressions from the 'outside world'.[16]

Husserl's phenomenology, then, was a major philosophical programme aimed at disclosing the absolute ground of human knowledge. His quest was based on a search for essences, which were seen as being unbound to the cultural or social sphere and thus not susceptible to the relativism and commonplace prejudices that characterize that realm. 'Husserl's fully developed philosophy', says Dickens, 'may be characterized as a philosophical hermeneutic aimed at disclosing the absolute grounds of human knowledge through a bringing to light of the unexpressed presuppositions which characterize that knowledge.'[17] Therefore, it is safe to say that, admittedly, the scientific status of phenomenologically informed inquiry is not based on the false guarantee of an absolute zero point as a starting point, but rather, it is the bringing to light of hidden biases and pretheoretical notions which constitute the objectivity of phenomenology-based inquiry. Because of the essentially historical nature of all understanding, the task of phenomenological clarification is always one of continuous criticism and re-examination. Husserl believed that a real and objective world exists, but because it is known only through subjective human consciousness, it is a socially constructed reality when it is interpreted. Phenomenology is considered a radical philosophical position which questions the empirical foundations of sociology as well as 'challenges the possibility of objective scientific knowledge, uninfluenced by the subjective consciousness of the investigator.'[18]

As we move from a brief but hopefully informative exposure to pure phenomenology in the domain of philosophy to that of applied phenomenology in the domain of sociology, we must remember that phenomenological sociology must be regarded as the antithesis of neopositivism. As noted above, the development of phenomenological sociology questions the empirical foundations of sociology, thereby challenging the adequacy and meaningfulness of traditional sociological knowledge. If phenomenological sociology is to have any claim to a distinctive perspective and any relationship to Husserl's phenomenology, Timasheff says that 'it must focus on the analysis of the structure of consciousness and relationship of the consciousness of the individual to the social fabric.'[19]

It should be emphasized at this point that Husserl actually knew little of the concrete or conceptual problems of the social and behavioural sciences. Yet, even though there is strong sentiment in certain philosophical as well as sociological circles that phenomenological sociology is simply not possible, there is a vocal, literate, and growing body of sociologists who are setting about the development of just this kind of approach, building primarily on the work of the German expatriate Alfred Schutz who is considered more or less the founder of phenomenological sociology, or at least responsible for the introduction and development of the sub-discipline on American soil. In his work, he attempted to clarify Max Weber's concept of 'action' and his method of 'ideal type' construction. Schutz, explain Heap and Roth, 'revealed the invariant formal structures of the life-world—the realms of manipulation and the system of relevance and typification.'[20] Before we discuss Schutz's contributions, it should be pointed out that early philosophically-inclined sociologists in Europe had already begun to explore some of the issues addressed in phenomenology, particularly the German sociologist Alfred Vierkandt (1867–1952), and the Frenchman Jules Monnerot of the same period. Vierkandt, whose books include *Natural and Cultural People* (1895), and *Theory of Society* (1922), believed that society is the sum total of human interaction (not a novel idea to be sure) and his method, called 'ideational abstraction' consisted of a quest 'for basic unreducible concepts clarified through contemplation'. This emphasis on the 'irreducible' and 'contemplation' plays heavily in Schutz's work. Monnerot, author of *Social Facts Are Not Things* (1946), was rabidly anti-Durkheimian as suggested in the title of his book. His work consisted of a study of social situations which precipitate immediate experiences analysable by sociology—a sociology built upon the conviction that 'social facts', as Durkheim called social phenomena, are really just humanly defined and perceived 'conditions' or situations, thus factual only in the sense that humanly contrivances might be considered facts.

Alfred Schutz (1899–1959) was a social philosopher who fled Germany in 1939 to escape the Nazis. Gifted and talented in banking and ingenuity, Schutz took a daytime position in a New York City bank to support himself and taught social philosophy classes in the evening at the New School for Social Research in 1943. Nine years later, he became professor of sociology and philosophy and continued to teach at the New School until his death in 1959. Schutz is generally credited with introducing phenomenology to American sociology. He assigned central importance to the meaning individuals impart to situations in everyday life and adapted Husserl's philosophy to sociology as well as incorporated Weber's concept of *verstehen* or subjective understanding into his system. In his attempt to apply Husserl's phenomenological philosophy to social science problems, Schutz found that Weber's concept of *verstehen* fitted nicely with his own emphasis upon individual consciousness. Schutz fundamentally believed that the 'experience and assumption of shared meanings built the foundation which made social life possible.'

The main source of Schutz's writings for a careful and systematic presentation of his system is *The Phenomenology of the Social World*, (first published in 1932 but recently reprinted by Northwestern University Press in 1967). His papers and lectures have recently been combined into three *Collected Papers*: Volume One, *The Problem of Social Reality* (1962); Volume Two, *Studies in Social Theory* (1964); and Volume Three, *Studies in Phenomenological Philosophy* (1966), all published by Martinus Mijhoff in The Hague. Two major elements in social relations which became the focus of Schutz's analysis are what he labelled 'uniqueness and typification'. All repetitive social situations constitute a process called typification-categorizing of situations and persons into types based on socially shared definitions and meanings. In face-to-face relations, typification is necessarily modified by unique situations. Thus, the rule of thumb is that the more personal the relationship, the more unique its character is bound to be; and the more impersonal the relationship, the more typified. For a critical discussion of this facet of Schutz's work, see Helmut R. Wagner's edited volume, entitled *Alfred Schutz on Phenomenology and Social Relations* (1970). For Schutz, the meaning that the individual imparts to situations in everyday life is of prime importance; he puts the spotlight on the individual's own definition of the situation. And he believes that the meaning an individual imparts to the interaction situation may be shared by the person with whom he is interacting; Schutz calls this 'reciprocity of perspectives'. An example Wallace and Wolf use to explain the idea is that of members in an orchestra. Because the musicians in an orchestra share their meanings of the situation with the conductor, the musicians could exchange positions with the conductor and experience the situation the way the conductor does. 'Shared meaning', Wallace and Wolf explain,[21] 'may be assumed and experienced in the interaction situation. In such situations, people are acting on the basis of taken-for-granted assumptions about reality.' Husserl spoke, in his system, of an 'ontology of the life-world', meaning, we assume, that *a priori* framework of the humanly experienced environment within which man lives his life. Schutz, not wishing merely to reiterate this philosophical postulate, 'sought to elucidate the *a priori* structure of the world in which sociological phenomena are apprehended.'[22] Therefore, we can assume that rather than seeking the 'essence' of, say, corporations or the state or religion, Schutz would rather turn to the structures of the life-world which those entities presuppose, such as a world of contemporaries beyond our reach grasped through socially distributed and pragmatically generated typifications. For Schutz, these structures inherent in social phenomena, i.e., *a priori* 'ontological' givens, included intersubjectivity of which he began but never completed, an interpretation through a kind of scientific methodology he called the 'constitutive phenomenology of the natural attitude'. This natural attitude, which intrigued him so much, is defined as that attitude of naive belief in the existence of the world as perceived and really believed to be 'out there'. 'Life-world', 'intersubjectivity', and the 'natural attitude' are the tripartite pillars of Schutz's theory of phenomenological sociology, and, claim Heap and Roth, 'the type of sociology founded on Schutz's phenomenology is constituted most notably by Berger and Luckmann'.[23]

Before further consideration can be given to Berger and Luckmann, who incidentally consider themselves phenomenological sociologists of knowledge, some attention must be focused upon Karl Mannheim who is to the sociology of knowledge what Schutz is to phenomenological sociology, and, as with the latter, so with the former, Edmund Husserl's philosophical system proved determinative in the development of their various schools of thought. Karl Mannheim (1893–1947), a German sociologist, was born in Budapest and died in London. He studied at Berlin and Paris, and at Heidelberg under Max Weber. His thought resembles that of such philosophers as Comte and Hegel, who believed that in the past man had been dominated by the historical process whereas in the future he would gain ascendency over it. In his first and most important book, *Ideology and Utopia* (1936), Mannheim asserted that the act of cognition must not be regarded as the effort of a purely theoretical consciousness, because the human consciousness is permeated by nontheoretical elements arising both from man's participation in social life and in the streams and tendencies of willing, which work themselves out contemporaneously in that life. Mannheim, therefore, argued for a new discipline to address this new level of understanding and analysing man's own knowledge, viz., the sociology of knowledge. According to Mannheim, this new discipline revealed that all knowledge, or at least knowledge of things human, was situation-bound (*situationsgebunden*)—that is, tied to a given constellation of sociohistorical circumstances. Each age develops its own style of thought, and comparisons between these styles are impossible, since each posits a different basic sphere. Even within each age there are conflicting tendencies toward conservation, on the one hand, and toward change on the other. Commitment to conservation tends to produce 'ideologies'—to falsify thought by excessive idealization of the past and overemphasis on the factors making for stability. Intentness on change is apt to produce 'utopias', which overvalue both the future and factors leading to change.

Mannheim suggested, by way of anticipating the later sociologists of knowledge such as Berger and Luckmann, that between ideology and utopia there is at least the possibility of completely realistic (*situationsgerecht*) thought that functions without friction within the given framework of life, and is set neither on pushing forward nor on holding back the development of society. But Mannheim places little emphasis on this possibility. He sees a very strong tendency toward the polarization of society into hostile camps. Only the comparatively uncommitted intelligentsia is likely to approach nearer the truth. From its special and particularly favourable vantage point, it could, and should, elaborate a 'total perspective' which would synthesize the conflicting contemporary world views and thereby neutralize, and to some extent overcome, their one-sided-ness. Such a 'dynamic synthesis', Mannheim thought, is the nearest possible approximation to a truly realistic attitude, within the limitations imposed upon a given epoch. He held, therefore, that every sociohistorical situation is located at a specific point along a unilinear, ever-progressing and never-returning temporal continuum— history. Each situation is, therefore, unique, and the knowledge to which it gives birth, and which is true within it, is equally unique, bound to its time and place, and relative.

However, Mannheim, as the father of the sociology of knowledge, was not primarily concerned with the truth of propositions. Rather, he operated with a radically different conception of 'truth'. To him, truth is an attribute, not so much of discourse, as of reality. The individual who is in contact with the living forces of his age has the truth, or better, is in the truth—a conception which shows at once Mannheim's Marxism, his historicism, and his pragmatism. He was moving close to the belief that the traditional correspondence of thought-and-reality should be replaced by a correspondence of thought-and-situation. Mannheim, in short, was interested in the genuineness, rather than in the truth *per se*, of a given world view.

As we have seen, Mannheim owes much to Husserl's phenomenology. Coser has pointed out that 'what impressed Mannheim in Husserl's phenomenology was not the attempt to penetrate to knowledge of pure essences ... but rather Husserl's emphasis on the "intentionality" of human thought.'[24] Husserl, as we noted earlier, has contended that the sharp separation between knower and known and the essentially passive conception of the act of knowing in most modern philosophy had to be abandoned in favour of an activist conception of knowledge through 'intentional' activity. Peter Berger and Thomas Luckmann's leading work in the phenomenological sociology of knowledge is their book, entitled, *The Social Construction of Reality* (1967). They are quick to point out their distinction from a more traditional sociology of knowledge, says Timasheff, because their emphasis has not been particularly concerned, as is the traditional sociology of knowledge, 'with epistemological questions about the validity of knowledge (i.e., the extent to which ideas or what people think they know are shaped by social and historical circumstances) and with the history of ideas.'[25]

Though Berger and Luckmann are more or less unconcerned with questions of the ultimate validity of knowledge *per se*, they are rather profoundly concentrated in their work upon the question of how whatever is accepted as knowledge in a society has come to be accepted as such. In other words, they are primarily concerned with 'the processes by which *any* body of "knowledge" comes to be socially established as "reality".' In their own writings, they have contended that the sociology of knowledge is concerned with the analysis of the social construction of reality. Thus, having departed from the traditional empirical foundation of scientific sociology, the phenomenologically oriented sociologists—under the various but everpresent influence of Husserl—hold the reality of the social world in abeyance, preferring to focus not upon 'social facts' so-called, but upon the structure of intersubjective consciousness and the creation of social meaning in human interaction. In a differentiated branch of phenomenological sociology, known as ethnomethodology, as we shall see later, concern is centered on the process by which commonsense reality is constructed in everyday face-to-face interaction.

Several concepts which, though not unique to Schutz and phenomenological sociology, have received special consideration and sometimes unique interpretations and usage should, for a moment, capture our attention. The meaning and use of the concept of 'reduction', though already mentioned earlier, deserves a further hearing because of its central place in Schutz's understanding of what phenomenological sociology is all about. 'The phenomenologist', he writes in 1962, 'does not deny the existence of the outer world, but for his analytical purpose he makes up his mind to suspend belief in its existence—that is, to refrain intentionally and systematically from all judgements related directly or indirectly to the existence of the outer world.'[26] This bracketing or suspending of judgement or holding in abeyance as best one can predispositions of interpretation in some ways is the core of phenomenological sociology. 'What we have put into brackets', Schutz goes on to say, 'is not only the existence of outer world, along with all the things in it, inanimate and animate, including fellow-men, cultural objects, society and its institutions ... but also the propositions of all sciences.'[27]

One of Schutz's and later phenomenological sociologists' problematical terms employed readily in philosophical phenomenology is the concept of 'essence', a term of questionable utility for the sociologist and one that requires definition. Heap and Roth, more so than any others since Schutz, have offered specific help in this matter. 'Essence', they write, 'may be taken to be that intuited invariant quality without which the intended object, the phenomenon, would not be what it is . . . . Essence has as its reference the *a priori* realm of possibilities which precedes that of actualities.'[28] Therefore, say the phenomenologists, essence is 'intuited' from the intended object—object as 'experienced', as 'perceived'. Schutz has explained that essence is 'arrived at' through the method of 'reduction' and 'imaginative variation'. An object's defining or distinguishing qualities and characteristics are arrived at *a posteriori*, through logical operations based on factual knowledge about actual objects in the taken-to-be-real world.

Another highly problematical but potentially useful concept for phenomenological sociologists discussed by Heap and Roth is 'phenomenon'. Present-day sociologists employing phenomenological language and method seem drawn to Husserl's dictum—'to the things themselves'—which seems to mean a return to the phenomena-as-given in the immediate consciousness. 'By phenomenon', explain Heap and Roth, 'Husserl meant that which, having been subjected to the phenomenological reduction, is purified from the reality attributed to it by "naive consciousness".'[29] A phenomenon as such only becomes available when we cease to treat an object as real, and begin to treat the object as meant, an intended, as it appears. Mention here of 'intend' calls to mind the role 'intentionality' played in Husserl's formal language and methodology. Though it is true that intentionality can be equated with 'purpose', it is so only at the predictive level of experience, that is, the level of judgement or of 'action' in Weber's sense. 'However', Heap and Roth explain, 'Husserl's theory of intentionality refers also to the pre-predicative level. This is the level of immediate experience, of perception, of so-called non-meaningful behaviour in Weber's sense.'[30]

When a phenomenological sociologist uses terms such as 'reality', 'subjective', and 'objective', the uninitiated should be careful in not assuming a particular taken-for-granted meaning. These terms for phenomenologists become specialized nomenclature in the sociological laboratory. Subjective reality, Timasheff has explained, means 'an individual's acceptance of a set of beliefs, expectations, definitions, meanings, and evaluations as his or her own view of the world which develops through the process of socialization', whereas 'Objective reality is socially shared reality; when meanings are shared by a group, they become objectified by virtue of being external to the individual persons who share common typification, i.e., common evaluations about types of persons and situations and the behaviour appropriate to them, share a common social world.'[31]

Thus, we can see that a social structure is the sum total of these typifications and of the recurrent patterns of interaction established by means of them. Finally, and in keeping with the specialized definitions of common sociological terms, we are able to define 'institution' in a phenomenologically correct fashion by saying that institution is a 'set of patterned (habitualized) reciprocal typifications.'[32] The individual experiences the institutional world as an objective reality but the apparently objective world is really a humanly constructed objectivity. A reflective consciousness, however, is able to superimpose the quality of logic upon the institutional order. And 'the logic by which the institutions of society are integrated is known as *legitimation*, which interrelates more limited meanings embodied in specific institutions by means of broader schemes of meaning.'[33] Thus, in keeping with the phenomenological spirit of Schutz's sociology, it can be said that all symbolic universes and all legitimations are human products; their existence has its reality or validity in the lives of concrete individuals, and has no empirical status apart from these lives.

Schutz specifically and phenomenological sociology generally have not gone without criticism—some severe and unjust, some productive and insightful. A strong critique of a single deductive model for the form of a theory, such as expounded in this school of thought, comes from Maurice Natanson, an existential and phenomenological philosopher and sound student of the social and behavioural sciences. In his critiques and formal writings, he has called upon social scientists to be more self-critical, more theoretical, and certainly more philosophically literate in their conception of theory and theory-construction, calling upon them to examine more internally critically the 'worldview' underlying their own arguments about theory and methodology. Warshay has provided an excellent example of both pro and con deductive models: '. . . tending toward the deductive model', he explains, 'is an "objective" worldview that, following a materialistic conception of consciousness, places the individual in the context of all natural phenomena,' yet, he counters, 'tending away from the deductive model, and from modern science as usually understood, is a "subjective" worldview that, following a phenomenological approach to social reality, sees natural science as but one aspect of the intersubjective world produced by the activity of consciousness.'[34] In spite of Natanson's criticisms of phenomenologi-

cal sociology, he has made significant contributions to its development and integrity in the scientific and philosophical communities,
especially in his edited volume entitled *Philosophy of the Social
Sciences* (1963). For instance, Natanson has employed the concepts
of social role and typification to analyse 'intersubjective consciousness'—Schutz's term. Individuals internalize conceptions of social
roles involving typification, i.e., socially shared expectations and
evaluations of behaviour in particular situations, which include
'self-typifications', that is, images and evaluations of the roles one
personally plays as well as role typifications of others. Natanson has
used extensively these concepts not only to analyse 'sociality', a
major concern of his, but also the relation of persons to science, art,
and religion. And as it stands now, Natanson's constructive criticism
of phenomenological sociology's weaknesses and his effective utilization of its strengths has served well the further development of one
of American sociology's most provocative and challenging theoretical
constructs and methodological programs since the appearance of
symbolic interaction.

Ethnomethodology

Growing out of the general developments of sociology of knowledge
came a widespread legitimization of fundamental questions about
the traditional discipline's presupposition about its subject matter,
its view of the world, and cognitive processes operative in human
behaviour. For example, How do sociologists and other groups of
humans create and sustain for each other the presumption that the
social world has a real character? And, as a result of posing such a
question, a more 'real' phenomenon revolves around the complex
ways people go about consciously and unconsciously constructing,
maintaining, and altering their sense of an external social reality.
'In fact,' Turner has pointed out in some detail, 'the cement that
holds society together may not be the values, norms, common definitions, exchange payoffs, role bargains, interest coalitions, and the
like of current social theory', rather he argues convincingly that it
may be 'people's explicit and implicit "methods" for creating the
presumption of a social order.'[35] These comments, of course, lead us
directly to a consideration of ethnomethodology which, as Zimmerman is quick to point out, 'is not a comprehensive theory of
society . . . (but rather) is an approach to the study of the funda-

mental bases of social order.'[36] Ethnomethodology concerns itself primarily with those structures of social interaction which would be invariant to the revolutionary transformation of a society's institutions. As a perspective, and as yet hardly claiming to be a 'sub-discipline', ethnomethodology has not concerned itself with such issues as power, the distribution of resources in society, or the historical shape of institutions.

Phenomenological sociologists understand the task of sociology fundamentally as describing precisely how we see the world, and although they emphasize that our perceptions are moulded intrinsically by our concepts, the phenomenological sociologists are not recognizably different from the sociologists of knowledge. The difference in emphasis, not in kind, seems to accentuate the domain of the ethnomethodologists. They all examine the ways we come to have similar perceptions to those of others—how we put together the phenomena we experience in such a way that we all construct a similar or shared 'everyday world'. Though ethnomethodologists really acknowledge their indebtedness to both phenomenological and the sociology of knowledge traditions, they are equally quick to emphasize their distinctive perspective.

The work of such sociologists as Schutz, Berger, and Luckmann is primarily philosophical and macroscopic, stressing the primacy of studying the processes of human consciousness, and concerned with the general nature of realities. The ethnomethodologists, on the other hand, have extended the concerns of symbolic interactionism and phenomenology, and focus on microscopic aspects of human behaviour. They are especially interested in the empirical analysis of the ways in which particular meanings are constructed. Yet, it must be noted that in the area of small group (micro) versus large group (macro) sociology, many sociologists, particularly ethnomethodologists, involved in micro-sociology do not accept the rationale for a separate theory of micro and macro analysis. The ethnomethodologists unreservedly acclaim the exclusive validity of micro approaches and contend that larger social structures can be meaningfully understood only by studying small groups and other face-to-face situations. For ethnomethdologists, the theoretical concern centres around the processes by which commonsense reality is constructed in everyday face-to-face interaction. With this focus, it is plain to see that ethnomethodology can quite rightly be judged a distinctive branch of phenomenological sociology, which, in common with other phenomenological forms in the United States, derived in large part from the work of Alfred Schutz, as discussed above. It is obvious that Schutz strongly influenced Harold Garfinkel, the founder of ethnomethodology, who sought to understand the methods employed by people to make sense out of their world.

However, before we take a closer look at Garfinkel's work, an overview of ethnomethodology seems in order. This approach to sociology studies the process by which people invoke certain taken-for-granted rules about behaviour with which they interpret an interaction situation and make it meaningful. 'To ethnomethodology', explain Wallace and Wolf, 'the interpretive process is a phenomenon for investigation.' They point out that 'ethnomethodology does not aim to "explain" human behaviour or to show why, for example, places and generations vary in their suicide and divorce rates, or why religion "really" exists.'[38] The emphasis, rather, in this perspective is on description (reflecting affinities with phenomenology), and the subject matter—people's methods of making sense of their social world—poses different questions from those asked by traditional sociology. Ethnomethodologists are, therefore, interested in the interpretations people use to make sense of social settings.

As we have seen, Harold Garfinkel is the recognized founder of ethnomethodology. Born in 1917, Garfinkel completed his Ph.D. (Harvard) in 1952, and aside from a couple of brief teaching stints at Ohio State and the University of Chicago, he has taught since 1954 at the University of California at Los Angeles. To date, he has published no single major work, but has had many of his best articles published in a collected volume, entitled, *Studies in Ethnomethodology*, by Prentice-Hall in 1967. Garfinkel's work differs considerably from Durkheim's over the issue of 'social facts'. Garfinkel saying no and Durkheim saying yes to their *sui generis* objective reality. Ethnomethodology, rather, sees the objective reality of social facts, says Garfinkel, as an 'on-going accomplishment of the concerted activities of everyday life.'[39] Much of the distinction in perspective between traditional sociology and ethnomethodology can be established in the definition of the latter term. The term's meaning can be understood in terms of a form of folk technique by which actors in social interaction 'think up' a series of accounts or verbal description that enable them to construct social reality as they perceive it. Ethnomethodologists, on the other hand, are interested in the ways in which people create a sense of reality. By 'making sense' of events in terms of preconceived order for society, people create a world that is indeed ordered.

The term 'ethnomethodology' itself was coined while Garfinkel was working at Yale with their cross-cultural files. During this time he was working on an analysis of jury tape-recordings when he came upon the file card categories of 'ethnobotany', 'ethnophysiology', 'ethnophysics', etc. He became extremely interested in how the jurors knew what they were doing in doing the work of jurors. In such things as the juror's use of some kind of knowledge of the way in which the organized affairs of the society operated, it occurred to him that on the jury deliberation project that he was faced with jurors who were actually doing methodology. 'He created "ethnomethodology",' explains Roy Turner, 'because "ethno" refers to the availability to a member of commonsense knowledge of his society as common-sense knowledge of the "whatever".'[40] Thus ethnomethodology is the study of 'folk' or commonsense methods employed by people to make sense of everyday activities by constructing and maintaining social reality.

Ethnomethodologists do not use a commonsense method, rather, they study commonsense methods of constructing reality. They use, explains Timasheff, the 'phenomenological frame-work' which is in essence the antithesis of the everyday commonsense interpretation of social life. The term itself, adds Mullins, was coined by Harold Garfinkel 'to reflect his belief that the proper subjet for social science is the way in which ordinary people establish rational behaviour patterns.'[41] Ordinary people use various methods to determine what is happening in society; 'this methodology', continues Mullins, 'is "ethno" in that, like "ethnobotany", it is derived from folk knowledge rather than from professional scientific procedures.'[42] Hence, ethnomethodology is the study of the methods used by members of a group for understanding community, making decisions, being rational, accounting for action, and so on.

Garfinkel has proposed the idea of an emergent, negotiable, shifting order in his ethnomethodological programme, emphasizing the vast web of commonsense understandings and folk classifications that all members of commonplace organized social situations take for granted—these are still in flux. There persists a preference for qualitative techniques in field research over the merely quantitative. Garfinkel stresses, Warshay points out, 'the common understandings underlying simple daily social conversations and transactions'.

Ethnomethodologists, he continues, 'study both biography and purpose of actors as well as analysis of the commonsense understandings of ordinary social life.'[43] It must occasionally be pointed out that, strictly speaking, ethnomethodology is not a new research method. It does not, for instance, seek to answer the question of how society is possible by introducing sociologists to new research techniques. Rather, explains Jonathan Turner, 'ethnomethodology is concerned with the study of a phenomenon that has received little attention within the intellectual confines of traditional theoretical perspectives. It seeks to study, Turner explains, 'this phenomenon by the use of many research strategies, including variants of observational and participant-observational methods.'[44] Garfinkel wrote a short paper, later included in Roy Turner's edited volume, *Ethnomethodology*, entitled 'The Origins of the Term "Ethnomethodology" ', in which the personal as well as the intellectual dimensions of the term's emergence are recounted.[45] Seldom are details such as these available to give posterity an exact account of a theoretical term's birth. Earlier, we saw how Husserl's work called for 'bracketing' or holding in abeyance the external world *per se* while studying 'pure consciousness'. But, with ethnomethodology, there is a specific bracketing of the social order while studying intersubjective consciousness in the interactive situation. Instead of studying the social order *per se* or empirically ascertaining objective reality, ethnomethodology seeks to understand how people in interaction create and maintain a conception of social reality. According to ethnomethodologists, what is most readily observable, and hence real, are the attempts by interacting humans to persuade each other that there is an order to specific social settings and to a broader society. 'What is "really real" ', then, explains Turner, 'are the methods people employ in constructing, maintaining, and altering for each other a sense of order—regardless of the content and substance of their formulations.'[46]

The sense of order is not what makes society possible, say the ethnomethodologists, but rather the capacity of humans to actively and continually create and use rules for persuading each other that there is a real world. They place much emphasis upon the necessity for understanding any situation from the point of view of the actors or interactional participants. 'Since meaning is seen as created in the process of interaction', explains Timasheff, 'its only reality is the interpretation given to it by the person involved in the interactive process, and this is what the investigator must seek to understand.'[47] As we have already seen, the ethnomethodologist is primarily interested in the world as perceived by people and as interpreted by them within social networks. The 'perceiving' component of this dual emphasis suggests affinities with phenomenological sociology, as we have seen already, and the latter is more suggestive of ethnomethodology's allegiance to the sociology of knowledge school. George Psathas has, in a rather fine way, articulated the nature and complexity of the relationship between these two fledgling schools in his essay entitled 'Ethnomethodology and Phenomenology'. For ethnomethodologists, what is directly observable are people's efforts to create a commonsense of social reality, and, explains Jonathan Turner, 'the substance of this reality is viewed as less interesting than the methods used by groups of people to construct, re-affirm, and alter a vision and image of what exists "out there".'[48]

Though ethnomethodology has not as yet refined or even identified its most effective analytical techniques, there are four more or less regularly employed methods evident in the work of most ethnomethodologists. Besides the tradition of participant-observation (well used in cultural anthropology and symbolic interaction), there is what is called the 'ethnomethodological experiment' which essentially calls for a disrupting of any interactive situation by acting (on the part, usually, of the researcher or one in his charge) incongruous with the situation's norms. 'Documentary interpretation', a third method, consists of taking behaviour, statements, etc., and other external appearances of the other (any other person or group) as a 'document' or reflection of an underlying pattern used to interpret appearances. And finally, a significant interest exists in linguistics as *communication of meaning*, with special attention placed upon the relationship between linguistic *form* and the *structure* of social interaction. The overlapping in methodological presuppositions and processes between ethnomethodology and phenomenology is reflected, as we said, in George Psathas' paper, and another comparative study appropriate to these methodological considerations is Norman K. Denzin's study of the similarities and dissimilarities between ethnomethodology and symbolic interaction, most recently discussed by him in his paper entitled 'Symbolic Interaction and Ethnomethodology: A Proposed Synthesis'. To the ethnomethodologist, symbols and meanings have no existence apart from their interpretation by persons in interaction. Ethnomethodology avoids the whole question of reality (a pitfall as these practitioners see it in virtually all traditional sociology), choosing rather to emphasize the study of the ways an image of social reality is created. 'Because they have rejected the basic assumption of empirical sociology,' says Timasheff, namely, that there is a real social and cultural world capable of being objectively studied by scientific methods, 'ethnomethodologists regard their approach as a radical break with all branches of traditional sociology and not merely another conceptual framework.'[49] One of the particularly problematical factors in their methodological process is their emphasis upon the uniqueness of each and every interactive situation and their suspicions about all generalizable similarities between interactive situations. Ethnomethodologists are interested in situations as 'creations' by participants who are viewed as having much freedom to alter, reinterpret, and change their social environment by acts of will.

Of course, their dubious feelings about all generalizations upon human behaviour are demonstrative of their ideological rejection of all metaphysical assumptions made by traditional empirical sociology.[50] The ethnomethodologist challenges traditional sociology's assumption that there is a sufficiently stable system of shared meanings in a society to provide a basis for meaningful responses to questionnaires or interviews or any type of research method in which the researcher fits subjects' responses or behaviour into predetermined categories. Wallace and Wolf, in their sympathetic defense of ethnomethodology have paid special attention to a concept employed in this kind of social analysis called 'accounting', which, in some ways at least, allows the perspective its skepticism about generalizations while not paralyzing its analytical interests. 'Accounting', they explain, 'is people's ability to announce to themselves and others the meaning they are getting out of a situation'. 'Accounts', they explain, 'involve both language and meaning; people are constantly giving linguistic or verbal accounts as they explain their actions.'[51] Garfinkel, for instance, has urged ethnomethodologists to call attention to reflexive practices, such as, when a child is asked to 'tell about' his or her own creative production and then proceeds to do so and to interpret the figures, shapes, and colours in the drawing to another person, the child is giving an 'account'. This technique, along with others mentioned earlier, has provided ethnomethodologists with the kind of practical research tools and topics which promise to advance the discipline through research and publication.

As might be suspected, the reaction of many sociologists has been to ignore, or misunderstand, or criticize, or in some happy cases integrate it into their own conventional approaches. Of course, as we have seen, a major criticism is ethnomethodology's neglect of what Berger and Luckmann call the objectification of social reality—a serious criticism by any standard and one which the discipline must come to grips with. And finally, from the macrosociologists, their rather formidable criticism is of ethnomethodologists' bracketing of the social order with major emphasis upon the interpretative situation, which precludes any adequate account being taken of such large systems as power or class structure. Needless to say, the ethnomethodologists have much work yet to do in the particular areas of criticism before they can become full participants in sociological research alongside traditional sociology.

NOTES

1. For a critical study of the literature on the crisis of meaning in contemporary society, see John H. Morgan, *In Search of Meaning: From Freud to Teilhard de Chardin* (Washington D.C., The University Press of America, 1977).

2. For a careful analysis of the concept of 'culture' in terms of its 'meaning-bearing qualities' as interpreted by symbolic anthropology, see John H. Morgan, 'Religion and Culture as Meaning Systems', *The Journal of Religion*, LVII, 4 (October, 1977), 363, 375.

3. A thorough investigation of the concept of man as an essentially interpretive animal is to be found in John H. Morgan (ed.), *Understanding Religion and Culture* (Washington D.C., The University Press of America, 1979).

4. Ely Chinoy and John P. Hewitt, *Sociological Perspective* (New York, Random House, 1975), p. 156.

5. Ibid.

6. Nicholas S. Timasheff and George Theodorson, *Sociological Theory* (New York, Random House, 1967), p. 352.

7. Karl Mannheim, *Ideology and Utopia* (New York, Harcourt, Brace, and World, 1949).

8. Gideon Sjoberg and Roger Nett, *A Methodology for Social Research* (New York, Harper and Row, 1968).

9. Ruth Wallace and Alison Wolf, *Contemporary Sociological Theory* (Englewood Cliffs, Prentice-Hall, 1980), p. 266.

10. Peter Berger and Thomas Luckmann, *The Social Construction of Reality* (New York, Doubleday, 1966), p. 19.

11. Peter L. Berger, *The Sacred Canopy* (New York, Doubleday, 1969), p. 45.

12. Ibid.
13. James Heap and Phillip Roth, 'On Phenomenological Society', *American Sociological Review*, 38 (June 1973), 288.
14. Ibid.
15. Timasheff and Theodorson, op. cit., 291.
16. James Edie, *What is Phenomenology?* (Chicago, Quandrangle Books, 1962), p. 19.
17. David Dickens, 'Phenomenology', in Scott McNall (ed.) *Theoretical Perspectives in Sociology* (New York, St. Martin's Press, 1979), p. 345.
18. See Timasheff and Theodorson, *Sociological Theory*, pp. 291–305. Also, for an informative discussion of Husserl's phenomenology with a sociological sensitivity, cf. Maurice Natanson, *Edmund Husserl Philosopher of Infinite Tasks* (Evanston, Northwestern University Press, 1973).
19. Timasheff and Theodorson, op. cit., p. 298.
20. Heap and Roth, op. cit., p. 287.
21. Wallace and Wolf, op. cit., p. 265.
22. Heap and Roth, op. cit., p. 287.
23. Ibid.
24. Lewis Coser, *Masters of Sociological Thought* (New York, Free Press, 1971), p. 454.
25. Timasheff and Theodorson, op. cit., p. 298.
26. Alfred Schutz, *The Problem of Social Reality*, Volume 1 (The Hague, Martinus Mijhoff, 1962), p. 104.
27. Ibid., p. 105.
28. Heap and Roth, op. cit., p. 283.
29. Ibid., p. 281.
30. Ibid., p. 280.
31. Timasheff and Theodorson, op. cit., p. 299.
32. Ibid.
33. Ibid.
34. Leon H. Warshay, *The Current State of Sociological Theory* (New York, David McKay, 1975), p. 112.
35. Jonathan Turner, *The Structure of Sociological Theory* (Homewood, The Dorsey Press, 1974), p. 321.
36. Don H. Zimmerman, Ethnomethodology', '*The American Sociologist*, 13 (February, 1978), 6–15.
37. The diversity of phenomenological sociology in the United States is brought out in the collection of essays edited by George Psathas, *Phenomenological Sociology: Issues and Applications* (New York, Wiley, 1973).
38. Wallace and Wolf, op. cit., p. 270.
39. Harold Garfinkel, *Studies in Ethnomethodology* (Englewood Cliffs, Prentice Hall, 1967), p. vii.
40. H. R. Wagner (ed.), *Alfred Schutz on Phenomenology and Social Relations* (Chicago, The University of Chicago Press, 1970), p. 16.
41. Nicholas C. Mullins, *Theories and Theory Groups in Contemporary American Sociology* (New York, Harper and Row, 1973), p. 184.
42. Ibid.
43. Warshay, op. cit., p. 37.

44. J. Turner, op. cit., p. 324.
45. R. Turner, *Ethnomethodology* (Balt, Penguin Books, 1974), pp. 16–17.
46. J. Turner, op. cit, p. 330.
47. Timasheff and Theodorson, op. cit., p. 302.
48. J. Turner, op. cit., p. 322.
49. Timasheff and Theodorson, op. cit., p. 301.
50. For a careful critique of this position, see Aaron V. Cicourel, *Method and Measurement in Sociology* (New York, Free Press, 1964).
51. Wallace and Wolf, op. cit., p. 272.

CHAPTER 10

Continuing Debate on Behaviourism, Structuralism and Quantitativism

I. *Behavioural Versus Structural Perspectives*

The most vexing problem in contemporary sociological theory concerns the relationship between individual and society. Theoretical orientations that conceptualize this relationship may be classified under four categories.[1]

1. *Nominalism.* The nominalist view, the oldest and the most extreme position, is that the group is not a real entity but merely a term used to refer to 'an assemblage of individuals'. In this perspective, the individual is the only real entity; general concepts such as society, group, culture and values are not regarded as useful in the study of human behaviour. The only thing that needs to be or can be explained is the behaviour of the individual. This is essentially the frame of reference of individual psychology which attempts to predict from one property of an individual organism to another, or to another set of behaviours and to formulate a universalistic explanation of a particular psychological process that holds for all men everywhere.

2. *Interactionism.* This perspective rejects the individual-group dichotomy and stresses, instead, the indivisibility of the two. Neither the group not the individual is real except in terms of the other and, therefore, interaction becomes the major concern. The interactionist doctrine combines biological, cultural, personal, and social explanations, and emphasizes the multiplicity of causative factors in the explanation of phenomena. Typical is Wirth's comment: 'Rather than settling the issue as to whether the individual or the group is the ultimate unit in terms of which social life must be analysed, the main stream of sociological and social-psychological thought has forgotten this issue and proceeded to analyse social phenomena as complexes of the meaningfully oriented actions of persons reciprocally related to one another.'[2] Interactionism is essentially the

social-psychological frame of reference which tends to ignore what is common to all men as well as what is unique to particular individuals but deals with what is common to classes of individuals in a particular culture or a particular social context.

3. *Neo-nominalism*. This is the reductionist perspective which accepts the existence of the group as an objective reality but claims that the individual is the more fundamental unit. Since society is made up of persons and of processes which have their locus and immediate origin in the person, social phenomena can be explained in terms of individual phenomena. Allport and Homans are two of the most ardent exponents of neonominalism. According to Allport:

The concept of a causal science on a purely social (non-psychological) plane is untenable, because in all science *explanation* is possible only by drawing upon the concepts of sciences at more elementary levels . . . The true basis for sociology is the social behaviour of the socialized individual, in other words, social psychology. The work of sociology is to describe collectivities of social behaviour and social change resulting from it in terms of the group, and to explain these phenomena in terms of 'the individual'.[3]

The neonominalists, reductionists or advocates of psychological sociology view social structure as 'a kind of convenient fiction or a shorthand designation for summarizing individual behaviour in aggregative terms'.[4]

4. *Realism*. 'This doctrine holds that (1) the group is just as real as the person, but that (2) both are abstract, analytical units, not concrete entities, and that (3) the group is understandable and explicable solely in terms of distinctly social processes and factors, not by reference to individual psychology. In short, modern realism is theoretical, analytical, and antireductionist.'[5] Durkheim and Radcliffe-Brown are only two of the most prominent masters of social thought who attest to the legitimacy and validity of the realist position.

We will concentrate primarily on neo-nominalism and realism. The former will be referred to as psychological perspective and the latter as the structural perspective. Let us consider the structural perspective first.

Durkheim viewed society as an entity *sui generis*. To him, the proper domain of sociology is the study of social facts which are the collective ways of acting, thinking, and feeling. 'These ways of thinking should not be confused with biological phenomena, since

they consist of representations and of actions; nor with psychological phenomena which exist only in the individual consciousness
and through it. They constitute, thus, a new variety of phenomena;
and it is to them exclusively that the term "social" ought to be
applied.'[6] Durkheim rejects the assumption that the ultimate
explanation of collective will emanates from human nature in
general and that, therefore, sociological laws are only a corollary
of the more general laws of psychology. Social processes are distinct in that they are external to the individual and independent of
his will. We can restrain our impulses because their process is
centrifugal, but the process of social restraint is centripetal.

Durkheim insists that social phenomena cannot be reduced to
individual phenomena. A whole is not identical with the sum of its
parts; society is not a mere sum of individuals. To argue that the
first origins of social phenomena are psychological because the only
elements making up society are individuals is like saying that
organic phenomena (human) can be explained by inorganic phenomena since living cells are only molecules of matter. The system
made up of individuals:

represents a specific reality which has its own characteristics. Of
course nothing collective can be produced if individual consciousnesses are not assumed, but this necessary condition is by itself
insufficient. These consciousnesses must be combined in a certain
way; social life results from this combination and is, consequently,
explained by it. Individual minds, forming groups by mingling and
fusing, give birth to a being, psychological if you will but constituting a psychic individuality of a new sort.[7]

Thus Durkheim contends: 'Since their essential characteristic consists in the power they possess of exerting, from outside, a pressure
on individual consciousnesses, they do not derive from individual
consciousnesses, and in consequence sociology is not a corollary of
psychology'[8]

The tendency to explain social life in terms of psychological
factors is often prompted by the assumption that certain qualities
such as religious sentiments, sexual jealousy, parental love, etc. are
innate in man, but, in reality these qualities result from the collective
social organization. Although collective life is not derived from
individual life, the two are nevertheless closely related; if the latter
cannot explain the former, it can at least facilitate its explanation.
Therefore, psychological training is a valuable lesson for the socio-

logist but he must free himself from it after receiving benefit from this lesson. He must go beyond it by special sociological training, abandon psychology as the centre of his operation and must establish himself in the very heart of social facts.

A variant of structuralism is the extreme view of cultural determinism suggested by Leslie White. According to him, human behaviour is made up of two distinct factors proceeding from two separate and independent sources—the organism and the cultural tradition. The infant organism could have been born into one cultural tradition as well as another, but from the point of view of subsequent behaviour, everything depends on the culture into which the baby is introduced by birth. White thinks that it is absurd to explain human behaviour in terms of psychological traits but holds that 'the differences of behaviour are simply the responses of a common, constant, human organism to varying sets of cultural stimuli. Everything that any people does—as *human* beings, that is —everything that he thinks, feels, and does, is culturally determined.'[9] White contrasts culturological and psychological interpretations of human behaviour and insists that instead of explaining culture in psychological terms, we must interpret human behaviour in terms of culture.

Culture is a continuum of interacting elements (traits), and this process of interaction has its own principles and its own laws. To introduce the human organism into a consideration of cultural variations is therefore not only irrelevant but wrong; it involves a premise that is false. Culture must be explained in terms of culture. Thus, paradoxical though it may seem, 'the proper study of mankind' turns out to be not Man after all but Culture. The most realistic and scientifically adequate interpretation of culture is one that proceeds as if human beings did not exist.

According to White all patterns of individual behaviour and social institutions are to be explained in terms of culture. Customs, political and social changes, revolutions, wars and organizations are no exceptions. War is a struggle between systems, not individuals. The attempt to explain a particular custom in a certain tribe in psychological terms cannot explain its absence in the neighbouring tribe. White adds:

To the culturologist the reasoning that says that one people drinks milk because 'they like it', another does not because they loathe it, is 'imbecilic',—to use Hooton's forthright term. It explains nothing at all. *Why* does one people like, another loathe, milk? *This* is what we want to know. And the psychologist cannot give us the answer. Nor can he tell us why a people does or does not avoid mothers-in-law, practice monogamy, inhumation, the couvade, or circumcision; use chopsticks, forks, the pentatonic scale, hats, or microscopes; form plurals by affixation—or any of the other thousands of customs known to ethnography.

Now let us look at the psychological perspective. In sharp contrast to Durkheim's assertion that society was an entity *sui generis* and that sociology was not a corollary of psychology, George Homans, the most outspoken advocate of neo-nominalism in contemporary sociology, insists that sociology is a corollary of, and can be derived from, psychology. Homans' brand of psychology is, of course, behavioural psychology, and hence what Homans advocates is a kind of behavioural psychological reductionism according to which behaviour and social processes can ultimately be reduced to the laws of behavioural psychology. He observes: 'The institutions, organizations, and societies that sociologists study can always be analysed, without residue, into the behaviour of individual men. They must therefore be explained by propositions about the behaviour of individual men.'[10]

It must be noted that Homans does not deny the reality of social institutions; he does not even concern himself with the question of whether the individual or social group is the ultimate reality. He is mainly concerned with how social phenomena are to be explained. The answer is obvious: the only plausible interpretation of social phenomena is in terms of individual behaviour. He writes:

I now suspect that there are no general sociological propositions, propositions that hold good for all societies or social groups as such, and that the only general propositions of sociology are in fact psychological. . . .no matter what we say our theories are, when we seriously try to explain social phenomena by constructing even the veriest sketches of deductive systems, we find ourselves in fact, and whether we admit it or not, using what I have called psychological explanations.'[11]

Ekeh points out that Homans' arguments for the reduction of social phenomena to behavioural psychological principles ignore two counter-currents in the philosophy of science. First, the growing dissatisfaction among established philosophers of science with the inadequacy and irrelevance of the traditional physicalist view of science has shifted the focus of inquiry from the search for 'process laws' to the 'problems of organized complexity'. 'This is saying that modern social science is a different type of science because the type of problems it faces require laws of organized wholes, not the nihilist reduction of organized wholes to their simplest units.'[12] Second, the phenomenologist view of the social sciences which insists that social scientists must include in their *action-meanings* the individual's *act-meanings*, i.e., the subject's own interpretation of what his activity means, militates against behavioural psychological reductionism. Other critics have charged that Homans has fallen into what the great philosopher Alfred North Whitehead called the 'fallacy of misplaced concreteness', which is the scientists' assumption that they could analyse the universe into its constituent parts and thereby eventually discover the basic elements and explain them—a fallacy because the assumption misplaces the concreteness of phenomena, ignores the relationships among parts forming a whole and treats the organization as a mere sum of its parts. Moreover, if we extend the logic behind Homans' assertion that sociological laws are reducible to those about men, then those about men must be reducible to physiological propositions which, in turn, must be reducible to biological propositions and so on.

There is also a great potential danger in adopting the reductionist strategy. Although reductionists admit the reality of groups, their research interests and theoretical orientations are likely to be focused exclusively on psychological and social-psychological phenomena. This may lead to the virtual neglect of macro-structures and the more complex sociological phenomena, resulting in one-sided research and theory-building in sociology. According to Turner, Homans' strategy amounts to pseudodeductions which consist in reducing certain interesting sociological questions, taken as given, to certain *ad hoc* psychological propositions without ever attempting to develop well-established sociological laws. A far wiser strategy would be to develop sociological laws first and let the issue of reductionism take care of itself when these laws are established. Turner observes:

. . . the use of Homans' deductive strategy will enable sociologists to define away as givens those sociological problems that need to be studied if true sociological laws are to be developed. Without these laws in the deductive systems advocated by Homans, such systems are logically inadequate and empirically confusing. A far wiser deductive strategy is to attempt to develop the 'laws of sociology' that, at some distant point in the future, can be subsumed logically by a more general set of principles—perhaps one similar to those advocated by Homans. To continue to pursue Homans' platitudinous recommendations for building sociological theory is to assure that such theory will not be developed.[13]

Warriner examines the basic arguments against the realist position advanced by neo-nominalists.

1. We can see persons, but we cannot see groups except by observing persons. This argument involves a confusion between the idea of *individual* and that of person. We see the former, the organism, but the person is observed only through a series of actions and behaviours. Moreover, the group is as real as the person. In fact, both are abstract, analytical units and we cannot see persons any more than we can see groups; they are realities which extend beyond the range of human perception.

2. Groups are composed of persons. This statement tells us nothing about groups except to draw our attention to the constituent elements, and, therefore, is not much different from saying that chairs are made up of atoms, a statement true enough but hardly adequate enough to be meaningful. Moreover, the statement reminds us of the 'fallacy of misplaced concreteness'. Just as in chemistry the characteristics of a compound are entirely different from those of its components, in the Durkheimian tradition of sociology, society is considered more than an aggregate of individuals. C. Wright Mills has observed:

The idea of social structure cannot be built up only from ideas or facts about a specific series of individuals and their reactions to their milieux. Attempts to explain social and historical events on the basis of psychological theories about 'the individual' often rest upon the assumption that society is nothing but a great scatter of individuals and that, accordingly, if we know all about these 'atoms' we can in some way add up the information and thus know about society. It is not a fruitful assumption.[14]

3. Social phenomena have their reality only in persons, this is the only possible location of such phenomena. This fallacy stems from:

the assumption that for a social phenomenon to be real it must be internalized by the individual, and results from a failure to make the distinction between knowing and internalization. It is clear that a person may know cultural forms, beliefs, and patterns and know when they are appropriate (much in the way an anthropologist knows a culture which he studies) without these becoming an integral part of his own personality.'[15]

Cooley insisted that the individual and society are two aspects of the same reality. Thomas and Znaniecki felt that we can say neither that the individual is the product of his milieu, nor that he produces his milieu, rather we can say both. And White has, as we noted earlier, claimed that culture, not the individual, is the only genuine reality.

4. The purpose of studying groups is to facilitate explanation and predictions of individual behaviour. If this is not a value issue, then, it is a totally erroneous assumption. The purpose of studying groups is to learn more about the structure and functioning of social systems, not to understand the individual. The purpose of studying money is not to understand coins, the study of a factory is not the study of individual workers, and the study of democracy is not intended to portray the characteristics of individual voters. James Coleman rightly observes: 'Social theory has, I think, allowed itself to be sidetracked off its main task, which is to develop theories for social systems—whether they be total social systems or systems of behaviour in small groups. Our attention is too often drawn away from the system itself to the individuals within it, so that we construct theories to account for some individual's behaviour.'[16]

Inkeles has proposed a viable alternative which incorporates psychological variables in sociological theory and research without indulging in psychological reductionism. He decries the tendency of many sociologists to analyse social phenomena with a method which strictly excludes psychological theory and data. He insists that:

adequate sociological analysis of many problems is either impossible or severely limited unless we make explicit use of psychological theory and data in conjunction with sociological theory and data. Indeed, I would assert that very little sociological analysis is ever done without using at least an implicit psychological theory. It seems evident that in making this theory explicit and bringing psychological data to bear systematically on sociological problems we cannot fail but improve the scope and adequacy of sociological analysis.[17]

Sociologists are generally inclined to study a social structure as a set of institutional arrangements; they ignore the meaning of those arrangements which are ultimately mediated through individual action and the key intervening variable, namely the human personality system. Inkeles illustrates his point with reference to different

studies that deal with rates of suicide and juvenile delinquency which
are variously attributed to normlessness or community disorganization without any reference to individual personality. Thus sociologists
begin with some rate (of a particular social problem such as suicide
or juvenile delinquency), find out the prior state of the social system
(such as community disorganization or broken homes) and formulate
a sociological S-R proposition in which S is the state of society and
R the resultant rate. According to Inkeles, both the sociological S-R
(or State-Rate) theory and its analogue, the psychological S-R
(Stimulus-Response) theory suffer seriously from failure to utilize an
explicit theory of the human personality.

The simplest formula, $(S)(P) = R$, although probably far from adequate, would nevertheless be greatly superior to the S-R formula, since
it provides for the simultaneous effect of two elements influencing
action. Without some general theory of the nature of human personality, it is impossible to explain why the absence of social integration
should in some cases produce, not Durkheim's egoistic suicide, but
mental illness or homicide—or nothing.

Inkeles insists that a theory of personality and knowledge about
the particular personality components in the population are fundamental to sociological analysis, for social conditions and personality
are distinct and, to some degree, independently operating determinants of social action.

Milton Yinger[18] cautions against confusing individual group facts.
To use the same term to refer to a state of social structure and the
psychic condition of the individual is to assume a one-to-one relationship between social and psychological phenomena. For example,
Durkheim's anomie refers to a social situation characterized by the
lack of cultural integration or the absence of consensus on norms.
It does not mean that every individual member in this society is
anomic. On the contrary, a wide range of different individual patterns
and behavioural responses can be found among the members of a
group that is anomic—responses that are both creative and destructive.

The confusion of social and individual facts is attributable to a
number of factors. First of all, it is related to the pattern of academic
training and boundary-maintenance between disciplines. Many social
scientists are unwilling to depart far from their 'home territory' in
order to benefit from, or integrate the perspectives of, different
disciplines. Secondly, our measuring processes, statistical averaging

and the practice of deriving group facts from the aggregation of individual measures have led to the equation of social and individual facts. For example, the discovery of a positive correlation between urban residence and mental illness, broken homes and juvenile delinquency, and high mobility and schizophrenic experience has sometimes led to sweeping generalizations that equate the state of the individual personality with the objective condition of society. Yinger also points out that the assertion, by psychologically oriented sociologists, that an aggregated fact has no importance in its own right since it is derived from a series of individual facts is obviously false; we may speak meaningfully of a 'peasant society' or a 'middle-class society'. Here the group designation is based on aggregated individual facts; but it is not confused with them. There are also structural properties of groups which are based on a relationship among the individual facts and thus cannot reside in them separately. Moreover, there are also some individual characteristics which make sense only in relation to others. Individual attributes such as 'shy', 'sympathetic' or 'outgoing' necessarily imply relationship with others. The thrust of Yinger's argument is that we tend to overlook so often the crucial distinction between individual and group properties because of an assumed parallel relationship between them.

Nominalism is now dead and neo-nominalism is on the ascendancy. However, with the recent developments in psychological reductionism, neo-nominalism has undergone a substantial metamorphosis. The question no longer is whether the individual *or* the group is real. There seems to be a general consensus that the group is as real as the individual. The controversy in contemporary sociology centres around the modus operandi: whether sociological phenomena can and must be reduced to psychological phenomena. In addition to the various criticisms already cited, it must be pointed out that there is no special advantage to be gained by resorting to the reductionist strategy. Rather, it only leads us away from the more genuine sociological concerns with structure and functioning of social system. And man is more than a psychological animal; he is also the product of his culture. Above all, society is more than a mere collection of individuals; it is an entity *sui generis* involving a qualitative jump from individual to society. Therefore, the contention that social phenomena can be reduced to individual phenomena is wholly untenable. The reductionist strategy cannot abstract the qualitative dimension inherent in the total action process. And, fortunately, it is not necessary to choose between the reductionist strategy and the Durkheimian contention of the primacy of society over the individual. We can account for individual and group facts as Yinger did and adopt a strategy that incorporates both sociological and psychological variables as Inkeles did.

II. *Neo-Positivism*

Erected on the analogy between physical and social phenomena, neopositivism has deep roots in sociological thought. Comte made philosophical positivism the corner-stone of his sociological thought. However, he recognized the importance of historical and comparative methods as well. But social physics or the school of neo-positivism that dominates contemporary sociology owes its origin primarily to the statistical tradition that may be traced to Quetelet rather than Comte's philosophical positivism.

Neo-positivism, probably the largest school in modern sociology, takes phenomena from the physical world as explicit models for social events and employs the laws of the former to explain the latter. It involves the direct application of explanatory models drawn from physical sciences to describe social phenomena. Neo-positivism asserts that sociology is, and should be, a science and its methods should follow those of the natural—especially physical—sciences. In the words of Wagner:

neo-positivism, as established and popularized in the thirties, purports to operate on the basis of a physical model. It largely identifies scientific procedure with quantification and measuring, and conceives of sociology as an applied science of social engineering. Many proponents of applied quantitative research operate without resorting to large-scale theory; the goal of the theoretical mathematization of sociological knowledge, however, is pursued independently. Advanced forms of neo-positivist theory are based on systems of interlinked causal (instead of functional) propositions which are expected to lend themselves to an eventual mathematical restatement of the theory.'[19]

Neo-positivists consider sound scientific methodology to be the first principle of sociological analysis, and what they consider to be sound scientific methodology necessarily involves mathematical and other formal models that feature formalization of variables, computer techniques and language, experimental logics, laboratory experiments and computer simulation of human behaviour. The great preponderance of articles in the mathematical-verification style in modern sociological journals attests to the current popularity of formalistic models. It seems there is a great rush to restate and adopt the philosophy of natural sciences to develop a formalistic and mathematical system for the 'interpretation' of social phenomena. Warhsay notes:

That formalistic and mathematical sociologists are positivistic (rather than, say, empiricist, idealist, or rationalist) can be seen in (1) their emphasis upon 'observable' data, including a wary view toward causation; (2) their use of formal devices to relate 'unobservable' terms to experience deductively; (3) their ready willingness to treat 'empirically observable wholes' in terms of 'constructs' that break the wholes into more 'handleable' parts; (4) their working assumption that science cannot deal directly with reality—and that the only alternative is to treat much of conceptual phenomena as 'constructs' and as nominal and operational definitions; and (5) the relative simplicity, circumspection, and intellectual conservatism of their work.[20]

Among the early masters Pareto and Giddings stressed the scientific nature of sociology and recommended the use of methods commonly adopted in the natural sciences. Lundberg, Dodd, Zipf, Ogburn and Chapin are, however, considered to be the leading exponents of neo-positivism. George Lundberg, the most articulate and influential spokesman of the school, rejected the distinction between qualitative and quantitative methods of study. Scientific generalization is always and necessarily quantitative, and all social sciences can and must be quantified, he insisted. Quantitative statements are absolutely essential for the exact description required of science. Lundberg considered quantitativism to be almost inseparable from behaviourism. He emphasized the study of observable behaviour and avoided any reference to mental facts. He went to the extent of asserting that a single principle borrowed from physics can explain a leaf flying before the wind and a man fleeing from a pursuing crowd.

The essentials of neo-positivism may be summarized as follows:

1. Positivistic epistemology. Neo-positivism rejects *a priori* definitions of the 'essential nature' of society, culture, social structure and institutions, and insists on operational definitions of concrete phenomena. The sequence of observable consequences that form a cluster of sense impressions is treated as the proper subject matter of sociology. Such a pragmatic philosophy, it is believed, necessarily

involves a sound scientific method. Mills has highlighted this position in his characteristic way.

As a matter of practice, abstracted empiricists often seem more concerned with the philosophy of science than with social study itself. What they have done, in brief, is to embrace one philosophy of science which they now suppose to be The Scientific Method. This model of research is largely an epistemological construction; within the social sciences, its most decisive result has been a sort of methodological inhibition. By this I mean that the kinds of problems that will be taken up and the way in which they are formulated are quite severely limited by The Scientific Method. Methodology, in short, seems to determine the problems. And this, after all, is only to be expected. The Scientific Method that is projected here did not grow out of, and is not a generalization of, what are generally and correctly taken to be the classic lines of social science work. It has been largely drawn, with expedient modifications, from one philosophy of natural science.[21]

2. Operationalism.   Neopositivists are not content with the vague definitions of theoretical constructs and concepts. Each term must not only be defined precisely but also be translated in measurable variables. Neopositivists usually claim that sociological theory is a systematic collection of concepts useful in the interpretation of statistical findings. Typical is Lazarsfeld's assertion:

We do call these concepts sociological *because* they apply to many varieties of social behavior . . . We assign to the sociologist the task to collect and analyze these concepts, which are useful for the interpretation of empirical results found in specific areas like the analysis of price or crime or suicide or voting statistics. Sometimes the term social theory is used for a systematic presentation of such concepts and their inter-relationships.[22]

3. Quantitativism.   Statistical analysis which involves enumeration and measurement is basic to neopositivism. Giddings viewed sociology as a 'science statistical in method' and insisted that 'a true and complete description of anything must include measurement of it'. And today, thanks to advances in computer technology, a variety of methods and techniques are available and these include factor and regression analysis, game theory, causal and path analysis, set theory, cluster analysis, latent-structure analysis, Markov chains, index construction, matrices and vectors, graph theory, stochastic models, etc. What is being attempted is to put together pieces of information pertaining to units of social structure into formal and

mathematical systems so that the relationships between different variables may be statistically ascertained.

4. Empiricism. Skeptical of 'armchair' theorizing, neopositivists undertake elaborate fact-gathering missions with 'sophisticated' tools, methods and techniques. They may set up elaborate administrative apparatuses or research institutes and serve as consultants to business corporations and governmental agencies. Whether it is survey research or experimental observation, the empirical work seems to fall into a standard pattern: pose a problem that can be investigated by a fact finding inquiry; formulate a set of hypotheses that can be tested on the basis of individual responses to a set of questions; collection of answers on an interview schedule, structured questionnaire, or an observer's notebook; the answers are then classified, coded and punched on computer cards; statistical runs are made utilizing various computer techniques. The results come out in neat computer print-outs showing all kinds of possible relationships between all sorts of variables. The researcher may interpret these findings in terms of simple satistical assertions. Or, the results may be combined in elaborate cross classifications or collapsed to form scales and graphs. In any case, specific findings are stated in systematically organized mathematical formulae and formalistic models.

5. Behaviourism. Because of their emphasis on operationalism and quantitativism, neopositivists tend to study observable behaviour patterns. They concentrate on specific instances of interaction, sometimes counting the frequency and patterns of repetition. Substantive problems of social structure and the history of institutions and ideas are often ignored; concrete behaviour of individuals becomes the focus of sociological inquiry. Accordingly, neopositivists develop non-subjective and non-voluntaristic theories of action and interaction. Based on mechanistic and field-theoretical conceptions, extreme variants of neo-positivism may border behavioural determinism.

6. Mathematical theory construction. Neopositivists have a commitment to formal theory construction. They claim that the strong symbolic representation of a theory in terms of the formal logic of mathematics necessarily increases the precision of theoretical propositions. The system of formal logic in mathematics enables substantive propositions to be couched in terms of exactly defined concepts and to state them with utmost logical coherence. In contrast, conceptual theories are thought to be vague, imprecise and

inconsistent. The advocates of formal theory construction also claim that only mathematical models can integrate theory and research. Without mathematization, they argue, the gulf between conceptual theorists who formulate substantive propositions of interpretative sociology and researchers who organize empirical findings into statistical models is bound to grow.

Formal theory construction appears in two different contexts. First, there is the formalization of well-developed substantive theories. For instance, there have been well-known attempts to formalize functionalism, system theory and symbolic interactionism. Second, specific finding of particular empirical research are codified in mathematical terms and then organized into a formal theoretical system which establishes the mathematical relationship between variables in symbolic terms. Most of the empirical studies undertaken by sociologists today fall in this category. However, the impact of mathematical sociology has been limited to a few substantive areas such as stratification, small group research, social exchange, coalition and demography.

Contemporary sociology seems to be preoccupied with formal theories and mathematical models. Zipf sought to 'integrate theoretically a number of social measurements'. He is best known for his postulate labelled as the 'principle of least effort'. This principle states that, given the alternatives, people will choose those procedures that result in the 'least average rate of probable work'. In other words, human beings always strive to minimize effort, which explains most patterns of behaviour as well as socal activities whether it is highway construction, migration to cities or the utilization of labour-saving devices. The underlying assumption, of course, is that men always act rationally and that human behaviour can be analysed according to this principle. Ogburn selected a wide range of technological and economic aspects of social phenonena, studied their mutual interdependence and made explicit use of the techniques of coefficients of correlation. Chapin refined the techniques of graphic symbolism and measurement by scale. His works are replete with graphs and charts. He also devised a number of scales for the measurement of various sociological concepts. Herbert Simon employed set theory in describing political power and authority. Caplow used similar equations to explain coalition formation. In chapter 6, we saw Emerson's formalization of exchange theory. Robert Bales studied interaction in small groups, counted and recorded acts directed toward each person in the group, and concluded that 45 per cent of all the acts that occurred in the group were directed toward the man who ranked first and about 6 per cent were directed toward the man who received the least attention. To find an impressive array of formal theories and mathematical models one need only refer to the multi-volume *Sociological Theories in Progress* edited by Joseph Berger and his associates.

We noted earlier that the enormous amount of empirical studies and mathematical models that appear in contemporary sociological publications is indicative of the popularity of neopositivism today. Inspired by the philosophy of the natural sciences and armed with the most sophisticated computer hardware, neopositivists insist that only quantification can make sociology a full-fledged science. Mathematically formalized theories alone are empirically verifiable, and verifiability is the most important criterion by which to evaluate the scientific worth of a theory. Formalization furnishes a rigorous logical framework that can provide the means for detecting inconsistencies in theoretical statements; it aids in uncovering hitherto unrecognized relationships. By making deductive propositions logically coherent and consistent, mathematical formulations can substantially aid the process of theory-building. Operationalism and quantitativism are known to enhance conceptual clarity and predictive validity. In the words of Treiman, the development of scientific theory 'requires, first, precision of measurement, and, second, precision in the specification of expected relationships among variables, that is, theoretical precision.'[23] Above all, neopositivists argue that a theory is valid and useful only if it is stated in law-like propositions and empirically verifiable statements of relationships between variables.

Although the proponents of neopositivism claim it to be the flowering of a truly cumulative and scientific sociology, its critics call it 'quantaphenia' or a meaningless jumble of numbers and formulas. C. Wright Mills calls neopositivists the 'science-makers' who want to be scientific and administrative at any cost and who are not touched by the most substantive problems of the discipline since they believe that their method can convert the philosophies into science. Because of their reliance on frequency and measurement, neopositivists tend to study social situations and problems which repeat themselves. They also display a strong a-historical bias because their techniques permit them to study only contemporary social problems, not historical social events. Moreover, they tend to choose those areas that lend themselves most readily to mathematical formulations, to the virtual neglect of more substantive areas of theoretical significance. Such a tendency, Coser warns, 'will result, in the worst of cases, in the piling up of useless information and, in the best of cases, in a kind of tunnel vision in which some problems are explored exhaustively while others are not even perceived.'[24]

Bierstedt has forcefully argued that an exclusive dependence on empiricism has neither historical nor logical warrants.

In the first place, as an epistemological doctrine empiricism has nowhere received the philosophic support that would justify its exclusive use in the social sciences. In the second place, the ultimate logical consequences of a pure empiricism are either Berkeleian idealism or solipsism. In the third place, it can be demonstrated, on logical grounds, that observation and experiment are never sufficient for the construction of generalizations, laws, and principles in any of the sciences, except in cases where the universe of data is so limited as to allow for a complete induction.[25]

The application of the laws of physics and all the sophisticated computer technology cannot illuminate complex social phenomena which have many layers of meaning and are mediated by the subjective experiences of creative individuals. In the first place, there is no reason to assume that the relations between the analogous elements in the social realm will be the same as in the physical world; in fact, they seldom are. Secondly, no amount of precise mathematical statements can give precision to imprecise data. Indeed, rigorous mathematization often obscures the weakness of the data. Thirdly, mathematical formulations are based on extreme oversimplification of reality. As Timasheff points out:

Proceeding by ingenious mathematical operations, social scientists are supposed to reach mathematical values that can safely be converted into real units, permitting the prediction of real events. This assumption, however, is dangerously ambitious for there are three languages— the mathematical, the operational, and the real (causal)—and these are not easily translatable into each other. Equations used operationally often express asymmetric (that is, irreversible) processes, whereas mathematical equations are symmetric (or reversible).[26]

Fourth, the statistical manipulation of depersonalized scores distorts meaning.

An oft-repeated criticism of neopositivism is that it is devoid of any substantive propositions and theories. Neopositivists can display an impressive array of mathematical boxes and graphic models but these are usually theoretically empty. Coser deplores the tendency to use new methods and techniques as 'magic helpers', as a shortcut to, or even replacement for, theoretical analysis. Such methodological inhibition can only breed 'a trained incapacity to think in theoretically innovative ways'. Coser is emphatic when he says:

The fallacy of misplaced precision consists in believing that one can compensate for theoretical weakness by methodological strength. Concern with precision in measurement before theoretical clarification of what is worth measuring and what is not, and before one clearly knows what one is measuring, is a roadblock to progress in sociological analysis . . . [Computers and other instruments of research] serve us well in certain areas of inquiry, but they can become Frankenstein monsters when they are applied indiscriminately and, above all, when their availability dictates the problem choices of the investigator so that trivial problems are treated with utmost refinement . . . . The sheer availability of new methods encourages their use and seems to release the user from the obligation to decide whether his problem or findings are worthy of attention.[27]

Neopositivists are never tired of claiming that if only they had more time and more money they could make their findings foolproof, accumulate adequate data to develop a systematic theory of social phenomena and eventually make sociology a full-fledged science. This line of argument, as Mills points out, 'assumes a view of the development of social science as a strange building-block endeavour'. The assumption, of course, is that data on specific units can be added up and fitted together to arrive at a coherent theory of social phenomena—an assumption which is obviously false. It must be remembered that what we get out of empirical research is information or pieces of information. To piece them together, if that is possible at all, we need a broader theoretical frame of reference, the kind of which the neopositivists abandoned in the first place. Thus empirical findings tend to become a jumble of facts and figures, unrelated to any meaningful theoretical system. Above all, it is helpful to remember Cameron's dictum that in sociology, unlike in the natural sciences, everything that counts cannot be counted and everything that is counted does not count.

However, none of these critical statements are intended to assert that computers and measurements have no place in contemporary sociology. Rather, these remarks are intended to express our concern with the growing abuses of these tools of research, the assumption that everything must be quantified to make sense, and the neglect of substantive theoretical areas and interpretative analysis.

NOTES

1. For a detailed discussion see Charles K. Warriner, 'Groups Are Real: A Reaffirmation', *American Sociological Review*, **21** (October, 1956), 549–54. Also reprinted in Milton L. Barron (ed.), *Contemporary Sociology* (New York, Dodd, Mead and Co., 1964).

2. Louis Wirth, 'Social Interaction: The Problem of the Individual and the Group', *American Journal of Sociology*, **44** (May, 1939), 966.

3. As quoted by Warriner, op. cit., in Barron (ed.), pp. 121–2.

4. Leo F. Schnore, 'The Myth of Human Ecology', *Sociological Inquiry*, **31** (1961), p. 135.

5. Warriner, op. cit., p. 122.

6. Emile Durkheim, *The Rules of Sociological Method* (New York, Free Press, 1950), p. 3f.

7. Ibid., p. 103.

8. Ibid.

9. Leslie A. White, 'Culturological Vs. Psychological Interpretations of Human Behaviour', *American Sociological Review*, **12** (December 1947), 686–98. Quotes from page 688.

10. George C. Homans, 'Commentary', *Sociological Inquiry*, **41** (Winter 1971), 231.

11. George C. Homans, 'Bringing Men Back In', *American Sociological Review*, **29** (December 1964): 809–18. Also reprinted in R. Serge Denisoff et al. (eds.), *Theories and Paradigms in Contemporary Sociology* (Itasca, F. E. Peacock Publishers, Inc., 1974), p. 369.

12. Peter P. Ekeh, *Social Exchange Theory* (Cambridge, Harvard University Press, 1974), p. 94.

13. Jonathan Turner, *The Structure of Sociological Theory* (Homewood, Dorsey Press, 1974). p. 257.

14. C. Wright Mills, *The Sociological Imagination* (New York, Oxford University Press, 1970), p. 163.

15. Warriner, op. cit., p. 126.

16. As quoted by Leo Schnore, op. cit., p. 130.

17. Alex Inkeles, 'Personality and Social Structure', in Robert K. Merton et al. (eds.), *Sociology Today* (New York, Basic Books, 1959), pp. 250–255.

18. J. Milton Yinger, 'Individual Facts and Group Facts', in Fred E. Katz (ed.), *Contemporary Sociological Theory* (New York, Random House, 1971), pp. 485–90.

19. Helmut R. Wagner, 'Types of Sociological Theory', *American Sociological Review*, **28** (October, 1963). Also reprinted in Denisoff, op. cit., p. 44.

20. Leon H. Warshay, *The Current State of Sociological Theory* (New York, David McKay Company, Inc., 1975), p. 91.

21. C. Wright Mills, op. cit., p. 57.

22. Ibid., quoted by Mills, p. 63.

23. Donald J. Treiman, 'A Comment on Professor Lewis Coser's Presidential Address', *American Sociologist*, **11** (February, 1976), p. 28.

24. Lewis A. Coser, 'Presidential Address: Two Methods in Search of a Substance', *American Sociological Review*, **40** (December, 1975), 693.

25. Robert Bierstedt, *Power and Progress* (New York, McGraw-Hill Book Company, 1974), p. 140.

26. Nicholas Timasheff and George Theodorson, *Sociological Theory* (New York, Random House, 1976, fourth edition), p. 216.

27. Lewis Coser, op. cit., 692.

CHAPTER 11

Two Macro Theoretical Approaches

I. ECOLOGICAL PERSPECTIVES

Although the term 'ecology' was coined in 1869 by a German biologist, Earnest Haeckel, human ecology as a social system approach was developed in 1921 by Park and Burgess[1] of the University of Chicago whose research interest centred around the growth of the city as a natural phenomenon. Park and Burgess sought to apply systematically the basic theoretical scheme of biological ecology—the science of the interdependence of plants and animals living together in a natural area—to the study of human communities.

Amos Hawley, one of the most influential pioneers, conceived ecology 'as a study of the morphology of collective life in both its static and dynamic aspects'.[2] According to him, the main task of human ecology is the analysis of community structure in terms of the organization of sustenance activities, that is, the way a population organizes itself for survival in a particular habitat. The key concept is ecosystem which is defined as:

a population comprising a set of species whose reactions to the habitat and coactions between each other constitute an integrated system having some degree of unit character. Coactions involve members behaving both with reference to their similarities in an *intra*specific relationship known as commensalism and with reference to their differences in what is called symbiosis, and *inter*specific relationship.[3]

The community develops from simple to more complex forms through a series of economic adaptations. Hawley made extensive use of demographic data and concentrated on the territorial aggregation of population as well as on the spatial distribution of different activities. Hawley's ecological approach—the study of the total community together with its habitat—is essentially macroscopic in nature. According to him, 'Human ecology seeks its explanations among variables that are structural properties, demographic attributes, and features of environment, including interactions with other systems.'[4]

Julian Steward developed cultural ecology as distinct from other approaches and defined it as:

the study of the processes by which a society adapts to its environment. Its principal problem is to determine whether these adaptations initiate internal social transformations or evolutionary change. It analyses these adaptations, however, in conjunction with other processes of change. Its method requires examination of the interaction of societies and social institutions with one another and with the natural environment.[5]

According to Theodorson, the primary areas of concern to human ecology may be subsumed under four general headings: (1) geographical, which includes climatic, topographic, and resource conditions; (2) economic, which comprises a wide range and variety of phenomena such as the nature and organization of local industries, occupational distribution, and standard of living of the population; (3) cultural and technical, which include, in addition to the prevailing condition of the arts, the moral attitudes and taboos that are effective in the distribution of population and services; (4) political and administrative measures, such as tariff, taxation, immigration laws, and rules governing public utilities.

Otis Dudley Duncan and Leo Schnore are two of the most articulate spokesmen of the ecological perspective in contemporary sociology. According to them ecology deals with society as the functional organization of a population in the process of achieving and maintaining an adaptation to its environment. They consider the ecological perspective to be central to sociological analysis because 'its view of social organization as the collective adaptation of a population to its environment avoids the reductionism of behavioural concepts and the etherealism of the "value-pattern" concepts of some culture theorists.'[6] What distinguishes human ecology from other perspectives is neither the phenomena it investigates, nor the factors whose importance it recognizes but 'its formulation of a problem and the heuristic principles employed in attacking that problem.' The central concern of the ecological perspective is the analysis of the problems of 'cultural diversity' and 'social change' in terms of the interaction between social organization and environment.

Duncan identifies four categories of variables that constitute 'the ecological complex' or ecosystem: Population, Organization, Environment and Technology. These categories can be remembered by using the mnemonic acronym of POET. It must be noted that these categories only 'provide a somewhat arbitrarily simplified way of identifying clusters of relationships in a preliminary description of ecosystem processes'. The ecosystem may be graphically presented as follows:

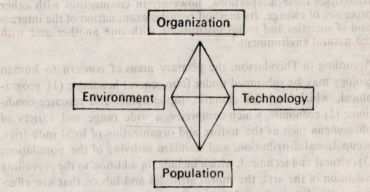

Figure 6. The Ecological Complex
(Hauser and Duncan, 1959. p. 683)

The four sets of variables are in reciprocal relationship and the lines in the presentation above are meant to suggest the idea of 'functional interdependence'.

Whether it is fruitful to regard this complex as a system with equilibrium-maintaining properties is a moot point of ecological theory . . . . It may be possible, however, to derive significant hypotheses from the assumption that the 'ecological complex' constitutes an equilibrium-seeking system whose path of change results from this tendency combined with dislocating forces impinging upon one or another point in the system.[7]

Duncan and Schnore recognize the distinctiveness of human population—its possession of culture—but reject cultural determinism and the anthropologists' global or generic view of culture. Their concern is 'not with culture as an undifferentiated totality but with aspects of culture as they play into the process of adaptation.' They regard population as an aggregate of individuals who establish viable relationships with environment, not independently but collectively, through the mechanism of a system of relationships.

The ecological perspective stresses the systemic attributes of social organization rather than the psychological mechanism of learning or aspect of social heritage stressed by culturologists. The ecologists view organization as a property of the population that has evolved and is sustained in the process of adaptation of the population to its environment, and tends to be investigated as a ramification of sustenance activities.

For the ecologist, the significant assumptions about organization are that it arises from sustenance-producing activities, is a property of the population, is indispensable to the maintenance of collective life, and must be adapted to the conditions confronting a population — including the character of the environment, the size and composition of the population itself, and the repertory of techniques at its command.[8]

The environment in the ecological complex refers to the natural unit in which the exchange of materials and energy between the living units and the non-living surroundings follows circular paths. The emphasis is on the reciprocal relationship between organization and environment. The ecosystem is viewed as an open system with a continual input of energy from an external source. Living systems are complex structures of matter maintained by energy inputs. Since 'information' is crucial for the maintenance of structures, every living creature is an information-gathering and information-processing unit. Information serves to control, modify and articulate the rate and pattern of material and energy flows between the organization and the environment.

The concept of "technology" in human ecology refers not merely to a complex of art and artifact whose patterns are invented, diffused, and accumulated (the processes stressed by culturologists) but to a set of techniques employed by a population to gain sustenance from its environment and to facilitate the organization of sustenance-producing activity.'[9] The ecological perspective considers artifacts and apparatus to be a part of the environment, and not merely factors that enable a population to control and transform the environment.

From the ecological point of view, the elementary unit of analysis is 'the pattern of activity' or simply 'activity'. The ecologists' system is 'an organization of activities, arranged in overlapping and inter-penetrating series of activity constellations, or groups.'[10] Duncan and Schnore reject the concept of role because of its psychological connotations. They consider the ecologists' primary concern to be the pattern of observable physical activity itself, not the individual's feelings of obligation concerning their roles.

The salient features of the ecological perspective may be summarized as follows:

1. The study of spatial relationship. In the words of Duncan and Schnore:

Although ecology is not to be identified with the study of area distributions, and its subject matter is by no means limited to the 'territorial arrangements that social activities assume', the study of spatial relationships continues to play a key role in ecology for several reasons. First, territoriality is a major factor giving unit character to populations. Second, space is simultaneously a requisite for the activities of any organizational unit and an obstacle which must be overcome in establishing interunit relationships.[11]

2. The interdependence of organism and environment. The crucial element that distinguishes the ecological perspective from other macro-sociological approaches is the reciprocal relationship between population and environment. It is not simply a matter of analysing the patterns of spatial distribution because of certain surface features, but of dealing effectively with the process of adaptation of the organism and the social organization to the environment by coordinating the flow of energy, information, and material.

The interaction of population and environment is seen as culminating in a system of relationships between differentiated parts which gives the population unit character and enables it to maintain its identity. As the property of a population, organization lends itself most readily to a morphological, or structural, analysis. The parts are the units—individuals or clusters of individuals—that perform functions and the relationships by which these units are linked.[12]

3. A holistic approach which views organization as the property of population taken as a whole and not of a collection of individuals. The ecological perspective is an aggregate, macro-sociological approach that deals with the community as a system and thus an effective counter to neo-nominalism. At the same time, it rejects the culturological interpretations which assign the organism and the social organization a passive role. Thus the ecological perspective 'brings sociological investigation down from the spaceless, timeless abstractions of culture theory but preserves it from the aimless

empiricism of detailing the manifold behavioural nuances of inter-personal relations.'[13]

4. The concept of equilibrium. Morphological change is assumed to be a movement toward an equilibrium state through a succession of ecological adaptations and continuous modification. However, unlike the equilibrium notion inherent in functionalism or system theory, the ecologists' usage of the term harbours no teleological overtones, claims Hawley.

5. Strong empirical base. Unlike the other general sociological theories such as symbolic interactionism, functionalism or system theory, human ecology has a strong data base. Indeed, it is more empirically grounded than theoretically sound. It is well known that the ecological perspective evolved out of a series of community studies, particularly studies of urban growth and settlement patterns.

6. Inter-disciplinary frame of reference. Ecological research has always been a cross disciplinary activity involving diverse perspec-tives from biology, economics, geography, demography, epidemio-logy, sociology and psychology. The fact that human ecology lends itself so well to fruitful exchanges among disciplines may be attri-buted to its strong empirical base and its relatively concrete view of society. As Duncan and Schnore point out, one need not even call oneself an ecologist to do ecological research or to employ essentially ecological concepts.

Now a brief note of evaluation is in order. In the first place, the theoretical framework of human ecology is extremely weak. Eco-logists have done a great amount of research but without the benefit of a sound conceptual scheme or a substantive theoretical frame of reference. They have yet to develop a system of definitions and measurement of their concepts. Terms like sustenance activity, social organization, ecosystem and human community are frequently used without conceptual clarifications or operational definitions. Kunkel notes:

In most empirical studies these terms receive a minimal definition and are measured in terms of available data ranging from census information to international trade statistics to ethnographic obser-vation. The conceptions of dependent variables are often quite gross, and in many cases it is not clear how the undifferentiated totality of 'social organization' is illuminated by the data of the analysis.[14]

Kunkel also points out that the ecologists have failed to specify the nature and operation of the link between the environment and social organization. They frequently use such terms as influence, adaptation, interaction, adjustment and flow but their studies are generally descriptive and result in merely intuitive understanding of the relationship. Finally there is a disturbing tendency for ecological research to be subsumed under community studies and urban sociology. This has, to some extent, prevented the fullest utilization of the heuristic value of ecology as a macrotheoretical perspective which Duncan and Schnore claim to be central to sociological analysis and even an effective alternative to behaviourism and functionalism.

However, the ecological approach has highlighted a very significant point: the need to study the community or a social system in its natural setting. In particular, the ecologists have contributed substantially to our understanding of the dynamics of land use, settlement patterns, population density, distribution and nucleation, centralization of specialized activities, segregation, functional interdependence of territorial units, permanence and composition of population aggregates, territoriality of societies, intersocietal relationships, cultural values and their impact on ecological organization, networks of community relationships, migration patterns and trends of community growth.

II. EVOLUTIONARY PERSPECTIVES

Sociological thinking during the nineteenth century was dominated by various conceptions of evolution which was thought of as an observable process that delineated man's march of progess from the most primitive to the most civilized cultures. Early sociologists and anthropologists were so preoccupied with the process of evolution that they laboured to show the lawful nature of societal growth through systematically defined stages, such as hunting-and-gathering, horticultural, agrarian, and industrial, that human culture treaded. The theoretical structure erected by the early evolutionists inhered the notion of cumulative development in human culture and considered progress, defined as an intrinsic goal, inevitable and universal. Although nineteenth century evolutionism has now fallen into disuse, the models of man and society derived from it continue to exercise some influence on contemporary sociology.

There are at least four variants of evolutionary theory.

1. *Unilinear evolutionary theory.* Based on the assumption that

human culture has undergone progressive and cumulative growth, unilinear evolutionary theory posits that man and society are progressing up definite steps of evolution leading to some final stage of perfection. This conception of evolution involves three essential characteristics. First, evolution is viewed as an irreversible process of unidirectional growth and development. Second, every society will go through a limited number of fixed stages of development. Third, evolution necessarily involves progress and every succeeding stage is considered to be better and higher than the preceding one.

Comte divided human history into three grand epochs or states of civilization: (a) The Theological and Military epoch. 'In this state of society, all theoretical conceptions, whether general or special, bear a supernatural impress. The imagination completely predominates over the observing faculty, to which all right of inquiry is denied.'[15] Social relations are exclusively military and conquest is the one permanent aim of society. (b) The Metaphysical and Juridical epoch. Possessing no well-defined characteristics, it 'forms a link and is mongrel and transitional'. Industry becomes more extended but has not yet acquired the upper hand. 'Consequently, society is no longer frankly military and yet has not become frankly industrial, either in its elements or in its *ensemble*'. (c) The epoch of Science and Industry. "All special theoretic conceptions have become positive, and the general conceptions tend to become so. As regards the former, observation predominates over imagination; while, in reference to the latter, observation has dethroned the imagination, without having as yet taken its place.' Comte had no doubt that the development of human race was towards a single design—the ultimate state of excellence, an utopia if you will, which the human mind and mankind will eventually reach. Every society will pass through the three great epochs and culminate in the inauguration of a scientific-industrial society characterized by progress in all aspects of life—social, technological, and spiritual.

Lewis Henry Morgan traced the unilinear development of societal progress 'from savagery through barbarism to civilization'. Savagery comprised stages of transition from the infancy of the human race to the development of simple tools, and the discovery of fire. The stage of barbarism was characterized by the invention of pottery, domestication of animals, cultivation by irrigation and improved metal tools. The invention of a phonetic alphabet and the development of language characterized the status of civilization.

In a sense, Marx and Engels also subscribed to the unilinear conception of societal progress. They identified three stages through which societies passed: Feudalism, Capitalism, and Communism. Each stage of civilization, which contained the seeds of its own destruction, prepared the ground for the next stage. Just as capitalism was founded on the ruins of feudalism, communist society will be borne out of the revolution which will destroy capitalism. The transition from one stage to another was considered historically necessary and inevitable.

2. *Universal evolutionary theory.* This perspective traces the development of human communities from simple to more complex forms with all its attendant consequences particularly those of increasing differentiation of parts and the integration of structure. It is not concerned with fixed stages or a unilinear sequence of development; nor does it assume that every society go through the same stages. The universal evolutionary theory posits that human society as a whole has followed a discernible path of evolution with varying consequences and patterns in different cultures. Spencer has summarized the process of evolution as follows:

Like a low animal, the embryo of a high one has few distinguishable parts; but, while it is acquiring greater mass, its parts multiply and differentiate. It is thus with a society. At first the unlikenesses among its groups of units are inconspicuous in number and degree; but, as population augments, divisions and subdivisions become more numerous and more decided. . . . As we progress from small groups to larger, from simple groups to compound groups, from compound groups to doubly compound ones, the unlikenesses of parts increase. The social aggregate, homogeneous when minute, habitually gains in heterogeneity along with each increment of growth, and to reach great size must acquire great complexity.[18]

According to Spencer, the knowable universe consists of material aggregates which are in a condition of incessant change. There is a universal tendency for elements to move from a condition of unstable equilibrium to a condition of stable equilibrium. The homogeneous is a condition of unstable equilibrium and must become heterogeneous; correspondingly, the simple must become compound and doubly compound and so on. Thus change involves transition from homogeneity to heterogeneity, and uniform to multiform. Spencer noted:

Social organization is at first vague; advance brings settled arrangements which grow slowly more precise; customs pass into laws which, while gaining fixity, also become more specific in their applications to varieties of actions; and all institutions, at first confusedly intermingled, slowly separate, at the same time that each within itself marks off more distinctly its component structures. Thus in all respects is fulfilled the formula of evolution. There is progress toward greater size, coherence, multiformity, and definiteness.

Different typologies of society may also be cited as examples of the variants of universal evolutionary theory. Durkheim enumerated two types of societies based on two types of social bond—mechanistic solidarity and organic solidarity—and the transformation from the one to the other is interpreted in terms of greater functional specialization, structural differentiation and the 'non-contractual basis of contract' as the foundation for individualistic and secular association. For Toennies, the process of evolution is from Gemeinschaft dominated by natural will, unity and sacred tradition, to Gesellschaft based on rational will, self-interest and contractual relationships. Redfield identified two types of societies—folk and urban—and the transition from the former to the latter involved growth in the size and complexity of social organization, greater functional specialization, improved technology, contractual relationships, increased interdependence and societal integration.

3. *Cyclical evolutionary theories.* According to this perspective there is no straight line evolution but there are discernible stages or cycles which a society or a long-enduring culture may go through more than once or even repeatedly.

The famous rise and fall theory of civilizations expounded by Oswald Spengler best illustrates the cyclical evolutionary perspective. Rejecting all previous conceptions of historical time, Spengler argued that there was not one linear time but as many times as there were historical civilizations. He identified eight great civilizations with a similar development and a similar destiny. He wrote:

Every culture passes through the age-phases of the individual man. Each has its childhood, youth, manhood, and old age. It is a young and trembling soul, heavy with misgivings, that reveals itself in the morning of Romanesque and Gothic. . . . Childhood speaks to us also—and in the same tones—out of early Homeric Doric, out of early Christian (which is really Arabian) arts. . . .The more nearly a culture approaches the noon culmination of its being, the more virile, austere, controlled, intense the form—language it has secured for itself, the more assured its sense of its own power, the clearer its lineaments. ... At last, in the gray dawn of civilization, the fire in the soul dies down. The dwindling powers rise to one more half-successful effort of creation and produce the classicism that is common to all dying cultures. The soul sinks once again and in Romanticism looks piteously back to its childhood; then finally, weary, reluctant, cold, it loses its desire to be and, as in imperial Rome, wishes itself out of the overlong daylight and back in the darkness of proto-mysticism, in the womb of the mother, in the grave.[17]

Thus each society, like an organism, has birth, adolescence, youth, maturity, decline and decay. The rising phase of society is referred to as culture and its declining phase as civilization. During the culture phase the society has a soul which nurtures the folk spirit, and all creativity occurs during this phase. As society grows to enormous size, large cities develop like cancer on its body drawing off its vigour and vitality by routinizing interpersonal relationships and by overinstitutionalizing social networks. Referring to the city's history, Spengler observed: 'growing from primitive barter-center to culture-city and at last to world-city, it sacrifices first the blood and soul of its creators to the needs of its majestic evolution, and then the last flower of that growth to the spirit of civilization — and so, doomed, moves on to final self-destruction.'

Where Spengler saw eight high civilizations, Arnold Toynbee, the English historian and author of *A Study of History*, discovered twenty-one cultures with a common pattern of growth and evolutionary history. The cumulative development of human culture is the result of the interplay between 'challenges' and 'responses'. Societies work out appropriate 'responses' to 'challenges' that arise first from the physical environment and later from social and political contexts. They may succumb to some of these challenges but they survive and progress as others are effectively met. The main thrust of Toynbee's work, however, is that while the course of its history as a whole is cyclical, every long-enduring culture climbs to great heights, each succeeding step a little bit better than the one preceding it. Hence, Toynbee's cyclical perspective is sometimes called the 'circular staircase theory of history'.[18]

Pitirim Sorokin sought to determine the 'constellation of conditions' governing 'supersystems' which integrate the various cultural elements in a given society. He discovered three general ontological principles that define the ultimate nature of reality and value:

(a) True reality and true value are sensory—the major premise of the sensate supersystems. (b) True value and true reality consist in a super-sensory, super-rational God, Brahman, Atman, Tao, or its equival-ent—the major premise of the ideational supersystem. (c) True value and reality are an infinite manifold, partly super-sensory and partly super-rational, partly rational, and partly sensory—the premise of the idealistic supersystem.[19]

Sorokin's theory fits the cyclical evolutionary perspective in that it describes the course of history as a continuous but irregular fluctua-tion between sensate and ideational cultures. Sensate systems are based on the testimony of our senses which dictate that nothing is true or genuine beyond what we can see or feel. Ideational systems are based on faith in supernatural forces and the perception of tran-scendental reality. Robert Bierstedt has beautifully summarized the two kinds of cultures in the following words:

A sensate culture is one in which all expressions—art, literature, religion, law, ethics, social relations, and philosophy—appeal to the senses and satisfy sensual needs and desires. An ideational culture, on the contrary, is one in which these expressions appeal to the soul, the mind, or the spirit. Sensate art, for example, is visual, sensational, and photographic; ideational art is symbolic, religious, and often abstract. Sensate sculpture emphasizes the nude human body in realistic fashion; ideational sculpture clothes the body in religious vestments. Sensate literature emphasizes the degeneracy of unimportant people, whereas ideational literature sings of the sublimity of souls and the sanctity of saints. Sensate philosophy invokes the truth of the senses (empiricism), whereas ideational philosophy relies upon the 'truth of faith' (fideism). Sensate psychology is behaviouristic; ideational psy-chology introspective. Sensate music, of course, is rock and jazz; idea-tional music reaches its height in the sacred choir and in the Gregorian chant. Sensate religion is of the lecture-hall variety and emphasizes social welfare; ideational religion is ritualistic and formal and gives its attention to heaven and to hell. Sensate ethics, law, and social relations are 'compulsory' and 'contractual' rather than 'cooperative' and 'familistic'.[20]

From the course of Western history Sorokin has singled out a number of cultures to illustrate his thesis. While the Medieval culture was undoubdtedly ideational, the twentieth-century American civilization is in the 'over-ripe' sensate phase. The Golden Age of Athens under Pericles was an idealistic system which is an integra-tion of both ideational and sensate cultures. Sorokin believed that the fluctuation between ideational and sensate cultures was inevitable.

A culture that develops into the extreme stages of either sensate or ideational phases, produces repercussions and counter-currents that push it in the opposite direction and the evolutionary change goes on.

4. *Multilinear Evolutionary Theory.* Contemporary evolutionists have abandoned the grand theories of evolution that make sweeping generalizations about the cumulative development of human civilizations; they focus, instead, on the processes and consequences of types of change in a given society. Steward has defined multilinear evolutionism as 'an ecological approach—an attempt to learn how factors in each given type of situation shaped the development of a particular type of society.'[21] Bellah observes:

Evolution at any system level I define as a process of increasing differentiation and a complexity of organization which endows the organism, social system, or whatever the unit in question may be, with greater capacity to adapt to its environment so that it is in some sense more autonomous relative to its environment than were its less complex ancestors.[22]

It must be noted here that very few sociologists now-a-days call themselves evolutionists. With the whole-scale repudiation of unilinear evolutionism at the turn of the century the entire evolutionary perspective fell into disuse. But in recent years the works of several leading anthropologists particularly Steward, White, Sahlins and Service, have largely revived an interest in the evolutionary perspective. Similarly in sociology, Parsons, Bellah and Eisenstadt have formulated explicit conceptions of evolution to explain the processes of structural differentiation and functional specialization. Then there are numerous sociologists, especially the proponents of various modernization theories, who use an essentially evolutionary frame of reference without acknowledging it. As Wilbert Moore puts it, 'What is involved in modernization is a "total transformation" of a traditional or premodern society into the types of technology and associated social organization that characterize the "advanced", economically prosperous, and relatively politically stable nations of the Western world.'[23] Similarly, Lerner defined modernization as 'the process of social change whereby less developed societies acquire characteristics common to more developed societies.'[24] Also, a vast number of other sociologists interested in the dynamics of modernization have established several correlates of 'development' that mark transition of developing societies from premodern to modern era. Smelser, for instance, identified four distinct but interrelated processes of modernization in the four principal areas of human endeavour: in technology, change from simple and traditionalized techniques towards the application of scientific knowledge; in agriculture, the evolution from subsistence farming towards commercial production; in industry, the transition from the use of human and animal power towards industrialization proper; and in ecological arrangements, the movement from the farm and village towards urban centers. Sahlins delineated three criteria of evolutionary progress: (1) the total transformation of energy involved in the creation and perpetuation of a cultural organization; (2) passage from lower to higher levels of integration, and (3) improvement in 'all-around adaptability'.

Parsons does 'not conceive societal evolution to be either a continuous or a simple linear process' but distinguishes three evolutionary levels called primitive, intermediate and modern. 'For the transition from primitive to intermediate society, the focal development is in language, which is primarily part of the cultural system. In the transition from intermediate to modern society, it is in the institutionalized codes of normative order internal to the societal structure and centers in the legal system.'[25] Parsons' paradigm of evolutionary change enumerates a number of processes central to the evolutionary perspective. The most important of all change processes is listed as '*the enhancement of adaptive capacity*, either within the society originating a new type of structure or, through cultural diffusion and the involvement of other factors in combination with the new type of structure, within other societies and perhaps at later periods.' Other processes include increasing structural differentiation, functional specialization, societal integration and 'the establishment of a version of the value pattern appropriate to the new *type* of system which is emerging.' Parsons attributes to advanced social systems a set of 'evolutionary universals' which he defines as 'a complex of structures and associated processes the development of which so increases the long-run adaptive capacity of living systems in a given class that only systems that develop the complex can attain certain higher levels of general adaptive capacity.'[26] Evolutionary universals most fundamental to the structure of modern societies are: stratification, involving a primary break with primitive kinship ascription, cultural legitimation with institutionalized agencies that are independent of a diffuse religious tradition, bureaucratic organization of collective goal-attainment, money and market systems, generalized universalistic legal system,

and the 'democratic association with elective leadership and mediated membership support for policy orientations.' Parsons writes:

Perhaps a single theme tying them together is that differentiation
and attendant reduction in ascription has caused the initial two-
class system to give way to more complex structures at the levels of
social stratification and the relation between social structure and its
cultural legitimation. First, this more complex system is characterized
by a highly generalized universalistic normative structure in all
fields. Second, subunits under such normative orders have greater
autonomy both in pursuing their own goals and interests and in
serving others instrumentally. Third, this autonomy is linked with
the probability that structural units will develop greater diversity of
interests and subgoals. Finally, this diversity results in pluralization
of scales of prestige and therefore of differential access to economic
resources, power, and influence.

In summary let us note that the evolutionary perspective has seen
at least a tentative revival in recent years. Although many sociologists would deny it, the advocates of structural-functionalism and
the proponents of diachronic theories of modernization often utilize
an evolutionary frame of reference. Of course, the unilinear theory
now stands discredited. The concepts of evolution and progress,
regarded as value-laden, were replaced by those of change and
differentiation, apparently value-free. But the evolutionary perspective provides a powerful conceptual tool for the analysis of the
processes and patterns of change. It has proved to be a big boon
to the now growing fields of historical and comparative studies that
deal with modernization. But as Eisenstadt points out: 'reappraisal
of an evolutionary perspective is contingent on systematic explanation of the processes of change within a society, the processes of
transition from one type of society to another, and especially the
extent to which such transition may crystallize into different types
or "stages" that evince some basic characteristics common to different societies.'[27] However, in another context, Eisenstadt cautions
that:

There is no reason why all societies should reach certain stages of
differentiation, or that they necessarily will develop the same types
of institutional contours once they attain such stages. The most that
can be claimed is that the processes of differentiation in different
societies exhibit similar formal and structural characteristics and that
these create somewhat similar integrative problems.[28]

Yet there seems to be general agreement that the evolutionary perspective can best illustrate the fundamental cumulative change processes such as differentiation, specialization and integration as societies move from simple to more complex forms. Moreover, the evolutionary perspective has provided a certain model of man and society, a philosophical conception that underlies theories of organic evolution and structural-functionalism. However, it must be emphasized that the evolutionary perspective is more a descriptive typological tradition than an explanatory theoretical system; it is primarily an approach to the study of social change in different societies, not a generalized theory of any particular social system.

NOTES

1. See Robert Park, *Human Communities: The City and Human Ecology* (Glencoe, Free Press, 1952); and Robert Park, Ernest Burgess and R. D. McKenzie (eds.), *The City* (Chicago, University of Chicago Press, 1925).
2. Amos H. Hawley, *Human Ecology: A Theory of Community Structure* (New York, Ronald Press, 1950), p. 67.
3. Amos Hawley, 'Human Ecology', in David Sills (ed.), *International Encyclopedia of the Social Sciences*, Vol. 4 (1968), p. 329.
4. Amos Hawley, *Urban Society* (New York, Ronald Press, 1971), p. 12.
5. Julian Steward, 'Cultural Ecology', *International Encyclopedia of the Social Sciences* (1968), p. 337.
6. Otis Dudley Duncan and Leo F. Schnore, 'Cultural, Behavioural, and Ecological Perspectives in the Study of Social Organization', *American Journal of Sociology*, 65 (September 1959), 135.
7. O. D. Duncan, 'Human Ecology and Population Studies', in Phillip M. Hauser and O. D. Duncan (eds.), *The Study of Population* (Chicago, University of Chicago Press, 1959), p. 684, 682.
8. Ibid., pp. 682–3.
9. Ibid. p. 682.
10. Duncan and Schnore, op. cit., p. 136.
11. Ibid.
12. Hawley in *International Encyclopedia*, p. 330.
13. Duncan and Schnore, op. cit., p. 144.
14. John H. Kunkel, 'Some Behavioural Aspects of the Ecological Approach to Social Organization', *American Journal of Sociology*, 73 (July, 1967), 13.
15. Auguste Comte, 'The Progress of Civilization through Three States', in Amitai Etzioni and Eva Etzioni-Halevy (eds.), *Social Change* (New York, Basic Books, 1973), p. 18.
16. Herbert Spencer, 'The Evolution of Societies', in Etzioni, Ibid., pp. 9–10, 13.

17. For details see Oswald Spengler, *The Decline of the West* (New York, Alfred A. Knopf, Inc., 1926). Quotes from Spengler, 'The Life Cycle of Cultures', in Etzioni, ibid., pp. 23–4; and Spengler, 'The Soul of the City', in Richard Sennett (ed.), *Classic Essays on the Culture of Cities* (New York, Appleton-Century-Crofts, 1969), p. 85.

18. Robert Bierstedt, *The Social Order* (New York, McGraw-Hill, Inc., 1974), p. 563.

19. Pitirim Sorokin, *Society, Culture and Personality* (New York, Harper and Row, 1947), p. 590. Also see his *Social and Cultural Dynamics* (New York, The American Book Company, 1937, 1941).

20. Bierstedt, op. cit., p. 564.

21. Julian H. Steward, 'Cultural Evolution', in R. Serge Denisoff et al. (eds.), *Theories and Paradigms in Contemporary Sociology* (Itasca, F. E. Peacock Publishers, 1974), p. 214.

22. Robert Bellah, 'Religious Evolution', in S. N. Eisenstadt (ed.), *Readings in Social Evolution and Development* (New York, Pergamon Press, 1970), p. 212.

23. Wilbert Moore, *Social Change* (Englewood Cliffs, Prentice-Hall, 1963), p. 39.

24. Daniel Lerner, 'Modernization: Social Aspects', in *International Encyclopedia of the Social Sciences*, p. 386.

25. Talcott Parsons, *Societies: Evolutionary and Comparative Perspectives* (Englewood Cliffs, Prentice-Hall, 1966), pp. 26, 23.

26. T. Parsons, 'Evolutionary Universals in Society', *American Sociological Review*, **29** (June, 1964), pp. 342, 56.

27. S. N. Eisenstadt, 'Social Change, Differentiation and Evolution', in Lewis Coser and Bernard Rosenberg (eds.), *Sociological Theory* (New York, Macmillan Company, 1971), p. 712.

28. S. N. Eisenstadt, *Readings in Social Evolution and Development*, op. cit., p. 1.

Subject Index

Alienation, 193–206; areas of its manifestation, 204–5; definition of, 204; literature on classification of, 201–3; Marxian concept of, 193–6; meaning of, 201–2; social conditions conducive to the development of, 200–1; a synthetic view of anomie and alienation, 203–6; see also anomie

Anomie, 177–93; of affluence, 188–9; and alienation, a synthetic view of, 203–6; and class structure, 185–6; definition and explanation of, 178, 180, 182–3, 191–2; and economic status, 187–8; and scarcity, 188; types of, 183, 186; see also alienation

Australian aborigines, marriage practices among, 145

Behaviourism, 148–54, 272; see also under exchange theory

Bureaucracy, 124–5

Chicago school of sociology, 231, 236–7

Class conflict; Dahrendorf's theory of, 126

Class struggle: and alienation, 116; and communist society, 118; crystallization of social relations into groups, 117; and dictatorship of the proletariat, 118; and economic determinism, 115; evolution of, 118–22; Marx's theory of, 114–22; pauperization of proletariat, 116; polarization of classes, 115–16; property, importance of, in, 115; and revolution, 117–18

Coercion theory of society, 110, 125

Conflict theory, 105–41; categories and types of, 108–11; of Collins, 134–5 and his formal, 131–7; and Coser's

conflict functionalism, 135–7; critical evaluation of, 138–41; of Dahrendorf, 125–8, 137–8; and dialectical sociology, 131–3; Frankfurt school, 128–31; and functionalist, 111; historical background, 105–7; and Karl Marx's theory of class struggle, 114–22; and Mills power elite, 122–5; postulates of, 113–14; and tradition of competitive struggle, 106; underlying assumption of, 111–12; varieties of, 128–38

Cultural determinism, 271, 275

Culture, 271

Deviant behaviour, 180–1, 189

Dialectic sociology, 137–8

Ecology, human, 288–94; salient features of, 291–3

Empiricism, 20–5; consequences of, 23–4, 30–3; see also research

Ethnomethodology, 244, 255, 258–65; concepts used in, 255–6; introductory discussion on, 255–6; see also phenomenology

Evolutionary theory, 294–303; variants of, 294–303

Exchange theory, 144–73; Blau's structural perspective, 155–62; collectivistic orientation in, 146; and distributive justice, 165–8; Homan's behaviourism, 148–54; institutional bases of, 147; intellectual background, 144–8; and norm of reciprocity, 162–4; viewed from various angles, 168–72

Exogamy, 148

Exploitation, 124

Functions: different connotations of,

Author Index

301
Ab15

67072

DATE DUE